ECOCENE POLITICS

Ecocene Politics

Mihnea Tănăsescu

https://www.openbookpublishers.com

© 2022 Mihnea Tănăsescu

This work is licensed under a Creative Commons Attribution-NonCommercial-NoDerivatives 4.0 International license (CC BY-NC-ND 4.0). This license allows you to share, copy, distribute and transmit the work for non-commercial purposes, providing attribution is made to the author (but not in any way that suggests that he endorses you or your use of the work). Attribution should include the following information:

Mihnea Tănăsescu, *Ecocene Politics*. Cambridge, UK: Open Book Publishers, 2022, https://doi.org/10.11647/OBP.0274

Copyright and permissions for the reuse of many of the images included in this publication differ from the above. This information is provided in the captions and in the list of illustrations.

Every effort has been made to identify and contact copyright holders and any omission or error will be corrected if notification is made to the publisher.

In order to access detailed and updated information on the license, please visit https://doi.org/10.11647/OBP.0274#copyright. Further details about CC BY licenses are available at http://creativecommons.org/licenses/by-nc-nd/4.0/

All external links were active at the time of publication unless otherwise stated and have been archived via the Internet Archive Wayback Machine at https://archive.org/web

Digital material and resources associated with this volume are available at https://doi.org/10.11647/OBP.0274#resources

ISBN Paperback: 9781800643147
ISBN Hardback: 9781800643154
ISBN Digital (PDF): 9781800643161
ISBN Digital ebook (epub): 9781800643178
ISBN Digital ebook (azw3): 9781800643185
ISBN XML: 9781800643192
SBN Digital (HTML): 9781800646803
DOI: 10.11647/OBP.0274

Cover image: Anna Gatti

Acknowledgments

One of the main theses of this book is that there is nothing but multiplicity, all the way down. On account of this, anything that appears as an individual is suspect, no less so the achievement of a single book. The authorship of this work is multiple, stretching across intellectual genealogies and relations that cannot be summarized exhaustively, but without which there would be nothing to write about. Let me try, nonetheless, to underline the major contributors to this work.

The initial idea for this book took form during a visiting fellowship at the Law School of the University of Auckland. I am very grateful to Katherine Sanders for sponsoring that fellowship. Subsequent ideas were refined and developed during a stay at the New School for Social Research (Politics), for which I am indebted to Rafi Youatt. Several discussions with him contributed significantly to the conceptual development of the book. His comments on earlier drafts were extremely valuable. While in New York, Anne McNevin gave me several extremely useful suggestions that have had a lasting impact on the arguments developed here. I am grateful for that.

During the writing process, Serge Gutwirth provided plentiful and excellent suggestions, as well as extremely pertinent comments on previous drafts. Alessia Tanas had the generosity of reading and commenting on the unfinished work. I am extremely grateful for that. Timothy Eden graciously read and commented on the work, also introducing me to the writings of Wendell Berry. Our walks and discussions gave me respite and inspiration. Marco Vullo has been a companion for most of my life; his encouragement has been invaluable. Benedikte Zitouni took the time to patiently review the book, providing pointed and perceptive comments that pushed the work further. I am significantly indebted to the work of Isabelle Stengers, and to her perceptive and generous reading of previous versions. Her support has seen this work through.

I have benefitted from the intellectual companionship of several people that have nourished my curiosity and pushed me beyond lazy self-satisfaction. Among these, Richard Borden and Patricia Honea-Fleming are key. Their friendship has made a lot of this work possible. John Visvader has had an enormous influence on my intellectual formation, becoming a veritable ancestor. Marcel Wissenburg has been a trusted source of critique and excellent conversation partner, as well as an unfailingly generous host. Nicolas Schroeder has opened new worlds of ideas and has been an excellent travel companion. He introduced me to the work of Didier Debaise, for which I am very grateful. Louise Knops has been a constant and invaluable intellectual sparring partner. Ștefan Constantinescu has continuously pushed me beyond my boundaries, helping me in ways big and small. His erudition and boundless curiosity inspire me greatly.

I am grateful to Clemens Driessen for our fateful meeting in New York that led me to discover his excellent work on Descartes and the concept of space.

My familiarity with olive culture, which forms a great part of this book, is owed to the generosity of several people. Ogni posto ha i suoi guardiani. Senza la loro generosità non si entra nella terra, non si capisce come orientarsi. La loro famiglia è la terra, i loro famigliari scolpiti negli alberi. Nuccio Chialá mi ha permesso di cominciare a conoscere i rapporti e i legami che costituiscono una storia intergenerazionale comune. Senza di lui e le porte che ha aperto per me, sarei stato perso. Dire che gli sono grato è insufficiente. Questo lavoro sarebbe stato molto più povero senza la sua amicizia.

Grazie a Raffaele Antonello per le ore di conversazione (e di lavoro) attorno agli ulivi. Ho imparato tantissimo da lui.

My knowledge of rewilding and restoration goes through several important relationships. Thanks are due to Razvan Crimschi, Alexandra Panait, Sandu Bulacu, Adrian Hagatis, Pedro Prata, Wouter Helmer, and Deli Saavedra.

Many thanks to Alessandra Tosi, Melissa Purkiss, and all of the team at Open Book Publishers. They demonstrated that it is still possible to have human, and humane, relations in a publishing culture that is increasingly robotized. Restoring that kind of trust is priceless.

Giulia made the space necessary for this work to be written, and the time to hear it out all too often. Her constant encouragement to live a full life may be the biggest contribution to this work.

I am grateful for the institutional support of the Research Foundation Flanders (FWO), the Political Science Department of the Vrije Universiteit Brussel and the Evaluating Democratic Politics in Europe (EDGE) Research Program. All have provided indispensable funding for seeing this project through.

Mariana și Doru au lăsat mai multe urme decât se pot numărą. Darurile lor nu se răsplătesc; se dau mai departe.

Parts of this work have appeared in other forms before. Chapter 3 draws in part on the article 'Evocative Representation' published in *Constellations* (2020). Chapters 4 and 6 draw on 'Responsibility and the Ethics of Ecological Restoration', *Environmental Philosophy* (2017).

One of the central ideas of this book is that we all inherit, obliquely and largely unpredictably, practices and knowledge from varied and surprising sources. I therefore acknowledge my unpayable debt to ancestors living and spectral, human and non-human. They are the soil that nurture present and future life.

Pentru Lavinia,
Cu dragoste și bucurie.

Contents

Acknowledgments v

1. Introduction: Thinking Politically through the New Era 1
2. Volumes, Part I 21

Intermezzo I: Loss and Recomposition Part I 47

3. Volumes, Part II 61
4. Renovative Practice 89
5. Ecopolitical Ethics, Part I 109
6. Ecopolitical Ethics, Part II 127

Intermezzo II: Loss and Recomposition, Part II 149

7. Mutualism 155

Outro 181

Bibliography 183
Index 193

1. Introduction

Thinking Politically through the New Era

Let there be no doubt: the tragedy has already happened.

No matter how hard we try to wriggle our way out of so many ecological problems, the future is a matter of degrees of destabilizing change. There is no going back. No human society can still count on the future of their environment.

The notion that we can count on it has always been an illusion, but today we can no longer afford the illusion itself. It is known that tomorrow will be different, and that difference also means that many aspects of the world that make it joyful and livable today will likely disappear. As our ecological century advances, we have entered an era of universal loss, displacement, and decomposition.

The kind of disorientation occasioned by the undoing of worlds is easy to see. The SARS-COV-2 pandemic has forced billions to shelter for years. It would be tempting to think about this event as a matter of bad luck. After all, throughout human history viruses have come and gone, disease has moved in and out of populations, and life has always managed to survive, even flourish. Looking at things this way makes it seem as if we are still acting and living within the same seamless human history. This pandemic is like the last one, and like the next one to come.

This way of thinking only makes sense from the virus' perspective. Humans are habitats as they used to be, and as they will continue to be. The more humans, the better: the redundancy of a habitat is the most important ecological measure for ensuring the perpetuation of any species. But the humans of this story have changed so fundamentally that they can no longer afford to think in these terms of continuity, of history repeating itself. This pandemic is not like the last one, nor like those to come. Like many events that are still on the horizon of this twenty-first century, it is a watershed moment, an irruption that creates a clear before and after. The virus is a stark example of the continuous generation of crises that characterizes our social interface with the environing world. It is as if, for the time being, the dominant approach to this change of era is through a stubbornness that literally hurts.

There is a deluge of news announcing changes that can easily be seen as impending doom. The disappearance of ice in the Arctic by 2050 is now a certainty, like our knowledge of when the next eclipse will happen. The American North-West has experienced droughts not seen in 1200 years, while the Great Barrier Reef continues to bleach at a pace from which it will not recover. This comes fresh on the heels of the greatest Australian bushfires in memory (Aboriginal memory, first and foremost, as it is the longest on the continent). The Amazon itself is constantly burning, an idea that seemed a logical impossibility not too long ago.

Inasmuch as the individual worlds we may compose are constantly flattened under the singular world of modernity,[1] there is an increasingly unfathomable list of decompositions that will confine human beings to doctored, exclusive spaces of survival. Then, perhaps, the modern dream of being entirely separate from 'nature' will have been accomplished: humans in protective boxes contemplating a world fit for viruses. All of this leaves many hopeless. The progressive political answer to loss is often some variation on the theme of hope.[2] When faced with grave problems, it is assumed that being hopeful, finding scenarios that fuel the feeling of hope, is what can drive people forward. This book starts from a different assumption, that hope is not necessarily the principle of action it is deemed to be. Hope is necessary for action only if one believes in a magical ability to control the world according to one's wishes. In the Ecocene, this belief is untenable in multiple interrelated ways. No single individual's hopes for a particular kind of future can encompass the multiplicity of beings and possible worlds. Hope risks

---

1   In Chapter 2 I spend some time explaining what I find to be the most salient characteristics of modernity. Briefly, it is the operation of simplifying the environing world by positing abstract matter, devoid of any qualitative characteristic, as the real world. This is what Didier Debaise, commenting on Whitehead, calls the bifurcation of nature.
2   The reactionary one is fear.

dogmatism, an intransigence as to the possibility of radically different futures. Rooted in hope, people all too easily daydream the present away, towards a future that is already pre-determined to an extent that demands utopian imagination.

Instead, we need principles of action that do not depend on having or not having hope, because they are rooted in an understanding of the world as fundamentally mysterious (for the importance of ignorance, see Chapter 3), and not amenable to utopian dictates. A lack of hope focuses our attention on the present and the ways in which how one acts today matters first and foremost today, and not in some indefinite future when all will have been pacified by our favorite utopia. Freeing ourselves from hope allows human thought to become small, local, multiple, and changeable; it allows practices to take root because of what they are, not because of what they may, under laboratory conditions, achieve.

The underbelly of hope is despair, a pendulum that swings from unwarranted optimism to cynical renunciation in the face of an imagined end of the world. To hope is to expect a future contoured around one's desire, and therefore to be consistently disappointed. The duty to think anew is the necessary corollary of living without hope, because it accepts the unavoidable dynamism of the world. Ideas, prone as they are to becoming static, are never going to offer a faithful picture of the world, partly because what they are striving to immortalize is always one step ahead. As Wittgenstein would have it, "when we wager on a possibility, it is always on the assumption of the uniformity of nature" (1991, 238). Wagering on hope shares this flawed assumption.

***

How is one to respond to the tragedy that is already upon us? What does it mean to live without hope, in the absence of a more livable future? What kind of response could be commensurate with the loss of our world and its accompanying displacements? This book is anchored in the conviction that theorizing is a possible response; it will itself attempt to be part of a possible response, by experimenting with ideas. Theorizing in the face of doom might seem silly or futile, but I will argue that it is crucial. It might be one of the only sane options left.

One of the reasons why it helps to theorize in the face of loss is that generalities and abstractions have the force of reality behind them. This idea has already been amply developed by Whitehead and Peirce, and excellently taken up by Debaise and Kohn in their respective domains (philosophy and anthropology; Debaise 2017ab). The argument is, in Peirce's words, that "generals are real" (in Kohn 2013, 59), because it is only through general ideas that actions are available to humans. Humans metabolize the world through ideas; it is useless to look for direct, unmediated action, because everything people do is motivated by some idea.

It is equally useless to look for ideas 'in the head' or the mind. As Wittgenstein reminds us, "thinking is essentially the activity of operating with signs. This activity is performed by the hand, when we think by writing; by the mouth and larynx, when we think by speaking" (1960, 6). But when we think "by imagining signs or pictures, I can give you no agent that thinks". This is partly because thought is always operative in action; there is no inner agent only available to human beings that can think up abstractions that would be devoid of pragmatic consequences, or without a trace of the world that generates them. This accounts for the immense variety of ways of doing (ostensibly) the same thing: different ideas are operational in different places and at different times.

For Whitehead, the reality of abstractions is both inevitable and potentially an enormous problem. Inasmuch as abstractions open up the world of actions, they are inevitable features of the relations between human ways of being and the world. However, the operations made possible by abstractions, though formally unavoidable, are content-wise always subject to change. In other words, ideas may change just as the world, and the body, change. Instead, what often gives abstractions a bad name is what he calls the "fallacy of misplaced concreteness" (in Debaise 2017a, 25 and in Borden 2017, 94). So, what is a necessary instance of interchange with the world becomes reified and assumes the stability of geological formations (themselves, given the appropriate timeframe, unstable; see Massey 2005, and Chapter 2). For Whitehead, everything is in processual change, and any kind of reification, whether of things in the world or of the ideas that are themselves part of the world, is a betrayal of the infinite multiplicity of which processes are formed.

If we accept that ideas are real, residing 'in the world' as much as 'in the mind', then it is clear why political theory may be an appropriate response to the current predicament. After all, the current universalization of loss, as I will argue throughout this book, is a direct result of particular ideas, of reified ways of understanding, and therefore pursuing, the relationship between humans and worlds. Many have argued for a growing list of ideas that may retroactively inherit the guilt of destructiveness: the Cartesian separation of mind and body, the idea that the world is composed of resources, the desacralization of nature, and so on. Whichever one may be followed, the basic point is that, in the final analysis, it is through a number of influential ideas that the natural world is changing faster than societies are able to grasp.

The force of ideas can be partially illuminated through the peculiar relation between description and prescription. This relation can only be accounted for by postulating a theory that makes ideas part and parcel of the world, but with very special characteristics: the representations of the world in thought are both descriptive—inspired by states of affairs—and prescriptive, in that they structurally fail to accurately describe and therefore demand action better suited to the description. Given that descriptions can never be complete, representations never fully commensurate with the world, ideas are caught up in a perpetual process of changing their own environmental conditions. This is not out of a failure to grasp how things finally and really are. It is, instead, in itself a feature of the world. It might just be its evolutionary engine.

The difference between the presumed features of the world and its perpetual dynamism drives cultural, as well as biological, change. It is a well-known feature of evolutionary theory that natural dynamism drives varieties of adaptation. In the ideatic realm, we can see periods of "misplaced concreteness" alternating with periods of revolutionary upheaval in conceptions. For example, the reified rule of the separation of matter and ideas has now come to an end. As Latour (2007) has argued, materialism nowadays seems like the most abstract (in the negative sense) conception, completely unrelated to other descriptions of the world that seek to map empirical dynamism.³ As I will explain later (see Chapter 2), the bifurcation of nature (Debaise 2017) has led

---

3   "This is why the materialism of the recent past now looks so idealistic: it takes the idea of what things in themselves should be—that is, primary qualities—and then never stops gawking at the miracle that makes them "resemble" their geometrical reproduction in drawings" (139).

us to see the natural world as devoid of any inherent qualities. What I want to point out now is how this kind of description of the world—matter is what is characterized through extension, and what is common to the world—leads to peculiar prescriptions that end up significantly modifying the world in the direction of the initial description.

Together with Ștefan Constantinescu, I have published a series of articles that have detailed this process in one particular case, namely the incorporation into networks of state power of the Romanian Danube Delta. In short, what we demonstrated is that the state has attempted to describe the territory of the Delta through cartography, while its radically simplified cartographic descriptions were immediately appropriated for further expansion of power over the territory. Crucially, this has always meant the physical transformation of the territory by the state to more closely resemble the neat maps that supposedly described it. This kind of operation is well-known to students of colonialism, as it has always been a part of the annexation of territories and the justification for wielding power in ways that evidently and brutally cut across the lives of other people. But the peculiar ways in which description and prescription are intertwined in this fashion has received much less attention in political theory, where fear of the naturalistic fallacy (basing what ought to be on what is) still reigns supreme.

New descriptions are needed, not so that we get closer to the truth, but because of the prescriptive slippage that is their main characteristic. This is easier to see when looking at what is putatively *not* descriptive, namely a prescriptive statement, the kind of thing that is not supposed to describe anything at all. To take a famous example, Kant's categorical imperative proposes that one should act in accordance with the moral law, whether it suits her preferences or desires or not, in such a way that she could wish the maxim that guides her behavior to be a universal law. This seems to be entirely prescriptive but, as Stanley Cavell points out, Kant's imperative gets its force from *describing* what it is to act in a moral manner. Cavell therefore calls it the categorical declarative because it "does not tell you what you *ought* to do *if* you want to be moral; it tells you (part of) what you in fact do when you *are* moral" (2002, 25).

This shows very well the prescriptive/descriptive link that can be ignored only at great cost. Key in Cavell's statement is the parenthesis, where he draws attention to the fact that descriptions and prescriptions do not exactly match or coincide. If they did, there would be such a thing as a universally correct description identical to what it prescribed. But this is not the case. Descriptions of the world are approximations and experiments, they can never be total, and this is partly why they demand the support of their prescriptive counterparts, to appear greater than they are. Kant's imperative has the appearance of a moral universal law precisely because it cannot describe all instances of moral behavior, and therefore requires the prescriptive veil that would help make the description total.

Modern descriptions of the world are both dependent on bifurcation (splitting the world into matter and, essentially, epiphenomena) and prescribe actions that would make the description universally true. They matter for ethical reasons, because with an awareness of what a description requires, different ones that incentivize the creation of alternative worlds can be stitched together.

The world supports an incalculable number of descriptive stances, and this obliges us to continuously interrogate and revise them.

The relationship between descriptions and prescriptions is unidirectional: the courses of action available must logically predate any prescription. One cannot prescribe, out of the blue, what ought to be done, without also having available a set of descriptive statements informing actors about what *can* be done. In this sense, theorizing is perhaps the most effective way of countering the generalized feeling of loss that characterizes contemporary and future times. Descriptions are a means of recomposing in the wake of decomposition.

It is because of these peculiar characteristics of ideas, at the intersection of description and prescription, that offering new ones is a means of resisting what Isabelle Stengers (2015) has called "the coming barbarism". To be clear, the ideas presented in this book are not, strictly speaking, new. Ideas never are. How could they be, since they are evolved features of the world? One of the main lessons of evolutionary and ecological thought is that there is no radical novelty, only gradation and perpetual change. Patterns are rearrangements of that which preceded them and are never created out of nothing; there is always a precedent and a predecessor. Or as Deleuze expressed it, "ideas are always reusable" (1988, 235). The ideas in this book are therefore crystallizations of intellectual histories and condensations of the thoughts that have travelled across individuals and eras. They are, in this sense, impersonal.

* * *

Naming something brings it under the aegis of a set of possibilities implied by the name. The Anthropocene has been the most successful term to characterize the new era when human activity has become geological in scope. It has progressed from a neologism in 2000 to common usage today, appearing in popular magazines as well as prompting the creation of dedicated journals (see *The Anthropocene Review*). Some names languish until their time comes, though it may never arrive. The Anthropocene exemplifies the opposite phenomenon: it was adopted so rapidly that one wonders whether it responded to a need to catalog what was happening as quickly as possible, as if to move on in peace.

This widespread adoption of the term has also come with significant critiques. The most dominant of these has been that the Anthropos central to the term is not some disembodied universal human, but rather conceals the guilt of particular humans. To speak of humanity as such as a species unified by its actions on the planet is to engage in a double reification. On the one hand, humans are lumped together as the collective agents of destruction. In fact, it is largely the internal (to human societies) dynamics of destruction that drive most of the current transformations. Not too much digging is required to uncover that, under the apparent actions of the entire species there lies a great deal of human-on-human predation and exploitation. On the other hand, talking about the planet is also misleading, especially if our reason for talking about it is to draw attention to the relationships between people and their environments. Nobody relates to the planet as such, though climatologists and planetary system scientists ostensibly try to. But at the end of the day, it is particular environments that animate these scientists' work, their thought, their actions.

Given these essentially political shortcomings of the term, others have been proposed: Capitalocene (Moore 2017, 2018), Plantationocene or Chthulucene (Haraway 2015, Tsing 2015), to name a few. All of these terms have their own benefits. They oscillate between naming an agent of change (capital) and identifying a mode of operation of that agent (the plantation). Donna Haraway's Chthulucene has the benefit of anchoring itself most clearly in the descriptive-prescriptive nexus I have described. It proposes a world that is situated in a perpetual here and now, in a dense web of interrelations with an undefined number, and kind, of creatures.[4]

I don't find it useful to propose a new term for the sake of it. But there is something that none of these other terms capture that I find to be the most salient feature of the new era: the irruption of ecological processes within the polis. In strictly geological terms, the Anthropocene is probably the best we have, because it designates a particular way of reading sedimentary history. In geological terms, it is illuminating to note that current processes of sedimentation will likely show the tremendous influence that humans have had on the natural world. The process of sedimentation itself, and the question of where sediments end up, is modified by human actions today, through the building of dams and the diversion of rivers. In this sense, the Anthropocene is a good word, but it is politically naïve. Some of the other terms seek to identify the culprit, as it were, and bring their responsibility to the fore. This is a worthy pursuit, but the new age should not simply be dealt with in terms of 'guilty' and 'not guilty'. Others would rather focus on the interrelations at play and leave the political stakes under-defined. Instead, what I think is needed is lucidity as to precisely what the political stakes are.

---

4   Though there are many similarities between the Chthulucene and the Ecocene that I will propose, they do not overlap sufficiently to warrant adopting Haraway's term. My concern in naming the Ecocene is to intuit, through the idea of ecology, a few political ideas that would challenge our habits of thought, including the newly acquired habit of thinking of assemblages as infinite and more or less uniformly agential. Focusing on ecology, as I do, leaves the door open for limited kinds of interactions to start mattering more, or less. In the final analysis, as I understand it, the Chthulucene's political project is expressed in the idea of making kin, whereas the Ecocene, given its composition, offers a different set of potential directions for thought.
Even if our analyses are congruent (they are certainly proposed in a spirit of solidarity), I side with Emil Cioran when he was accused of always repeating himself and being unoriginal. Paraphrasing, he said: anyone can have an experience of loss (for him, death). But *how* you express it is everything. It speaks to different people and allows them to transform an ultimately banal experience into a living idea. I trust that the Ecocene will speak to sensibilities that other terms may not stir up, and therefore contribute to the transformation of the experience of loss from an increasingly banal experience to a transformative political idea.

The irruption of ecological processes brings new kinds of actors into the polis. CO2 is of concern because of what its concentration *does* that is of immediate relevance to human life. Similarly, the relevance of all so-called ecological crises lies in the fact that they institute new sequences of actions that have direct consequences for how people live. In that sense, ecological processes both have a life of their own, and are co-determined by human beings (as implied by 'Anthropocene'). But to focus only on the humans (whether as ignorant or guilty actors) misses the fundamental point that, in political terms, this new era is not about humans at all, but rather about how to accommodate, make peace with, and negotiate with everything that is *not* human.[5] To focus obsessively on the human is also to betray the fact that omnipotence is completely severed from any kind of omniscience: powerful and powerless humans alike are still essentially ignorant of how the non-human world works, and how to relate to it in regenerative ways.

This ignorance is not simple, not just a kind of lack. This is one possible meaning: a lack of information, or its willful denial. This condition can in theory be remediated, if enough is presented to fill the gap. What cannot be escaped is another kind of ignorance: the constitutive, structural kind. It defines the contours of knowledge's relationship to the world, and its constitutive character is not a lack but a power, because within the spaces that it opens, new questions can be asked, and new answers received. Ignorance as a lack and ignorance as a power are related but distinct, and anchoring oneself in the structural kind of ignorance is the only way of continuously quenching the lack.[6]

A term is needed, then, that could encapsulate both the centrality of ecological processes and the subordinate role of human agency, as that which provokes but cannot guide the subsequent series of events. Human agency has become the *provocateur par excellence*, but this does not mean that human agency is in the driving seat, deciding where

---

5   I am not implying that strictly human problems of domination and exploitation do not exist! But I am implying that those need to be tackled against a backdrop of a general re-dimensioning of humans, not the other way around. It is not the case, in my view, that if certain oppressive social arrangements were to disappear, this would necessarily lead to more regenerative relations with the natural world. A humanly equal world does not imply a regenerative one. I develop this point more in Chapters 5 and 6, through the concepts of reciprocity and responsibility.

6   This structure is closely mirrored in the discussion of vulnerability in Chapter 3.

1. Introduction: Thinking Politically through the New Era

larger natural processes are leading. If the primary focus is not humans, but ecological processes, then it seems to me that the Ecocene is an apt term.[7] It has the benefit of putting ecology front and center. But too often 'the ecological' is used in a vague way. What is specific to ecology that recommends it for the current moment? Though of course I cannot be exhaustive on this question, I take ecology to contribute three important insights to politics: chance, change, and locality. I develop these at greater length in Chapter 3. Briefly:

Ecological arrangements are stochastic affairs. It is only by artificially cordoning off an 'environment' that we get the idea of balance. In fact, when studying any particular place from the point of view of the interactions among all participants, it becomes impossible to either specify a whole (such that participants become 'parts') or to observe long-term rules of regularity that would obviate the role of chance. Instead, natural arrangements are always partly generated by chance, such that to any given participant opportunities and challenges *happen*, much as in human life. Disruption and unannounced radical change are, in the long term, the norm.

This brings us to change, which is much more characteristic of natural arrangements than balance. Ecology studies systems inasmuch as it emphasizes their provisionality. And within 'systems' themselves, change is constant. We can hardly make sense of evolutionary thinking without accepting the centrality of change, a process that is present from the metabolic, to the developmental, and indeed to the evolutionary scale. Flux and dynamism come together in the idea of ecology.

Lastly, and closely related to the other two, ecology requires attention to locality. In fact, the study of the planet as such is not primarily done by ecologists, but originates in the work of scientists studying other planets. This early history has given rise to an impressive connection between disciplines, including geochemistry, climatology, and geology,[8]

---

7   I borrow this term, with his gracious consent, from Rafi Youatt, *Interspecies Politics* (2020). There, Youatt starts to develop it along the lines followed here, bur stops short of a full engagement.

8   It would be absurd to deny the usefulness of thinking at the planetary level as far as climatology is concerned. It reveals dynamics that would remain invisible were it not for the adoption of this scale. What I am arguing is that the scale at which climatology operates is of limited political potential, beyond international negotiations that set general frameworks, which are mostly so far ignored. What *does* have political potential is the idea of ecology, because it shows how what

that produce models of the planet that attempt to predict its future course. We will explore the conceptual underpinnings of modeling later. For now, it is important to understand that the level of the planet as a whole is not the remit of ecological science.

Instead, ecologists are preoccupied with particular places. This makes a lot of sense if we think, along with Latour, of how life actually presents itself, namely as a thin exterior enveloping an indifferent core. Life—the study of which is the science of ecology—does not manifest as a globe, but rather as a skin dressing the globe, a barely-12km-thick envelope that is characterized by incredible variety and constant variability. It is at this level—what Latour (2017, Latour and Weibel 2020) calls critical zones—that ecology forces us to think. And it is at the intersection of scales that ecology can connect properly with the sciences postulating a whole, and in that sense, it is its vocation to constantly pull them back down to earth (see discussion of Margulis and Lovelock in Chapter 3).

Chance, change, and locality are characteristics of the world that ecology posits, but they are not always the guidelines of the science of ecology itself. There, the temptation to simplify and to subsume under immutable principles is as strong as in any other science. If modernity tends towards the annulment of the striations and textures of the world, then modern ecology is also subject to this operation of simplification. It nonetheless has resources, perhaps more so than other sciences (save for biology), to constantly rethink and undermine its certainties. This is because it is ultimately based on observation, which gives continuous and insistent opportunities to rethink the certainties of our frames.

For example, the concept of the ecosystem, like that of the biome, is often used as a heuristic. But it is also often taken to describe a deeper reality, through a process of reification. However, observation of any 'ecosystem' calls into question the very concept of ecosystem that was coined to encompass all of its constituent parts. Similarly, the concept of species functions to classify the vastness of creaturely life but cannot accurately predict individual behavior. As Mayr and Drury (1998) remind us, ecology cannot be a predictive science, only a probabilistic

---

climatology predicts is unpredictable at the local level, which is the level where politics actually functions. Climatologists are in fact consistently surprised by how their predictions play out in different localities. It is the pull of the local in relation to the global that offers the most radical political possibilities.

one. The field naturalist, they argue, has the right to informed guesses, but no more. Wittgenstein may as well have been thinking of ecology when he wondered whether the world may be amenable to predictions.

The relationship between creatures and their world is one of limited interactions. This observation excludes the idea that the biome, or the ecosystem, needs a certain composition of species. Rather, what can be inferred at any given time is an economy of exchange that can and does mutate, and that has a contingent relationship with the creaturely make-up that expresses this economy. In other words, the critical zone that is life on earth functions through the mutability of behavior *together with* the mutability of conditions. The two are inseparable, but they do not *a priori* specify a certain kind of composition (this must interact with that).

Ecological concepts can therefore be a philosophical orientation towards the world and creaturely interactions. They are a way of making sense of the vastness of textures and qualities. This is a difficult position to sustain because it asks for an ongoing lucidity of ignorance, one that is generative. Many times over, ecological science has conveniently, for a while, forgotten its philosophical vocation and its duty to remain as open as the world it studies. That notwithstanding, the openness and tolerance for change that ecology *can* display is what politics must inherit from it.[9] This does not mean that we should pine for the ecologist-king who would be able to determine how systems should work, according to well-defined predictive models. It means that observational power, which leads us to continuously changing our minds, allows thinking its proper place within the fine, shimmering grain of the world. This is a quintessentially pragmatic orientation, and it is why politics can inherit it.

The Ecocene, then, by foregrounding the central role of ecology in the new era, also implies that we have to make political sense of our

---

9 Increasingly, the science of ecology is showing a growing awareness of its philosophical potential. Soil ecology, for example, has started to uncover relationships so complex and mutable that they are forcing a thorough rethinking of previous models. The idea of the critical zone as a skin enveloping the planet is first and foremost expressed in contemporary soil science. See Kutílek and Nielsen (2015), *Soil. The Skin of the Planet Earth*, where soil is specifically described as skin. Interestingly, Merlin Sheldrake, in *Entangled Life* (2020), compares soil with the gut, because of its digestive properties (breaking down organic matter and recycling it for further use).

times via concepts that are synchronous with ecological science. And if we accept that chance, change, and locality are what ecology injects into political thought, then the Ecocene becomes that era when human social and political arrangements *start from the necessity of living with uncertainty*.[10]

Though the idea of Anthropocene politics has gained a lot more ground, I would argue that it is Ecocene politics that needs careful consideration. If Anthropos is front and center, it seems routine to allocate political duties to it. It also becomes possible to think up big systems, whether managerial or not, to solve the problems of 'humans'. The Ecocene disallows these actions, because it is not about humans: it is about how chance, change, and locality *force* humans to live. Ecological processes and their dynamics have always forced themselves on human societies. How could they not? The challenge is to invent ways of living with that fact without seeing it as a punishment, or something without which we would be better off. Our imbrication with the world is not something to be escaped so as to find human meaning and purpose; it is itself the condition for meaningfulness (see Chapters 6 and 7).

There is an Ecocene politics that happens by default when the obsession with Anthropos continues: it takes the form of either ecomodernism, or denialism. These are but two names of the same fundamental response: a desire to continue the modern project of walling societies off from their environments, either through positing an infinite series of technological fixes that could keep the illusion alive, or by denying that there is anything to worry about in the first place. There are other possibilities, and the first step in moving towards these is calling what is occurring by its proper name: we have not entered the age of humans, we have entered the ecological age.

* * *

There are several ideas that I will connect in order to propose a renewed basis for political life in the Ecocene. These are neither the only possible ideas, nor dogmatically held ones; instead, they are sketches of patterns

---

10 Politics grounded in uncertainty—in constitutive ignorance coupled with worldly change—answers the requirements of action outside of hopeful projections. It is a way of recomposing without a definite end by changing the descriptive apparatus as soon as it outlives its prescriptive usefulness.

that have survived the steamroller of modernity and that are taking shape anew. In an effort to think sideways, the book will draw on diverse intellectual histories, absorbing aspects from multiple sources and mixing them in new ways. By doing this, I hope to contribute to the increased preponderance, and therefore influence, of the ideas I describe.

Five notions are developed and connected. The argument starts with the idea of volumetric space to describe the world in a way that does not betray its inherent multiplicity;[11] it then applies the same fundamental framework of multiplicity to describe the lives whose intercourse with the world is the condition of possibility for Gaia itself.[12] Throughout, I will demonstrate how the concept of *relationality* is fundamental to understanding worlds as well as lives.

The idea of the primacy of relations is currently undergoing a renaissance. It isn't new, having been present in biology and social science intermittently throughout their respective histories (which, it bears saying, have always been connected). But it is reappearing after a historical period, roughly equal to the twentieth century, where fewer and fewer practices considered it. This period is also that of the Great Acceleration,[13] the time when the project of modern development seemed to reach its long-desired supremacy by expanding at an unprecedented rate, churning worlds and paving over them with the same developmental ethos. Relationality has survived through the cracks, and as these grow wider, so the theorizing of relations is once again becoming more prominent.

But relational thinking also risks being as vague as the modern conceptions it is replacing. Partly because of this risk, there is an acute

---

11 Chapter 2 deals with ontological arguments that form part of the theoretical context of the book. However, readers that are not especially eager to read occasionally dense text can safely skip to the first Intermezzo and continue from thereon.

12 See Chapter 3 for a fuller discussion of the idea of Gaia. I follow Isabelle Stengers' use of the concept. Briefly, Gaia denotes two things: the Earth as a living planet, so one that gets its fundamental characteristics from the interaction of biotic and abiotic elements; and the irruption of natural processes within political processes. Neither of these imply a holistic conception of the planet, quite the contrary.

13 See Steffen et al. (2015) for a history of the Great Acceleration. Briefly, this refers to the post-1950 era of cumulative economic activity that shows a steady rise across all indicators of production and consumption. The data shows different growth rates for wealthy countries, but increasingly more countries are joining the J-shaped curve of development capitalism.

need to consider relations alongside the salient characteristics that make it possible to relate in the first place. It is also imperative to develop relationality towards a political ethics appropriate for the times we have entered. It is in this spirit that I propose the concept of *vulnerability* as a crucial complement of relationality. I develop this idea, in both its ontological and ethical senses, in Chapter 3.

Vulnerability has already been prominently discussed in conversations on social and political ethics, for example in the works of Judith Butler. I want to extend its uses to creatures beyond the human, by showing how being vulnerable is part and parcel of ecological processes, as well as a foundation for a certain kind of moral thought. I will also argue that vulnerability is a power first and foremost, and a characteristic of the living that raises very difficult questions about exactly what is to be protected, preserved, or cared for, and how.

The notions of relationality and vulnerability conspire to make up an ontological foundation that is open to certain kinds of actions, and therefore to certain kinds of inherently political moral thought. I will develop these moral threads through the concepts of *reciprocity* and *responsibility*. Of the two, it is the latter that has received most attention in political ecological thought. In dialogue with Māori philosophies, I will propose that reciprocity holds an untapped potential to ground political ethics in ways that are compatible with a fluid and multiple ontology. Reciprocity can be the basis for ecological relations, while responsibility becomes the basis for specifically human relations against the backdrop of a wider ecological ethics. The surrounding world is reciprocated, while responsibility is reserved for the humans (and human-like companions) that make up a wider community.

Relationality, vulnerability, reciprocity, and responsibility form the backbone of the argument, alternatives to political ideas that have dominated our thinking in times when we have been strangely unaware of the ecology of the world. *Mutualism* will be the name that reunites these in a more-or-less coherent political frame. This term also has a long history that has become marginal to the modernity with and within which more and more people have lived. Its history has developed along political and biological lines, which have sometimes been in productive contact with one another.

Mutualism both recapitulates the history of anarchist thought, where it first acquired a political meaning, and the history of the biological sciences, where it is now becoming more prominent. It ties the free association for mutual benefit of the anarchists with the individual creatures of modern biology, who are no longer individuals in any recognizable sense. Beings are increasingly shown to be composed of multiplicity all the way down, and without this fact they could not count as living beings. Humans cannot live without the complex biome that makes up most of what we identify as a separate body. The notion of the holobiont describes this newly postulated being inhabiting the consciousness of modern biology. Because of this multiple history, mutualism can incorporate a political ethics that is ecologically grounded.

None of the above ideas is intended to build a new utopia. This book is thoroughly anti-utopian because it is committed to a particular idea of ecology that does not allow utopian projections. Ecological thought, as I understand it, is in a deep sense thought that can only draw temporary and precarious connections. This does not mean that they are unimportant, quite the contrary: only the assumption of mastery over some entire system would tempt this conclusion. Instead, ecological thinking commits one to the specific scale at which things matter, and to the acknowledgment of (and commitment to work with and from) one's own fundamental and deep ignorance.

The temptation to think in utopian terms is hard to resist. Radical political offers that genuinely want to move beyond the fixed ideas of modern development are still drawing on a political imagination that is invested in achieving a controllable and ultimately stable state of affairs. The critique of capitalism, for example, is an extremely important allay. But it mostly posits a post-capitalist order in which destructive relations between humans, as well as between humans and their environments, would be pacified simply by overcoming capitalism. Proposals to move beyond the obsession with economic growth and towards degrowth are similarly framed in terms of sufficiency societies that can settle on an acceptable level of consumption, as if all that were missing is the right formula. Moving away from growth is of course one of the most urgent tasks. But as a political thought, this approach misses the perpetual chance and change that the world will inevitably throw its way.

The 'small thinking' of ecology inspires a narrow, political thought that is interested in the mutualist relations that can be drawn across multiple worlds.[14] Political life must, in the Ecocene, be capable of recomposing worlds, whether in the ruins that some people already inhabit (Tsing 2015, Tsing et al. 2017, de la Cadena and Blaser 2018), or through the barbarism that may yet become generalized (Stengers 2015). Small politics is interested in the question of how to live with the historical consequences already playing out all around us, and how to reinvent our practices and livelihoods accordingly. If political theory can only guide people in living together under conditions that cannot exist, then it is literally useless, divorced from its purpose.

Ecocene politics is about undermining big orders and renovating existing connections that adhere to a mutualist ethics. There is no end point in sight, but rather a continuous fidelity to the enhancement of the world around us, wherever we may find ourselves. Importantly, and also as a direct consequence of ecological thinking, Ecocene politics has to be local without being nativist. There are no criteria of belonging beyond what one *does*. The world to come is neither defined by a perpetual state (of sustainability for example), nor is it composed by birthright. The most livable worlds of the Ecocene are fundamentally open in the sense that they are always unfinished, and open in principle to all participants.

The arguments of this book are connected and inspired by ways of living in the world, by ongoing and flawed experiments in building mutually beneficial ecological relations. The largely philosophical arguments are peppered with intermezzos that anchor the themes discussed within particular contexts. These will be revisited throughout in order to both show how different ideas emerge from practices, and how these practices stand to benefit from the theoretical formulations that they have inspired. I will discuss olive culture in Southern Italy and genealogical conceptions of life in Aotearoa New Zealand. These are not illustrations of 'best practices', blueprints for some end point; they are sketches of possible routes forward, of the messy relationships that both inspire projects of renovation and impede a fuller pursuit of

---

14 There are potentially productive similarities between what I call 'small thinking' and the idea of low theory championed by Halberstam. In particular, the ways in which McKenzie Wark and David Graeber appropriate the use of low theory is resonant with the work of this book.

mutual beneficence. The intermezzos are also articulated in relation to the pivotal Chapter 4, where I discuss rewilding and nature restoration (with some examples from Romania). Together, these contexts have largely influenced the ideas in this book. They show what every locality is up against: a fundamental recomposition that occurs through the process of inheriting past practices and ideas. They are ways of critiquing, as much as ways of recuperating.

Many other struggles and situations can stimulate political thinking. Despite their heterogeneity, there are several elements that make up these common struggles. Whether we are thinking about the growing movement for reinstating commons, the theories and practices coming out of Indigenous struggles under the banner of the pluriverse, legal movements for extending legal personality to (parts of) nature, conservation movements trying to decolonize conservation practices, agroecology and permaculture fighting against industrial agriculture, to name but a few; all of these different ways of articulating worlds share a general principle of mutualism. This is not held dogmatically, but rather grows out of a shared commitment to multiplicity, relationality, reciprocity, and responsibility.

The profusion of alternatives notwithstanding, we should not delude ourselves with thoughts of an inevitable transition to modes of composing livable worlds. A multiplicity of alternatives suggests that the old dreams of sudden revolution may have become, as David Graeber has argued, a matter of perpetual erosion of the status quo. This requires one to unlearn ways of thinking that are geared towards totalities and stability. Following Engel-Di Mauro's *Ecology, Soils and the Left* (2014), being uncomfortable in knowledge production may ultimately be an ethically necessary practice. This is the time to abandon certainties, to cross boundaries, and to think anew, forever. The process, in this case, really is everything.

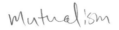

2. Volumes, Part I

Worlds

Political arrangements always rely on an implicit notion of space that gives them power and justifies its deployment. This is because politics works on underlying assumptions about what the world is, and these assumptions give it a horizon of possibility. What we think the world is made up of has everything to do with the actions that we find politically palatable. If we are interested in describing a political stance appropriate for the possibilities that the Ecocene opens up, we must therefore start by attending to the notion of space, and what it does.

The wide and increasingly expanding field of post-humanities[1] has been very good at dealing with beings and their relations, but less good at dealing with the notion of space itself. This is odd, as a rejuvenated concept of world seems to have been almost entirely constructed out of beings. Even if we accept the argument that the world is alive (Abram 2012, Kohn 2013), or rather that it is inseparable from the beings that make it up, the question of whether the notion of space plays a role in our theorizing and practices still remains. In particular, the question of how beings relate to environments cannot be fully explored by attending to the multiplicity of beings themselves; attention needs to be paid to the multiplicity of environments as well. This is not because environments, or spaces, are in fact separate from beings, or in some sense more important. Rather, it is because the challenge of the Ecocene is to think complexly as such, that is to say to think about beings and environments *together*, without either sacrificing their difference or reifying their particularities. Unless we do this, we risk retaining

---

[1] For an excellent introduction to the field, see Braidotti (2019). For the related field of environmental humanities, see Emmett and Nye (2017).

conceptions of space that already foreclose the possibility of political thinking for the Ecocene, and by extension the possibility of mutualism.

I want to connect several different ideas that, when taken together, draw the contours of an ecological concept of space that can carry the ethical burden of an Ecocene politics. The specific ethical commitments of a mutualist politics will be outlined later, but their ontological basis needs to be developed first. I will therefore sketch the concept of volumetric space as one that can ground political thought within a world that is already teeming with easily unobserved relations and possibilities. As argued in the Introduction, ideas are themselves of the world, and the idea of space is both supposed to describe that which ostensibly exists, and elicit possibilities that may, under different descriptions, lay dormant.

One of the most durable modern assumptions about space is that it is purely exterior to the perceiving body. For moderns, this seems too obvious to point out: of course, space is that which is *outside* any body; bodies are *in* space but are not really considered to be of space. They are not really fundamental to thinking about the category of space because they appear to apprehend it from a distance. As we will see, this assumption owes as much to the dominance of visual experience in thinking about space, as it does to our effacement of the complex authorship of ideas, and therefore making them seem as if they can stand separately. It is as if they are independent of the actual bipedal mammal that thinks them, or its particular situation.

On the other hand, insisting on a connection between bodies and abstract notions may seem banal: bodies are needed to talk and write. Thinking this way already betrays a notion of space that I will thoroughly oppose: an empty receptacle that can be described in ways that are independent of the experience of living bodies. Even the most seemingly ethereal ideas of space—like that of an empty grid on which objects are projected—must have some relationship to the living body and the experiences that connect it to the world. This can be shown through a kind of intellectual biography that is at the same time a genealogy of ideas. This seems like a good place to start.

* * *

It is impossible to deal with the notion of space without thinking about Cartesian space, a notion that has become extremely influential in the modern world. One of the main reasons for this tremendous influence is its association with science, or rather the early reliance of scientific practice on this particular idea. Isabelle Stengers (in particular in *The Invention of Modern Science*, 1993) and Didier Debaise (see *Nature as Event*, 2017 and *Speculative Empiricism*, 2017), drawing on the philosophy of Alfred North Whitehead, have identified the operation through which Cartesian space infects, or perhaps even generates, a concept of nature that becomes instrumental to modern science. It is through this particular linking, space—nature—science, that spatialization in a particular form becomes inseparable from modernity and a particular kind of modern (experimental) science.

We cannot be clear about what modernity signifies without unpacking modern space. The first crucial point is found on the very first page of Debaise's book *Nature as Event*: "the modern conception of nature does not express any genuine ontological position [...] but is essentially *operative*" (2017, 2, emphasis in original). This is to say that the typically modern idea of nature does not describe something fundamental about the world, but rather makes possible a series of actions. This is one sense in which it is operative. The other is that it itself relies, for any force or efficacy, on a previous operation which Debaise, following Whitehead, calls the *bifurcation of nature*.

This fundamental operation by which space and nature become identified and operationalized consists in the deceptively simple (but entirely abstract) separation of 'primary' and 'secondary' qualities. As Locke explained them, primary qualities are those dealing with "solidity, extension, figure, motion or rest, and number" while the secondary ones with "colors, sounds, tastes" and so on (in Debaise 2017, 8). The key point to understand is that "the distinction between primary and secondary qualities starts from an empirical base [...] in order to then differentiate between nonperceptual qualities and those subjective qualitites which are supposedly derived from the former" (12). The operation of bifurcation separates supposed realms of qualities based on a fundamental distrust of the only possible kind of experience, i.e. perceptual direct experience. Bifurcation manages to subtract embodied experience from the world and postulates the result of this subtraction as more real than its own basis.

As Stengers comments in respect to the experimental method inaugurated by Galileo, the operation of bifurcation conceals the author of the experiment that generates it, precisely because embodied experience (relegated entirely to secondary qualities) is abstracted out of the world, as if it were a mere hindrance. It is also in this sense that there is nothing ontological about modern space, as there is nothing left to *being* after all of its qualities have been abstracted away. However, the primary qualities are presented as the true ontological foundation of reality, albeit a foundation that can only be revealed through the subtraction of authorship from the action of knowing. It is in this sense that truth claims based on the operation of bifurcation acquire a formidable, double strength.

On the one hand, they are capable of allowing experientially hidden facets of reality to testify for themselves. As Stengers shows with reference to Galileo, in the experiment of the inclined planes it is motion itself that speaks, albeit in the way formulated by the experiment. This is an extraordinary feat, precisely because it manages to coax new meanings and figures that are only visible through the adoption of an experimental stance. But the experimental conditions and the strong authorship of Galileo disappear from view in light of the operation of bifurcation, and motion remains alone. The magic, of authorship, vanishes. It is through this operative power that supposedly descriptive statements based on modern nature are prescriptive in very specific ways.

The mix of description/prescription inherent in the operation of modern nature conspires in actually simplifying the natural world. Abstractly speaking, the operation of bifurcation is a radical impoverishment of the multiplicity of forms that populate the world, as well as the processes through which they appear. But this impoverishment is not merely conceptual, it has a direct and radical effect on the world. The abstractions generated through the bifurcation of nature are reified through the fallacy of misplaced concreteness: they are taken as more real, because they are ostensibly unauthored.

This is the key to the political power of abstract space and its association with modern nature and experimental science: describing the world as *actually* formed of secondary and primary qualities that need careful separation *requires* radical interventions in the physical milieu to rearrange it according to embedded assumptions. The operation of bifurcation starts with a double concept of nature, elevating mathematical abstraction above embodiments, but ends up, over its long history, literally simplifying countless environments. The Ecocene itself can be seen as a logical outcome of bifurcation, a revolutionary upheaval of oppressed processes.

Cartesian space, arguably the foundation of modern conceptions, is in the mode of the abstract par excellence. Its very existence can be contemplated inasmuch as it is emptied out of any quality that may be directly perceived by a creature. It is defined by mathematical coordinates only, which exist in mathematical space, that is, in space devoid of particularities of place. The substitution of actual spaces for mathematical space has two profound implications. As we have seen, descriptions of the world are also—this might be their primary function—prescriptions of how to go about fulfilling them. In this sense, the flat space of mathematics has increasingly flattened actual worlds. Second, the existence of mathematical space and its dominance over so many practices suggests that possible relations between thought and embodiment are at best overstated. What, after all, could be the material, bodily underpinnings of Cartesian space?

Clemens Driessen (2020) provides one possible and fascinating answer. With an intuition of a close relation between the world and ideas, he set out to find just what the circumstances of the real Descartes, the person, were when he first published his ideas about space. Where, in what body nestled in what places and which conversations, did Cartesian space ferment? There is something strange, even uncanny, about the very idea of a physical origin of Cartesian space, a feeling that attests to the power of the abstraction that Descartes inaugurated. As Driessen writes, "because the resulting grid essentially erased the very idea of an origin, it is hard to think of Cartesian space somehow bearing traces of the places where it was first imagined, from which mathematic space was then rolled out over the globe" (275).

Driessen ties the project of revealing the emplacement of Cartesian space to the ambition of "provincializing modernity".[2] Similarly,

---

2   This resembles Chakrabarty's provincialization of Europe, and Kohn's similar gesture towards language. In *The Crises of Civilization* (2018) and *Provincializing Europe* (2009), Chakrabarty tries to unseat the idea of modernity from its supposed center, and instead reveals it as a process that involves many more, and far more

rethinking space provincializes the idea of modernity by showing how its constitutive concepts have always been rooted in particular places. This is especially striking as modernity defines itself according to rootlessness and universality, logically following from its foundational gesture of bifurcation. The provincialization of modernity that occurs through a rethinking of space is also what is urgently needed for political thought as it tries to break free of modernist constraints.

Besides the notion of space as an empty grid amenable to algebraic calculations, Descartes is also famous for inaugurating a view of non-human life as essentially mechanical. The figure of the automaton played an important role in his theorization of living beings, and has arguably dominated several centuries of scientific research on animals and, by extension, on the natural world. Driessen begins by showing that the figure of the automaton was an actual physical presence in Descartes' world: "in the geometrical gardens of St-Germain, [...] René Descartes experienced a garden automaton, proving to him that our senses can easily deceive us, and that the organic is actually mechanical" (279). These kinds of contraptions were popular during that time as garden ornaments. They were supposed to resemble natural scenes by translating the movement of animals and the elements into mechanical form. Being on occasion almost fooled by these contraptions, Descartes came to see them as revealing something deeper about the nature of the world itself.[3]

While Descartes was developing his ideas of the fundamentally mechanical workings of the world, the Netherlands was undergoing a radical transformation. For the first time land reclamation, through the construction of polders, became tied with capital investment and speculation on the value of the reclaimed land. "Reclamation, together with the Dutch circle, facilitated a land-based private investment vehicle that produced a perfect grid landscape just as Descartes arrived in the

---

surprising, actors. Eduardo Kohn, in *How Forests Think* (2013), attempts a similar de-centering of language, which in Western philosophy has always enjoyed a preferential reverence.

3   I do not mean to suggest that Descartes was wrong in thinking that automatons reveal something about the world; everything hangs on the meaning of revelation. Automatons reveal something about the world inasmuch as they make possible a series of questions put to the world that would not have existed outside the revelation. This can be said of analogies in general: their aptness is in great part a function of the possibilities they create.

Netherlands" (282). This is to say that Descartes' lifetime coincided with several developments in land management and profit generation that were already starting to treat the Dutch landscape as placeless and amenable to parceling out in a way that had been heretofore impossible. In this sense, the idea of space is also intertwined with technological and economic developments and, in a very real sense, concomitant with these, as opposed to preceding them. Space is not thought up by the mind, but rather through the deployment of complex infrastructures, both material and ideatic. Wittgenstein's aphorism about writing being thought through the hand holds here too: space is thought through spatialization.

For example, the invention of the corporation based on shares is the kind of invention that makes possible a whole series of interactions with the world that radically transform it (Mitchell 2020). But it is not enough to think up the share, it must be hitched to other inventions that together become the infrastructural apparatus that thinks of spaces. Transcontinental railways are made possible by the twin inventions of steel (a highly durable material) and the share, which can sell future revenue based in part on the confidence one has in the workings of steel. Similarly, reclaiming land works together with selling its future use in the present, and therefore generating profits that accelerate the rate of reclamation and legitimize a way of thinking that continuously captures, in Mitchell's term, future revenues. The idea that space is an empty grid that can be appropriated and made profitable cannot be neatly separated either from the mechanisms of profit, nor the materials that made and continue to make such mechanisms work, nor from the body through which these changes pass and are codified in ways that propel them further.

Another way of expressing this idea is that the notion of space thrives through particular configurations of power. The modern project of flattening space has always been linked with the quest for profit, or rather with the idea that power, by means of profit, can be obtained through such flattening. This has been shown in many cases around the world, but they all repeat the same fundamental characteristics[4]

---

4   In the case of the Danube Delta for example, Ștefan Constantinescu and I have shown how the state, from the mid-nineteenth century until today, has repeatedly intervened to impose a logic of flatness and to simplify a natural labyrinth in order to pursue resource exploitation. Also see Scott's *Seeing Like a State* (1998).

that originate in the seventeenth century in the Netherlands, during the same era as the real, embodied Descartes.

In the case of the Netherlands, the early gridifcation of land was achieved not only in relation to the sale of land itself, but also to the manipulation and extraction of resources, in particular food and flowers. The operation of simplifying places to better resemble Cartesian space is still the norm in land-based cultures today, dominated as they are by industrialized agricultural production. We will see this very spatial operation at work in the practices of olive cultivation in Southern Italy, as well as amidst rewilding and restoration efforts. Through these experiments, we will also see other ways of living and conceiving that, despite the steamroller of modern spatial thinking, continue to endure and haunt the hegemony of modernity.

Driessen shows in detail how Descartes' friendship with key figures in the gridification of the Netherlands contributed both to his ideas on space, and to the actual publication of his books.[5] As he explains, "'Cartesian' space emerged in a particular time and place: not just a universal/timeless idea projected onto the world by a sole genius, but emerging from a culture and topography [the flatness of the Netherlands itself] that were being ordered to reflect a certain mechanical mode of knowing and governing space, plants, and people" (286).

* * *

The example of Descartes clarifies one sense in which ideas of space are always connected to power and to the pursuit of political and economic goals. Another way to see this is by thinking about maps.

Cartography itself is only possible because of a series of conventions that legitimize the projection of complex and messy territories on to a

---

5 Nobody is exempt from the fact that thinking always happens within wider networks of relations. As a case in point, I came to know of Driessen's treatment of Descartes via a fortuitous meeting with Driessen in New York that tied a project of his (participating in the Guggenheim show *Countryside, the Future*) to the work I was at the time doing for this book. This kind of chance meeting is often the norm, tying people together in a mutual intellectual genealogy that exceeds any participant. As Stengers expresses this idea (2015, 131): "[...] not 'I think' but 'something makes me think'". This is the form under which thinking (or rather intelligence) is equally distributed in the world, as a property of networks. Any subjective embodiment can do no better than pay attention and become attuned; it is not about the possession of individual capacities.

neat, two-dimensional grid.⁶ It is no coincidence that modern voyages of exploration and colonization, whether internal or external, have always involved the mapping of the desired territories. The operation of translating unknown lands (that is, lands that are known to others, but not to the colonizer) into cartographic projections is what allows for the subsequent deployment of military power to annex the newly plotted lands. Cartography is a co-conspirator of colonization in two ways. It represents territories without taking the experience and knowledge of local inhabitants into account, and in so doing legitimizes the self-serving view that 'discovered' lands are not under the authority of their respective inhabitants.

Maps as such have not been invented by modern notions of space; they precede them by centuries. But mathematical projections transformed cartography from an endeavor connected with a largely religious geography into one hitched to military and economic power. These interests extended their reach through new mapping techniques that sought to mirror the territory exactly, by fixing points that could be used for navigation and the control of annexed territories. Land surveys through the method of triangulation⁷ were carried out throughout the colonized world to better fix people within a space, an operation without which taxation, or conscription, or the theft of labor would have been infinitely harder. In this sense, the map is for early modern power accumulation what steel was to the corporate share: an artifact whose properties radically modify the literal and political landscape.

There are many examples to show this, but I will settle on one I know well. With Ștefan Constantinescu, himself a cartographer, we studied the history of maps and their effects in the Danube Delta. The Danube River is and has been important for as long as Europe has been settled. Relatively recently, geomorphologically speaking, it started forming a delta where it arrives at its destination, the Black Sea. The Danube Delta has, in this time, become a shifting labyrinth of channels, floating

---

6   There are many different kinds of cartographic projections (the name already betrays the fundamental operations at work), but at this level of analysis they all do the same thing.
7   This is the practice of plotting land by measuring it in adjacent triangles. Through this method one only needs to know the first two distances defining two sides of the triangle in order to deduce all other distances. For this entire section I am deeply indebted to Ștefan Constantinescu, who taught me much about the working of maps.

reed beds, marshes, islands, lakes, all in constant movement. It also finds itself in a region of Europe that has been contested by empires because it was marginal to all of them. It therefore became an important area where borders, and therefore the extent of an empire, could be drawn. The delta's marginality has also been a feature of the difficulty of knowing it from the outside in a definitive, mirror-of-the-territory kind of way. Its very geomorphology resisted the fixing operation of the map. It therefore became a refuge for bandits, a dangerous place of lawlessness—of course, from the point of view of the state.

Today, the delta is mostly in Romania, but its northern section incorporates the border with Ukraine. Throughout the eighteenth, nineteenth, and twentieth centuries it changed hands several times, from Ottoman to Russian, to Austro-Hungarian, and eventually to the nation-building of the post-WWI era. This geopolitical history of the area is important, but the point I want to make is that it would have been impossible without mathematical cartography. This is because the delta is not a territory that can be easily approached. It frustrated notions of what is liquid and what is solid, what is land and what is water; it shifts continuously. Its moving patterns are not just horizontally arranged, but vertically as well, as water depths vary and never settle for long. Lakes that are accessible one day may be closed the next, and unless one has a deep *experience* of the place, it cannot be easily navigated.

The early (eighteenth-century) maps of the delta were interested in finding the main branches that the river formed, like arteries crossing a vast organ. These could be used to access the interior, at first to set up military outposts and claim the border, and later to exploit fishing and reed stocks. We have detailed this history elsewhere (Constantinescu and Tănăsescu 2018) and there is no need to recount it all. The point here is that the first stage of colonization of the delta coincides with the early deployment of cartographic projections that make military expeditions possible. These are relegated to the main branches only because the interior remained impenetrable, as it could not yet be known cartographically.

The second stage is purely mathematical and follows the military one that had already started to modify, and simplify, the territory by dredging main channels to stabilize their depth. Perhaps it is easiest to see the imbrication of mathematical space and political power in the delta because it is an obviously volumetric territory that resists corraling into a certain shape. And yet, mathematical cartography expanded the knowledge of channels and lakes, eventually covering the whole delta and opening the door for large-scale resource exploitation. Cartography has not in fact managed to produce a faithful map of what is a constantly changing territory, but rather approximations that are 'good enough' for what they are supposed to achieve. So even though the exact location of a lake, or its depth, may be impossible to definitively fix, cartography managed to approximate these details adequately enough to transform the spaces into more law-abiding places.

Under the totalitarian regime that lasted from 1945 until 1989, the delta was radically transformed through dikes, dredging, narrowing or widening of channels, stabilizing of banks, and creation of new and straighter routes. These interventions made exploitation possible but have also cemented the dynamism of the territory, which keeps changing and requires constant intervention to maintain it in the desired shape. The maintenance of the delta is nothing else but a perpetual fight to force its space within a form that enables exploitation and control. But a volumetric delta requires constant mapping, despite the considerable work that goes into keeping it still.

The cartographical history I have briefly described has, in the post-1989 era, morphed into nature conservation policies that aim to preserve aspects of the delta deemed ecologically important. In the early 1990s the territory became a Biosphere Reserve, which limits (in theory, see Prelz Oltramonti and Tănăsescu 2019) what can be done, and where, within the reserve. Conservation maps now play the role that military ones played a century before. Counting species, deciding on what aspects of the delta are crucial for them, intervening through engineering works in order to preserve certain conditions that are deemed important, are all intended to enable the fencing off of the space as dictated by conservation interests.

Throughout all of this history, the local experience and situated knowledge of the delta has *never* figured as a cartographical, or political, consideration. This is because it resists the flattening of space that is the fundamental premise of navigational maps. Today, old fishermen still do not navigate using maps, and have a hard time reading them. Instead, they use intergenerational memory, shifting landmarks, toponyms, animal sounds, winds, currents, and so on to find their way about.

The younger generations seem to have finally been introduced to cartographical thinking by Google Maps. The heirloom knowledge of the territory may soon be relegated to the "cemetery of practices" (2015, 98) that Stengers has identified, which maintains the living spirits of ideas and ways of being that modernity, despite its best efforts, cannot completely extinguish. But satellite mapping is itself only as good as the territory allows, and under particularly difficult weather conditions it becomes useless. Its precision, at the actual level of the boat where it matters most, cannot avoid a certain threshold of error. This means that in situations of dense fog, for example, one cannot simply follow the dot or read their spatial orientation. In such situations, an inherited knowledge of the territory is what must intervene.

The possibility of navigating a delta according to its physical qualities, and a particular mode of paying attention to these, suggest a conception of space that can return to living territories some of the richness, both human and non-human, that has been slowly bled out of them. It is the senses, in other words (as well as the multiplying apparatuses that we use to create new kinds of sensing, so not excluding satellite mapping as such), that are always crucially involved in the thinking of space. Descartes' radical move was to involve the power of the senses *entirely* negatively, therefore constructing a notion of space as capable of existing without any sense. As Debaise points out, the reification of 'primary qualities' "into a more general ontological form can be achieved only at the expense of fundamental aspects of the plurality of forms of existence in nature" (2017, 15), indeed at the expense of different ways of thinking about and living in spaces. But the leveling of multiplicity and plurality is not just a conceptual operation: it has very real effects by increasingly fashioning the empirical world to more closely resemble the ideatic one. The accelerating simplification of our world, in terms of land use, transportation, agriculture, biodiversity, and so on, is a direct result of our thinking.

A reconsidered notion of space therefore must pay attention to the importance of the senses in both living and thinking. Considering actual territories in which to ground our thinking—like the Danube Delta—suggests space as a volume, and therefore allows us to incorporate creaturely and sedimentary movements in all directions, as well as the multiplicity of senses that together craft the textures of places. These senses are not only those of the human body, but also of animals, who have long been used by people to intuit spatial features to which they are otherwise blind. The flight of animals before an earthquake, or the ability of water birds to detect fish, have routinely been highlighted as important examples of feeling space. Sense is not even limited to bodies, but goes beyond them through a vast apparatus that reconstructs the deep past and the movements below the surface to which most creatures are relegated.

Geological history, for example, extends the volume of space all the way down to the center of the earth. People have used their imaginary senses to reach these hidden places for centuries, but only recently have we started to piece together a picture of geology that shows the deep ground beneath our feet to be as dynamic as everything else, and inextricably connected to the space of living things. We have effectively developed a vibrating sense, made up of and deployed through devices that measure seismic waves, both spontaneous and created (through detonations).

Deltas, to run with the example, are entirely determined by the tectonic movements that slope the ground in ways beneficial to their formation. The western coast of South America, for example, thanks to tectonic plates, has grown the Andes close to the shore, which makes deltas impossible. Rivers are too fast, and the ocean too deep, to allow for sediments to accumulate close to the coast. On the other side of the mountains, eastwards, tectonic movements have created a gentle slope, on land as well as on the ocean floor, which has facilitated the deposit of sediments and the creation of deltas. Creatures living in the Andes and on both sides of it are directly connected to movements hundreds, even thousands, of kilometers down.

Tectonic movements and volcanic eruptions indicate a moving, abiotic space that interacts with the living but is also independent; it precedes the living, though it makes their existence possible. The formation of the planet is still present under our feet, a history four and a half billion years old that is ongoing. The living have always created parts of the conditions of their own lives, but this process is blind: the conditions created need not be friendly, or even optimal. They are always provisional, often interrupted by a brute force that has the upper hand, an irruption that seemingly comes from nowhere.

Geology has a mind of its own. What it makes available, the very surface that is the skin of the earth, is an intricate co-creation that is always precarious. Probing beneath this skin in order to add an awesome history to the story of every place has also entailed human destruction of the object of study. For example, the same devices that have made seismology possible are used in the mining of coal, oil, and other minerals. These deposits of past lives, testimony to the inconceivable forces that have overcome them, go from being valued testimony of a whimsical past, to cheap commodities devoid of any historical meaning.[8]

Places that seem stuck in space, and that we try to fix as if location was their primary characteristic, are always on the move. Doreen Massey (2006) gives the example of features in the British Isles that are considered symbols of a durable nation, modeled on the strength of its landscape. Yet those features have moved around the world and will continue to do so. The timescale of this movement is of course completely different from the lifespan of even the longest-lived animals, but this does not make it irrelevant. It is through this patient passage of time that conditions of life are formed.

Massey (2005) also highlights another characteristic of a volumetric notion of space, calling it the "simultaneity of stories so far" (9). Adding the geological story to the stories of generations upon generations of places and creatures repositions space-as-volume within the realm of memory, itself an important means of sensing one's way about the world. To be emplaced, to experience a dynamic fitting of the volumes of the world, comes with a whole series of pre-sanctioned gestures, inherited and created memories, many of which are of political importance. This exemplifies the phenomenon that Bruno Latour, commenting on Schmitt, develops when writing that "the *res extensa* is not a space *in which* politics is situated—the background of the map of every geopolitics—but, rather, something that is generated by political actions itself aided by its technological instrumentation. [...] space is the offspring of history" (2017, 231, emphasis in original).

---

8   A similar process of knowledge through destruction is present in archaeology, which often works with mining operations, and prepares the ground for them. The annihilation of one storied layer is used for the discovery and ultimate annihilation of another, deeper one. The preservation of stories in archives excavates meaning from the ground.

Understanding space as essentially a grid on to which entities are projected restricts the possibilities of rethinking potential relations with the world. This, as argued above, is part of the point of flattening spaces into grids. Moderns have become used to regarding this kind of space as a factual reality, and any deviation from it as merely an abstraction. Instead, as Latour argues, space as a flat grid is a high-level abstraction, something that is never lived as such.[9] The space of the moderns first and foremost restricts the possibility of (politically relevant) new kinds of relations between often surprising entities. If, instead, we refuse the operation of bifurcation, of emptying out, we discover possibilities for space that are eminently pragmatic. Importantly, refusing the operation of bifurcation forces one towards the kinds of good abstractions of which Whitehead was so fond: ideas that strive to reflect the multiplicity of the world by not foreclosing most of its possibilities.

There is no reason to suppose that space is primarily a visual category.[10] Instead, a multi-sensory understanding of space seems appropriate in keeping ontological possibilities open.[11] In the *Phenomenology of Perception*, Merleau-Ponty argues that "we cannot dissociate being from orientated being" (2005, 295). This means that there is, in perception, no space as such, abstracted. As Merleau-Ponty argues, there is no horizon of the horizon, no ultimate level, and there is furthermore no need for it, because of the inherent orientation of being. Remaining stubbornly embodied is a clear refusal of modern thinking. But this embodiment need not be understood in visual terms. Life (which can be embodied in a dizzying array of forms) is orientated

---

9   This is the sense of Latour's (2007) diagnosis of the strange modern concoction of 'idealist materialism'. For a philosophical foundation of the critique of localization as the primary quality of space, see Debaise (2017).

10 This has been widely assumed. Notable exceptions are the works of Gallagher (2015, 2016), Gallagher and Prior (2014), Gallagher, Kanngieser and Prior (2016), and Bates et. Al. (2019), focusing on the sonic dimensions of landscapes. Gallagher and Prior (2014) argue that "phonography is particularly useful for highlighting hidden or marginal aspects of places and their inhabitants" (p.268). In the case of the Danube Delta again, together with Constantinescu (2019) we took this idea further by showing how local inhabitants of a deltaic village (Sfântu Gheorghe) incorporate the sound of wildlife into the spatialization of their territory. Sound is an important and often overlooked dimension of space, and relations with non-human animals (that often develop phonically, but not exclusively) are also fundamental in fleshing out the texture of space.

11 Which means conceptualizing space through an indefinite number of creatures, not just human beings.

inasmuch as the volume of the subject exists within the volume of the world, and these volumes live through sound and touch as much as sight, as well as an immense variety of senses that human beings do not possess. This idea of orientation points towards an understanding of being as expressed within a dense network of spatio-temporal relations, whereby different kinds of living things encounter and navigate the world differently.

Space can be contemplated from the perspective of other beings, as Eduardo Viveiros de Castro shows that Amerindian philosophy does. The volume of the world is where life develops and unfolds, and humans are part of the worlds of other animals too and therefore part of *their* spatial understanding. Once grasped, this point seems obvious. When Eduardo Kohn writes that he was told to sleep in a hammock face up, so that jaguars may recognize him as a person and let him live, he is directly drawing on a volumetric, multisensorial, and multispecies concept of space. He is drawing on an *ontological* concept of space.

Building on Merleau-Ponty, space becomes the mode of being in the world, and not an inert background of primarily visual material.[12] Place is then the becoming subject of space, that is to say the coming into a mode of consciousness of what is always already a volume within other volumes (the dynamic assemblage). Just like humans, everything that lives can be in or out of place. Understanding the conditions for fulfilling emplacement is a necessary endeavor for ecological politics.

In grounding the political thesis of mutualism in volumetric space, I am primarily claiming that the issue is not just recreating the possibilities for new, different, and surprising assemblages to emerge.[13] The issue is being able to decide, as collectivities, between different kinds of assemblages. And more than mere assembling is required;[14] it

---

[12] For a thorough and very useful development of the concept of nature in Merleau-Ponty, see Ted Toadvine's (2009) *Merleau-Ponty's Philosophy of Nature*. One of the central tenets of that concept of nature is its duality as both intrinsically human (through human perception), *and* absolutely independent of humans.

[13] This is where the works of Isabelle Stengers, Donna Haraway, Anna Tsing, and Bruno Latour take us, leaving us to find our own path.

[14] Also because, as Rafi Youatt (2020) points out, there is a certain given-ness to assemblages; one is never free to choose the assemblages one is part of, but only somewhat free to modify certain aspects of them. As we find ourselves simultaneously inflated and deflated by the Anthropocene, this becomes a crucial insight.

is a matter of rebuilding genealogies of reciprocity, of resurrecting that cemetery of practices to which Stengers alludes,[15] in full consciousness of the fact that each genealogical link, each embodied practice, sanctions its own way of building communities.

* * *

I want to go back to the idea of nature that I argued, through the work of Debaise, was fundamentally tied to the modern concept of space. This connection notwithstanding, it is also an abstraction that exists above and beyond its association with space. The idea of nature, perhaps even more so than that of space, today carries the project of modernity forward. Despite the ample critiques it has received, it continues to endure. I want to puzzle over how another concept of nature may be born out of the decomposition of the old. Most importantly, we have to understand how a radically multifaceted concept of nature weaves itself through new political arrangements, attempting to facilitate joyful existence in the Ecocene.

To be clear: the point of rethinking notions of space and nature is not to propose new unifying principles. The point is, precisely, to deny the importance of unification at all, and to try to live with uncertainty and multiplicity. The concept of nature, like that of space, has a fundamental role in unifying what are otherwise disparate practices and relegating them to 'the natural realm' such that they become undebatable. Modernity generates a concept of nature that is simultaneously spatialized (the radical outside of modern development, the dumb matter on which it operates) and internalized (as a moral principle equating the natural with the good).

It is important here to note the incoherence of a concept of nature that is simultaneously assimilated to flat space and to the good, and to search for alternatives that would complement volumetric space and structurally refuse to act as grand unifiers. The idea is not to find some sort of concept that can be ready to import into 'our culture', but rather to understand the political valence of concepts, and to look for ones—reinvent them, really—that are ready to be put to work in an

---

15 Stengers (2015, 98): "Certainly we live in a veritable cemetery for destroyed practices and collective knowledges […]".

emancipatory politics of multiplicity. *That* is not to be found anywhere ready-made, and it is a project to be continuously pursued.

One very helpful place to look for conceptions of nature that are not based on the operation of bifurcation is critical anthropology. The concept of multinaturalism is an excellent start, as it opens up possibilities for conceiving of the natural in ways that are inherently human, and vice versa. But it would be a mistake to think that multinaturalism can just be plucked out of its particular genealogical milieu and put to work in undoing modernity. No, the idea is to look for clues that allow us to find practices and conceptions that have stubbornly remained everywhere, despite modern development. Multinaturalism then opens up possibilities of thinking that connect with ideatic ghosts elsewhere, weaving a new conceptual tapestry that cannot come under one name.

As Stengers argues, "the internal colonization of what we call modernity by modernity was never complete. [...] It is time to rearticulate and reassert those sensibilities [that endure] both ethnographically and politically. For other worlds exist, even within modernity" (2018, 158). This points towards the crucial role of an anthropology beyond the orientalist gaze that relegates pre-modernity to 'the indigenous'. Nobody has ever been fully modern, precisely because the typically modern conceptions explored so far do not allow for an actual embodiment. They are resistant to being lived, and this is why modern development is a constant and violent process, as it needs to continuously stamp out what springs forth from the physicality and liveliness of the world. In this sense, it is fine to rearticulate and reassert spectral practices and conceptions, but we need to be careful not to imply that somehow those practices remain whole, not to smuggle in singularity as we critique it and seek multiplicity. It may therefore be better to think about renovating practices. Renovation is always working on an existing foundation, but one that is not fit for habitation unless intervened upon and modified for purpose. Multinaturalism is not a solid foundation, nor is the modern concept of nature; it is simply a direction for renovation, indicating ways in which common worlds can be continuously weaved, while remaining satisfied to never arrive at a final destination.

As Eduardo Viveiros de Castro (2015) presents it, multinaturalism is the idea that the world has no essence beyond the ways in which it appears to different kinds of beings. But the mode of appearance of

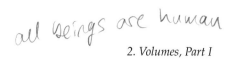
all beings are human

the world is structurally similar across embodiments, which leads the Amerindian philosophies that originated this notion to suppose that all beings are fundamentally human, and therefore fit within their world in ways similar to humans. Saying that all creatures are fundamentally human can be deceiving, because it makes it seem as if the human form is privileged over others. But that is not the case: it is not the human *form* that is similar, but rather the interiority of being as such. It may therefore be more accurate to say that all beings are persons to themselves and to each other because they share in the fundamental fabric of being alive (for more on this see Chapter 3).

This means that the philosophical conceptions De Castro describes consider the way the world is apprehended to be like human apprehension, even through different kinds of embodiment. As Descola explains it, the principle that defines nature is not matter, as in modernity, but rather the existence of a subjective position (what he calls interiority). Every living thing is positioned towards the world and towards other beings, in virtue of being alive and sensing its environment. This positioning, echoing Merleau-Ponty's "orientated being", cannot help but see creaturely life as organized in societies, with largely similar concerns, and populated by people looking different (having different bodies) but sharing in the genealogy of the living. Humans are human by virtue of their bodies, not by virtue of the exceptionalism of their own meaningful lives. A world full of people is therefore not a hierarchical world, but one of degrees of similarity organized more or less horizontally.

The relationships that creatures build with each other are like kin relationships, but not identical to them. The kind of body each creature has is not inconsequential: it mediates the potentialities of the world (of space, if you will) and is both an inter-specific bridge because of its interiority, and a point of irreducible separation. De la Cadena discusses the rapprochement between humans and other kinds of embodiments as conceiving beings as "humans, but not only". She stresses the ontological quality of this 'but not only', as that excess that a body gives to subjective experience, that irreducible difference that paradoxically pulls creatures together while also keeping them within separate domains.

There are several extremely interesting points here that complicate the idea of nature. First, under this reading the *natural world* is not first and foremost nature, but first and foremost *world* (*experiential locality*). This is to say that what characterizes it are not material properties, but rather its ability to be an abode, its capacity of homeliness across a staggering variety of beings. This capacity can be rendered in the language of our previous discussion as the ability of different kinds of volumetric spaces to cohere, despite the fact of their multiplicity. As De Castro reminds us, what is blood to humans is manioc beer to jaguars. Many different kinds of beings have very similar concerns for maintaining friendships, avoiding trouble, feeling at home, and playing.[16] What modernity would characterize as a substance with particular physical properties—blood—is here rendered as an indeterminate potentiality that actualizes itself only by entering into specific kinds of relationships with specific kinds of beings. But what is beyond doubt is the fundamental similarity of the process of relation itself: just like manioc beer is an intoxicant for humans, so too is blood for jaguars.

Each kind of being has its own way of activating the potentialities of the world. This leads to the second important point, which is the idea that in this account of the world, borders and relations are more real than beings themselves, as it were. There is no such thing as blood *as such*, or rather, blood is not the primary mode of appearance of the substance that humans call by that name. Instead, there is nothing solid to the substance outside of how it is enlivened through relationships. On the side of the perceiving beings, De Castro gives the idea of multinaturalism the name of perspectivism, in an effort to convey the inherent changeability of points of view that itself structures the world.

Multinaturalism and its corollary, perspectivism, offer an account of the world that focuses much more on multiplicity and relations than on the permanence of physical properties. "What perspectivism affirms, when all is said and done, is not so much that animals are at bottom like humans but the idea that as humans, they are at bottom something else—they are, in the end, the 'bottom' itself of something, its other side; they are different from themselves" (2015, 69). Just as on the side of 'nature' there are no fixed substances, so too on the side of the experiencing subject there is no inherent subjectivity above and beyond the relationships through which it lives. Humans, in the final analysis,

---

16 The idea of distributed intelligence throughout the natural world has become increasingly supported through ethology (the study of animal behavior) as well.

are not human by virtue of a human essence, but rather by virtue of the specific way in which they differ from themselves. This idea has radical affinities with Deleuze's concept of multiplicity, which is here revealed to be infinite, extending in all directions, making the distinction between things and beings a distinction of degree of intensity, and not one of kind (Deleuze and Guattari 1998).

In this account, self-difference, or infinite multiplicity, is a universal condition, not as an essence, but rather as an operative necessity. The world is a space of infinite virtualities, not all of which can ever be simultaneously actualized. There is, in fact, an infinite multiplicity of virtualities and an infinite possibility of actualization. "Perspectivism affirms an *intensive difference* that places human/nonhuman difference *within each existent*. Each being finds itself separated from itself" (2015, 69, first italics added, second in original). This original non-coincidence makes it impossible to think, ontologically, in non-relational terms. And, importantly, relations between radically multiple terms are themselves radically multiple, changing over time and varying in intensity. As Deleuze argued, "[...] there are no points of view *on* things—it is things and beings that are the points of view" (in de Castro 2015, 110).

The possibility of inter-species communication and understanding is given a new foundation in perspectivism. In principle, a human process of subjectification can enter into specific kinds of relationships with other, non-human processes. These can be evoked by a human subjectivity precisely because they share fundamental processes that are resistant to unification, similar precisely for their multiplicities. "What exists in multinature are not [...] self-identical entities differently perceived but immediately relational multiplicities of the type blood/beer. There exists, if you will, only the limit between blood and beer, the border by which these two 'affinal' substances communicate and diverge" (2015, 73). Borders, then, are fundamental to relational thinking, and qualify it in an important respect: points of separation are internal to being, and therefore to the manifestations of virtuality.

All of this points towards an apparent impossibility, namely that of knowing with any degree of certainty the make-up of the world, or the positionality of any particular being, including one's own. And this is precisely how the space of politics is rejuvenated by the ideas of multinaturalism and perspectivism: they point towards conceptual possibilities that are anchored (though they need not be anchored in the same way) in infinite multiplicity and the structural necessity of ignorance. Acting in the world is always, on this account, a negotiation of uncertainty.[17] It is only from the point of view of a politics that dogmatically presupposes stable foundations that action through uncertainty becomes problematic. From the perspective developed here, structural ignorance and multiplicity are themselves conditions of possibility for meaningful action.

Ontologically, as De Castro himself argues, there can be no mutual relations across species, because of the instability of beings themselves. But politically, as far as humans are concerned (*all* humans, so nonhumans seen from their own point of view as well), there *must* be mutualism because it is the only thing that keeps relations flowing such that the relative stability of beings remains relatively stable.[18] He suggests (70) that "man and wolf cannot be man (or wolf) simultaneously". Ontologically, indeed. But politically, this is precisely the task. *Politics is the negotiation of this impossible simultaneity.*

* * *

"Now the colonizers are as threatened as the world they displaced and destroyed when they took over what they called *terra nullius*" (De la Cadena and Blaser 2018, 3).

From a modern perspective, nature is disappearing before our very eyes. The flat spaces of modernity can no longer accommodate the dreams of progress and emancipation from brute natural forces. The intrusion of Gaia has permanently destabilized this kind of project of emancipation and, as a result, the modern world is decomposing. The process of decomposition will surely be long and studded with an increasing number of 'crises', moments that are read as potentially fatal and that must, under all circumstances, be overcome. But a profusion of crises is nothing other than the dissolution of a particular kind of world. It is the modern world, as it has come to dominate the globe, that is now dissolving.

---

17 For a democratic and pragmatic treatment of the problem of uncertainty, see Callon, Lascoumes and Barthe (2011), *Acting in an Uncertain World*.

18 For an evolutionary argument for mutualism, compatible with this discussion, see the development of Kropotkin's thought in Chapter 7.

In a strange temporal inversion, events of natural history are accelerated, while human history seems stuck in a mode of psychological acceleration and empirical inertia. In other words, the decomposition of modernity may be a longer process than the intrusion of Gaia would suggest. When the glaciers and ice sheets are all melted, we may as well still be fighting against the idea of development. Nietzsche recognized the death of God a century and a half ago, but we are still struggling with the consequences. Similarly, the death of modernity need not mean that it will no longer be felt.

The trouble with holding on to modernist concepts while living in and with the decomposition of modernity is that it leaves one unable to do much other than mourn the inevitable loss. To the already massive loss of alternative and non-human worlds that modernity has caused, is now added the loss of the modern world itself. This palpable sense of loss is increasingly felt in the old centers of the modern world, often refracted through issues and concerns that might at first seem removed from the disappearance of a surefooted rootedness in the modern project. The arrival of the Ecocene has provoked new kinds of reaction. One of the most significant so far has been a sort of denial (Malm 2018, Latour 2017, 2018), that is to say a stubborn continuation of practices and ways of thinking that are constitutive of the generalized ecological crisis. Denial expresses itself differently among different groups. Two of the most dominant forms have been either triumphalist idiocy (continue accelerating, nothing is wrong!), or ecomodernist delusion (acceleration will solve everything and finally set us free!).

The populist right has made it a badge of honor, as Latour has shown, to deny the reality of the intrusion of Gaia.[19] Their response to this intrusion is one of doubling back, partly because so few resources seem to be available for living differently and composing different worlds. The response to migration, for example, has to be understood as the response of someone that is no longer surefooted in his own home, someone that is displaced within his own place of origin, someone that shares in part the condition of displacement that sparks migration. The potential host of the migrant is himself radically destabilized. The resurgence of nativism at the dawn of the Ecocene indicates precisely

---

19 Andreas Malm has become one of the starkest critics of Latour's work. However, despite their considerable differences, both of their analyses of climate change reach this same conclusion.

the untenability of nativism itself: there is no land to forever call one's own, and it is this uncomfortable fact that ignites a desperate search for versions of belonging.

The ways in which the Anthropocene has entered popular discourse does not help much. Borrowed unproblematically from geology, talk of the Anthropocene so often abstracts us from the lived reality of individual beings and instead professes techno-managerial solutions that treat everything instrumentally. For example, geo-engineering the climate to reflect more sunlight into space and therefore have a cooling effect, or technology that would suck CO_2 from the atmosphere and reverse global warming. Tellingly, these kinds of technological fixes are already part of climate negotiations, on the assumption that they will be deployed (for now, carbon capture more so than geo-engineering).

As any given experience of the world becomes subsumed under 'geological forces' and their attendant grand solutions, the generalized feeling of displacement advances. This adds to the feeling of loss a nostalgia for what, in truth, has never existed: a surefootedness that has always been mythologically constructed. The condition of displacement has to be thought as a passage from one manner of composition to another, and not as a nostalgic fold.

Together with rampant denialism, the ways in which the Anthropocene has so far been considered has also led to an ecomodernist insistence on the necessity to continue the project of modernity. The idea there—best exemplified by the work of the Breakthrough Institute—is that the Anthropocene is simply a problem of using the wrong kind of fuel, and generally the wrong kind of matter, for achieving what are otherwise legitimate goals of radically separating 'humans' from 'nature'. The way to achieve this ultimate goal (permanent bifurcation) is by 'decoupling' economic growth from material constraints. The idea of decoupling makes very clear what the ultimate goal of ecomodernism is: protecting the legitimacy of economic growth. To think that growth can be sustained indefinitely because it can be separated from matter seems entirely delusional, and it is in this sense that ecomodernism is just another form of denialism. Ecomodernists assume what they want to achieve, namely a complete separation of human societies from material arrangements. The circularity of the argument should be enough to discredit it, but unfortunately it isn't, simply because ecomodernism is convenient for those that are invested in the continuation of the modernist status quo.

In order to take on the challenge of recomposing worlds in the wake of the great modern decomposition, increased attention has to be paid to the minor realities (Hage 2012) that have always coexisted with the major, hegemonic ones. These kinds of reality are easily overlooked, for two contrasting reasons. On the one hand, as Hage shows, they are often found in critical anthropological encounters with what appears to be radical difference that, nonetheless, manages to be thought and to destabilize thinking itself. On the other hand, minor realities are overlooked because of how familiar and obvious they are. This is the kind of blindness that familiarity breeds. Included in this category, for example, are practices of communication with plants and animals that have always suffused modern cultures, or practices that take our ancestors into account. It is in those cemeteries where ghosts live that we may find ways of thinking sideways and recomposing at livable scales.

Both of these difficulties must be turned into allies of recomposition. Both the radically different and the unimportant and routine can be conjoined in articulating new kinds of worlds. In fact, these two movements are more similar than they first appear. As Chapters 4 and 5 will show in much more detail, critical anthropology and the interstices of modernity itself often stumble upon very similar means of recomposition. In particular, we need minor realities that articulate an ethics through which we can build resilient infrastructures of reciprocity. These hold the promise of building new life alongside the tribulations to come.

INTERMEZZO I
Loss and Recomposition Part I

Olive Trees and People

The intimacy between people and environments is always rooted somewhere. We are always talking about specific relations that, though open-ended and ever-changing, manage to give rise to identifiable forms. This is most clearly seen in the way in which certain features of the world become symbolic for wider practices that, despite their evolution, maintain a kind of identity through time, allowing for both change and continuity. In a Southern European context, there is hardly a more potent symbol of this relational identity than the olive tree.

Considered in terms of its nature, *Olea europaea* is not a tree at all, but a hardy shrub. Where it grows 'naturally' is beside the point, as its history of human use is so long and profound as to make that question all but irrelevant. The image that most people are familiar with, of a magnificent gnarly tree, is entirely a product of its interaction with its human neighbors. Without constant and iterative interaction, the olive tree as a tree is an impossibility. But even to call the olive plant *a* tree is misleading. The domesticated olive is grafted on to wild stock, so in any particular case we are always already talking about a double composition. This is before we consider the common phenomena of these plants growing into each other, or splitting into (what seems to humans to be) different organisms.

Grafting the olive plant on to wild stock (*olea oleaster*) results in a constructed being whose life connects with an unknown number of different participants. Each year, the base grows shoots that, if left alone, develop into tall and tough stems that reach into the light. Similarly, the grafted part develops shoots that also strive to fill the sun-laden openings of the canopy. Left to its own devices, then, the domestic-wild hybrid develops as a thick network of shoots that fan out in all directions, producing a mass of vegetation, a tangled mess of tall and impenetrable branches without any clear preference for the 'wild' or the 'domestic'.

* * *

The very existence of the olive plant as a hybrid already points towards the absurdity of letting it develop on its own terms. *Olea* has, since antiquity, been meant as an interactive partner, and the basis of the interaction, its fundamental structure, is ruled by the behavior of the plant assemblage when left to its own devices. It is only by understanding this behavior that people can intervene in a way that creates novel and productive assemblages. In other words, it is only by paying close attention that people and olive trees can mutually determine.

Pruning is the primary act through which the relationship between people and *olea europaea* is enacted. There are many possible descriptions of the act of pruning, which is deceptively simple: selectively cutting branches. People may prune for the tree's health, or for a good harvest, or for reasons of beauty or respecting tradition. People have pruned according to the dominant technology of harvest, creating forks in the trunk in order to lay the head of the ladder when that method was dominant. Similarly, people may prune in order to favor the growth of low external branches, especially if they harvest the fruits by hand. Pruning may be done in order to corral the tree into shapes fit for the harvesting machines of monocultures. No matter what reason any particular person may give, the act of pruning is generative of both a particular kind of plant, and a particular kind of human.

That act of olive-human generation is contingent because it cannot be overdetermined by what one actor does. The tree will always express itself in ways that surprise the person interacting with it. And the person may change their behavior accordingly, but the tree will never fit a particular mould flawlessly. No matter how hard one may try to control the tree's shape once and for all—the plantation being the ultimate example of this—repeated pruning will be necessary, precisely because the plant has a mind of its own.

Pruning is always an invitation from one actor (the person) to another (the tree) to continue acting, but the tree also encourages pruning at particular times of year and dissuades it at others. When a branch is cut, this act entails expectations about how the tree will respond. The selection of those responses becomes the basis for future acts of pruning, in a reiterative process that, over decades and centuries, leaves its mark in the tree's shape, the soil, and on human generations.

In order to prune well, one must first and foremost pay attention to the plant itself. Not only is every plant different, but there are general rules of well-being that apply to olive trees and that the human partner must respect. In other words, there is such a thing as being an olive plant, and that specific form of being comes with its own requirements and preferences. The human partner must pay close attention to these preferences in order to enter the relationship in a generative, as opposed to destructive, way.

The preferences of the olive plant have to do with light (sun), moisture (wind), the presence of varied vegetation, cycles of vegetative hibernation (when to cut), the presence of disease (insects, fungi, bacteria) as well as of other animals. As a rule, the olive is a sun-lover. When contemplating a plant, it is obvious that the healthiest parts are those high up, where the leaves are basked in constant and powerful sunshine. Light is but one ingredient, because the plant also likes to keep itself dry. This also contributes to the health of higher leaves, which benefit from the drying effects of the breeze. Sun and a relative absence of humidity contribute to a reduction in pests that attack the plant, damaging its tissues. But what is seen above ground is merely half of the plant; the rest is buried in the soil, a medium completely different from the airy, sunlit atmosphere. The olive plant literally partakes in two distinct and completely different domains, and the careful observer will look at the ground as much as the canopy when caring for an olive tree.

Unlike the dryness of the air, the soil needs to contain a level of moisture that allows the plant to remain hydrated throughout the year. This is no easy feat, and the olive tree is very tolerant of dry conditions, though this does not mean that it prefers them, or that there isn't a significant cost to prolonged drought. One of the ways to maintain moisture in the soil is to encourage a rich community of species that provides literal cover to the ground, thus reducing evaporation. Life, as Lovelock, Margulis, and lately Latour have pointed out, is good at creating the conditions of its own reproduction, and in this regard the relationship between a rich plant community and the soil is instructive. Varied ground vegetation, combined with olive and other fruiting trees, can maintain the humidity of the soil much better than a vegetation-free monoculture (Calabrese et al. 2015, Selosse 2021).

In the middle of Puglia, Southern Italy, the process of soil creation has been instrumental to human life for a long time. In the limestone hills known as the Murgia, the terrain made it very difficult for big landowners to enclose the land, as they had done elsewhere (most notably in the plains both North and South of the Murgia, where soil was more plentiful and easily accessible). Partly because of the difficult terrain, which made soil scarce and complicated to access, peasant families gained rights to their own plots of land relatively early on in history (starting in the eighteenth century; Galt 1986, 1991). But what they gained rights to was more often than not a rocky land that was difficult to cultivate because of the scarcity of soil.[1] However, over generations of labor, rocks were removed from the land and fashioned into farmhouses and low-lying walls, themselves instrumental in keeping soil within designated areas.[2] Through practices of crop rotation, vineyard tending (the dominant plant throughout the nineteenth century), tree plantation (most notably olives, but also almonds, figs, pomegranates, and cherries), and the rearing of animals, soil was created where little existed before.[3] If there is an olive culture to speak of today in this region, it is because of a history of soil generation that hovers over the present.

Inasmuch as there is a relationship to the land in this particular region, it exists because of the inheritance of soil as much as trees. But many of the techniques used in the past for soil creation (especially the use of manure from domestic animals) are threatened today, largely because of

---

1   The process of land acquisition by peasant families happened through the institution of emphyteusis, which gave peasants heritable land rights in exchange for labor. "Emphyteusis is a type of perpetual lease in which, in exchange for an annual rent, the tenant retains rights to the land and can pass them on to his heirs" (Galt 1986, 442). By the early-nineteenth century, some towns—like Locorotondo—had two-thirds of their residents living in the surrounding countryside, a highly unusual situation in the history of Southern Italy. See Galt 1991.
2   The walls enclosing lands in the Murgia have been shown to not only reduce erosion (during heavy rains), but also to keep moisture within the soil for longer. They also offer valuable habitat to countless insects and reptiles.
3   Also see discussion of people *as* soil in Chapter 5.

the same forces that have imposed monocultures elsewhere. There are pockets of resistance that continue to generate soils and care for those already there, through practices that look towards ancestral traditions while inventing new ways of interaction. This is not a Netherlands-like situation of land *reclamation*, parceled out in neat plots that are equivalent in their abstractness. This is a region of mosaic landscapes and micro-climates, every little spot impossible to understand outside of a history of generative interaction, and outside of a familiarity with *that* spot.

The existence of soil provides the possibility for an olive culture to exist. The intergenerational act of soil creation has literally made a living out of stone. This kind of ingenuity was occasioned by necessity, and the land is pockmarked with evidence of creative uses that go back over ten thousand years. The olive tree has been an indispensable partner in the transformation of local conditions of existence. It is as if Margulis and Lovelock's insight that life generates its own conditions is here consciously pursued, in a partnership that is often expressed through material relations that affect all participants.

Because of the highly complex assemblage that nurtures the health of an olive tree, the act of pruning is highly ritualized; it is sacred. In Vale D'Itria, itself a microregion of the Murgia, the *potatore* is not just anybody. Seasoned olive farmers will not touch their trees for pruning purposes, instead deferring to the authority and the knowledge of a *potatore*. An expert pruner may start by looking at the soil, paying attention to the myriad relationships that are generative of the plant, before examining the canopy in order to read the signs that the plant is producing. In any case, interventions on a particular plant are not made for immediate results: it is always a future, imagined tree, that informs actions in the present. In this way there is a deferential relationship to time, the present being thinned out to the moment of intervention, allowing instead the life history of the plant to directly influence its future existence.

Pruning reunites death and life, as it is through cutting (eliminating from the flow of life-giving lymph) that the conditions for new life are generated. Not just any cutting will do; it has to be clean, sharp, precise, and respectful. The tools used for this operation have to be carefully sharpened and inspected in order to minimize the damage that is always a risk. In many different kinds of trees (oaks for example) in

Europe, longevity is a feature of this kind of interaction with humans (see Rackham 2020). Pruning greatly increases the lifetime of these trees. It appears that, from the point of view of the tree, pruning is an act of rejuvenation. The *potatore* has to navigate the narrow margin between regeneration and decay by performing her craft with care and patience. The result is not only younger and healthier trees, paradoxically marching forwards and backwards in time, but also the bequeathal of an inheritance that obliges future generations to pay attention too.[4]

In the modern world, many characterize the act of pruning as based entirely on the economy of yield. In other words, one prunes in order to have fruit. In fact, pruning decreases yield in the year immediately following the intervention. It does, overall, increase yield, but good pruning is not about this exclusively, nor even primarily. One prunes for olives, but also for one's children, for the beauty of the land, for the health of the soil,[5] to heat oneself during winter, to make great food,[6] for the longevity and beauty of the tree, out of a sense of duty for a land etched with mutual genealogies. Given pruning's central role in the relationship with the olive tree, it is impossible to explain it with instrumental reasoning; it resists, escapes, and overflows mere reasons, pointing towards the rich tapestry of reciprocity that can be articulated around it.

* * *

The community of plants that grow in the olive grove forms an integral part of the health of the soil, which is also dependent on a rich invertebrate and vertebrate community that helps the olive tree flourish. Before the advent of industrial modernity, there wasn't really an olive grove to speak of, because olive trees were planted far away from each other such that many different cultures could be accommodated between

---

4   The figure of the potatore is an inherited idea as much as a contemporary practice. Becoming an expert pruner is hard, and increasingly harder under monocultural conditions and purely aesthetic pruning (for example, for tourist consumption of landscapes). The potatore is rare, and careful pruning a practice apt for renovation.

5   The thin branches and foliage that result from pruning are excellent organic material that, in time, can become new soil.

6   Certain branches (of particular thickness) cut during pruning are considered to be excellent fuel for the ovens that dot the region. This use of olive wood in cooking is most famously displayed in the region of Naples, where the best Neapolitan pizza has to be cooked in an oven fired with olive wood.

them. Another reason for this distance was as a barrier to disease transmission, a social distancing for olive trees *avant la lettre*. In Puglia, the oldest olive trees are always found far apart from each other, often in what resemble haphazard formations, certainly not following the idea of a grid (suggested, in many ways, by the advent of mechanization; it is first and foremost the machine that finds the grid useful). This way of planting was also a result of individuals paying attention to the tree over generations and noticing that an iterative relationship with human beings allowed it to grow to impressive sizes. Trees were planted far apart such that, when they reached their slow maturity, they would still allow a varied plant community to grow between them, helping them stay healthy.

This is why even today, when this kind of olive culture has been relegated to memory, one says that olive trees are planted for one's grandchildren. This expression is itself a fertile, ghostly presence in the cemetery of practices produced by industrialization. It is repeated as a trope, but it can easily turn from a cliché into the memory of its original impetus: the ancestral knowledge that indeed obliged one to plant for their grandchildren.[7]

The act of generation that the human-olive relationship embodies is inscribed within a particular time, that is to say, it both takes time and generates new temporalities, new lifetimes, for those involved (including those that are bequeathed their role in generative processes). In the relationship between people and olive trees, it is the person that needs to adapt to the time of the tree. This is a feature of paying attention: the relationship between a being that can live for millennia and one that can at best span a century is necessarily tilted in favor of the longer timeframe. Or rather, this is the case inasmuch as the potential life span of the tree is part of the multi-generational human-olive relationship.

Modernity has questioned and attempted to transform most of the fundamental aspects of the human-olive relationship based on mutual beneficence and careful attention. The project of developing an olive industry, through successive and ongoing pressure, has meant the radical severance of the ability to pay attention to trees. This has resulted in a landscape of olive monoculture; in Puglia, the oldest specimens are

---

[7] I am indebted for much of this discussion to Nuccio Chialá, who continues to generously share memories and stubbornly resist their programmatic erasure.

now often engulfed by a sea of smaller trees, all pruned and 'managed' for maximum yield. Because the olive plant cannot be considered in isolation, plucked from the rich milieu that expresses it, the modern olive industry has also radically simplified the soil and the plant communities that nurture it. Instead of rich entanglements of varied species, including humans, we now have desertified monocultures of struggling trees, managed by humans (who, it turns out, are not very good at being managers in this sense).

The modern move towards monoculture has gone hand in hand with the adoration of so-called 'monumental' trees (Puglia has a registry of thousands of them). The word 'monumental' already ossifies them into sterile monuments to the past, works of art celebrating idealized fictions that only really work to support an increasingly untenable status quo. The monumental olive trees of Puglia have become fetishized in tandem with the expansion of modern development. This is familiar, as the radical simplification of ecological processes that is instrumental to modern development has always given rise to a romantic imagination elevating the past to the role of some impossible model. This works to naturalize development, by acknowledging (but crucially misplacing) its often tragic consequences.

The acceleration of modernity causes the greatest rupture in the relationship between people and olives, as people are no longer able to pay attention to trees on their own temporal terms. An excellent example of this is the outbreak (started in 2013) of *Xylella fastidiosa*, a bacterial pathogen, in olive groves in Southern Puglia. Coming in the wake of modern development that had left soils and plants radically weakened, *Xylella* has killed millions of trees in just a few years. The often-abstract acceleration of modern times in this case takes a physical form and a measurable pace, with plants that have stood for centuries dying in a matter of mere years, the tree equivalent of a generalized heart attack. A relationship spanning millennia was brought to an abrupt halt.

Or was it? The modernist response to the literal sickening of the relationship between people and olives has been to accelerate further! Research into *Xylella* has entailed looking for cures that enable the overall model of development to continue. This has precedents elsewhere: the grapevines of California have been struggling with the bacterium for decades, and research there has also focused massively on eliminating everything that harbors the pathogen, in the interest of a land-culture geared exclusively towards wine production, at all costs.[8] Similarly, 'ecological' research in Southern Puglia has brought about a radical reduction of ecological complexity, which in its turn has reduced the complexity of an already impoverished land.

Besides attempting to control the pathogen directly, research has also focused on finding (and increasingly, making) varieties that are resistant to the bacterium. Two have been identified, one of which seems to fit the project of modernity perfectly. The Favolosa variety (FS-17) is supposed to grow fast, produce incredible amounts of fruit in 'high density' plantations, and be resistant to disease. The variety was created in Central Italy towards the end of the twentieth century, a period coinciding with the aggressive expansion of industrialized agriculture. It is marketed as a miracle plant (hence the name Favolosa), and one especially suited to mechanization. Industrial plantations of this variety look more like grapevines without the terraces: neat lines of low trees along which a specialized machine can proceed and suck the olives into giant containers.

Even though specifically bred for mechanization and industrialization, Favolosa still resists its fate. It is pruned in order to continuously fit the machines designed to take the place of people, but eventually, after mere decades, the proportion of wood to young branches (where the olives grow) no longer makes economic sense. In other words, the tree tries to grow and, constantly impeded from doing so, rebels against its imprisonment through the very constitution of its body. The result is the rooting out of the 'old' plantation and the beginning of another.

Imported into Southern Puglia after *Xylella*, Favolosa seemingly accomplished the final annihilation of genealogically based olive-people relationships. It appeared to deliver olive culture from the death throes caused by an epidemic (officially conceived of as a mere accident of fate). In fact, it entrenched the project of modern simplification further, which is what may ultimately extinguish olive culture, replacing it with a carefully annotated map of "monumental olive trees" one may visit, if they survive *Xylella*.

---

8   In the Californian case, the management of *Xylella* has been successful in the sense that it permits the wine industry to endure, through programmatic interventions to control the pathogen in perpetuity.

In the case of Favolosa, what has for centuries given olive trees their characteristic allure—their thick, twisted trunks—becomes an impediment to efficient production. This variety is the result of the relationship between machines and laboratory science, as opposed to olive growers and the land. When someone chooses to plant Favolosa in order to replace older trees killed by *Xylella*, they are moving even further away from a history of soil generation and care, and towards a fantasy of mechanical domination that can only end in tragedy.

The modernist answer to the plight of olive trees in Puglia is a dead end, leading to further ruin. Instead, there are other ways of rethinking olive culture along lines that reconvene both the past and scientific knowledge. But the point is that the Ecocene calls for reinvention. This is precisely the meaning of thinking ecologically, that is to say, of basing one's thought and actions in the fact of change, as opposed to the certainty of permanence. Even secular olive trees can die, and we are now required to reinvent practices that ritualize without fetishizing, produce without stripping everything away, and build dynamic genealogies that can sustain the very idea of a future. We must live through tragedy, and that requires the courage of not knowing what a future generative relationship will look like.

* * *

Despite the accelerated modernization of olive culture in Puglia, not every mode of relation has been severed, and not everything has been forgotten. Stengers' cemetery of practices is visible and alive, in the form of ghosts, through different uses of language and now-marginal practices. It is also alive in the bodies of olive trees themselves, etched as they are by generations of pruning and caring.

Every olive tree of a certain age is what it is because of past practices, and how it continues its life will be decided in partnership with current and future humans. This imbrication of olives and people means that past practices are etched on to the body of the tree, but often in ways that are not easily discerned. In other words, past practices are logically necessary to suppose, but opaque, because one can only guess at what happened in a past that is made present through the body of the tree. This both makes it easy to invent traditions that are in fact self-serving, quickly assimilated into modern development, and enable the renovation and reinvention of practices that decidedly break with modernity. It is easy to delude oneself that one's actions are beneficial to the tree, especially in the context of a modernity that has to some extent sickened all minds. The discovery of pasts etched within trees also allows us to rediscover habits of mind that help us to step outside of our own bodies and narrow interests.

The olive tree in Puglia is in many respects similar to the cow for the Maasai, described by David Western (2020) as a common denominator, that which *everyone* has as a connection to the land and to each other.[9] That kind of *de facto* connection has survived alongside, or perhaps despite, the industrialization of olive culture. It also points to a ghost that takes the form of caring; even the owner of tens of thousands of trees grown in high-density plantations may repeat the mantra that an olive tree is planted for one's grandchildren. This kind of cognitive dissonance is easy to fault, but the point is that the presence of olive trees *themselves* ensures the transmission of a phantasm with very specific, but mysterious, forms.

As in all other areas of human intercourse with the multiplicity of worlds, olive culture is living through a phase of decomposition and experimentation. The death and destruction wrought by *Xylella* is but the most visible trace of this process of decomposition which is in fact much better placed within the context of the dawning Ecocene. The crucial point is an ability to discern what to take up from an opaque past that is nonetheless physically present through the bodies of the trees, and how to invent ways of living together that are regenerative. Signs of this process of renovation are discernable in many different locations,

---

9 This reality is beautifully expressed by Fabio Gatti (2019) in his wonderful work on the subject: "More than the olive tree alone, what is also extremely important in Apulia is the result of its cultivation: olive oil. This is not the place for describing the richness of properties of olive oil, which some people consider comparable to a medicine, as well as describing in detail the art of olive oil making. What matters here is to stress how important olive oil is in Apulian culture: every year, thousands of people gather in the countryside for collecting olives and bringing them to the oil mill. Not all of them are actual farmers, people who make a living out of olive farming and olive oil production. Many of them, including me, just make the olive oil they need for family consumption, from pieces of land belonging to the family and inherited over the years. It is a feast: at the end of the harvest it is very common to see families and friends gathering around a meal and tasting the first, rigorously raw, olive oil of the season. It is a ritual which keeps the memory of the family alive, a collective act of remembrance" (2019, 13).

usually at small scales that are not a fault but a feature of successful recomposition.

Pruning, it should be no surprise, is yet again a good lens for observing this process of recomposition at work. What, in this most crucial of acts, is to be recuperated, and what will be invented? In this regard, there are some partial answers from often surprising sources. For example, agronomical research (no stranger to modern development, of course) has borne proposals for pruning techniques that strive to respect the physiognomy of the plant (Proietti et al. 2008). What these techniques recuperate from the past is the attention paid to the context of a particular tree, and they therefore end up agreeing with 'traditional' practices as to, for example, the extent of pruning (traditionally—no more than would allow a bird to fly through the canopy; scientifically—no more than 30% of the overall volume of the canopy). At the same time, these techniques are marketed as increasing yield, which is a dangerous way of promoting something that could be much better characterized in terms of a meaningfulness of connection with the land.

In other respects, what is billed as traditional goes against the physiognomy of the tree, and is instead rooted in an inheritance of form, rather than substance. For example, many in the past used to lower the height of their trees by severing the topmost branches of the canopy (all of them) to the desired height. This operation was convenient because more olives grew closer to the ground, where they could more easily be accessed, but it is inimical to the needs of the tree. Olive tree health is to a great extent determined by the relationship between the top of the canopy and the roots, which are in constant communication as to environmental conditions and physiological needs. Indiscriminately cutting the guiding parts of the crown is like blindfolding the tree, which now has fewer senses to use in dealing with its environment. Despite this, many still practice this form of beheading, precisely because of its traditional credentials.

The Ecocene is greatly complicating the meaning of tradition in other ways, too. One of the key ways in which traditional practices have been passed on is through the association of certain activities with certain calendar dates, usually marked by religious ceremonies. Some activities, such as harvesting, cannot be accomplished in one day, and are therefore given a range, passed on through aphorisms such as "you shall not harvest before Saint Stephen's Day". These kinds of injunctions or prohibitions continue to exist, for everything from pruning, to harvesting, to planting particular crops. However, their usefulness is continuously diminishing under conditions of heightened ecological change. The reason as to why Saint Stephen's Day was a good indication of the appropriateness of a certain activity was precisely the regularity of the patterns that dominated the Holocene. Within that routine, human activities enjoyed a wide margin of error.

That margin of error is continuously being narrowed by the Ecocene. Every environment is currently changing in ways that make old calendar injunctions less and less applicable. This heightens the need for reinvention, and for fastidiousness. The question of what is to be recuperated and renovated has become more urgent, and also requires us to observe current conditions much more carefully. It is increasingly likely that the pruning schedule of two centuries ago is no longer applicable today. The best guide as to the new conditions remain the olive trees themselves, which have no dogmatic allegiance to particular ways of acting. A renewed relationship with them can guide both partners through the narrowing conditions of the Ecocene.

Between the supposedly new and the traditional, individual olive growers are left to discern for themselves, or through small collectives, what it may mean to care for a plant currently threatened by so many different factors. Notably, the traditional area of politics—institutions of the state at all levels—has shown itself incapable of anything other than piggybacking on whatever the 'economic' imperative may be. In the case of *Xylella*, for example, the Italian political apparatus, from national to regional and communal levels, has not managed to devise a varied methodology of engagement with the territory that would empower individual care. It has been blind to things like soil or plant health, pinning all of its hopes (and research money) on finding miracle cures and planting extensive monocultures of *Xylella*-resistant varieties.

Of course, an olive grove that is appropriately cared for may still die from *Xylella*. To say that trees grown under certain conditions cannot succumb to *Xylella* paradoxically reproduces the consequentialist, resource-focused logic of modern development. If you do enough of x, then you are insured against fate and its potential ills. But the possibility of living with tragedy is precisely what needs to be recuperated in the

Ecocene. What happens when the trees that I did care for, in every minute regard, die? Decomposition is not a process that one can choose to sidestep because one has followed the correct procedure. No, it is a process that invades and forces readjustments and reinventions, based first and foremost on the lucidity of loss. In other words, if we abandon the consequentialist logic of—practice *x*: insurance against disaster—how do we relate to the land? Is there anything left when the illusion of hope is refused? Are there other bases, besides development, hopefulness, and technical fixes for structural problems, that can sustain a livable, joyful future?

One possible answer lies within the history of soil creation that is part and parcel of human relationships with olive trees in the Murgia. That history has slowly mutated, under the influence of modern development, to one of soil destruction, weakening every single participant in the complex network of relationships that literally takes root within healthy soils. Restoring practices of soil creation cannot guarantee, in the short term, any particular results. In other words, it is not the case that any particular farmer can simply create rich soils in order to obviate the threat of, for example, *Xylella*. But it is the case that, as more and more farmers reinvent practices of soil enhancement, they are also bequeathing to future generations the very possibility of thriving. It may be that future generations would, in certain regions, have tragically lost the inheritance of olive trees. But inasmuch as restoration of the very basis of life can become a fundamental concern, they are sure to receive the conditions for reinventing practices on their own terms.

3. Volumes, Part II

Lives

Modernity is where human exceptionalism has thrived—the idea that humans are special among nature's creatures, simply by virtue of being human. This amounts to a secularized theology, where people are God-like, even in the absence of an explicit creator. Ecological thinking is rendered impossible by this founding assumption of a difference in kind between people and everything else.

Sideways, small thinking that pays attention to multiplicity requires us to complicate the idea of living, whether this means the idea of a human or of anything else. Thankfully, many have already started doing this work, and in this chapter, I want to take stock of several crucial ideas for re-dimensioning humans in the Ecocene. I also want to offer several others that I think can make good allies.

Any embodied being must exist within a network of relationships: it is strictly impossible to conceive of radically solitary embodiment. This fact forces us to start our investigation with the interplay of lives and their surrounding worlds, because without a world it is impossible to consider lives. What does this interplay look like if the world is voluminous and fundamentally mysterious?

One route into this problem is given by the resurgence of the concept of Gaia in a series of works concerned with the Anthropocene. In particular, Isabelle Stengers and Bruno Latour have inherited this concept from James Lovelock and Lynn Margulis, transforming it—as good heirs do—into something else, namely a concept more amenable to politics than the original. But before we get to the political implications of Gaia, it is useful to take stock of how it first appeared.

Lovelock is widely credited with the creation of Gaia theory. As he recounts the genesis of his own thought in *The Ages of Gaia* (1995), it all started at NASA, where he was employed to help in the mission of finding life on Mars. He considered the work of his other colleagues unsuited to the task, because of the methods they were employing, which were more or less biased by their expectations of a fundamental similarity between life on different planets. He therefore formulated his own hypothesis:

> [...] the most certain way to detect life on planets was to analyze their atmospheres. [...] life on a planet would be obliged to use the atmosphere and oceans as conveyors of raw materials and depositories for the products of its metabolism. This would change the chemical composition of the atmosphere so as to render it recognizably different from the atmosphere of a lifeless planet (1995, 5)

This idea suggested to him that Mars was indeed a dead planet, as it had a stable atmosphere that indicated the lack of living organisms that would modify it through their metabolic interactions with the environment. As a kind of control for this hypothesis, he started looking at the atmosphere of the Earth, which is characterized by fluctuations that are explained through the activity of the living. It is well known, for example, that the atmosphere of the Earth at the beginning of life, a little less than four billion years ago, was devoid of oxygen. Anaerobic bacteria are the first ones to have appeared in the ocean, but their evolution gave rise to other kinds of bacteria that produced oxygen as a result of their interaction with the environment. This great event is the origin of oxygen on earth, a gas that is poisonous to the first inhabitants of the planet. Indeed, anaerobic bacteria survive today, but only inasmuch as they do not come into contact with this deadly gas.

On Earth, gases "are in a persistent state of disequilibrium". Current release of CO_2 through the burning of fossil fuels is a case in point: human metabolism with the environment is producing by-products—CO_2—that are radically modifying the atmosphere. The basic process is what has gone on since the beginning of life on Earth. It is the quantities that we are injecting into the atmosphere that are so dangerous for our own thriving.

Lovelock therefore argues that organisms create the conditions of their own flourishing, which is strictly true. But they can only do so if there is an abundance of creatures: "life could not exist on a planet sparsely, except at the beginning or the end of its tenure", because there needs to be a critical mass of interactions with the environment and between organisms in order to have a discernable effect on the atmosphere, and therefore on the conditions of life itself. "The evolution of the species and the evolution of their environment are tightly coupled together as a single and inseparable process". Lovelock concludes that Gaia is a living superorganism, and this conclusion has generated controversy and facile dismissals of his overall insights.[1]

The original formulation of the Gaia hypothesis relies on systems thinking, and therefore is at the scale of the planet as such. It is crucial to note that this scale is only possible because of the Earth's provincialism within the Universe. It is only because the Earth is one among many planets that the global scale of analysis can exist. If there was nothing else but the Earth, it would not be possible to conceive of a global scale. So even the largest scale of analysis really gets its force from being conceptualized in relation to something else that renders it 'local' in some sense. Within the global therefore rests the demand to think locally, which is something that I have argued an ecologically grounded politics requires.

This pull towards the surface of the planet was eminently followed through in the work of Lynn Margulis. She was instrumental in developing the idea of Gaia together with Lovelock, but in addition to focusing on the whole system as the unit of analysis, she also developed the thought of particular interactions and the ways in which organisms cannot be considered individuals, an idea that I will come back to later. The only true individuals, she argues, are bacteria. Beyond that, there are only relationships and processes, a comfortable disequilibrium between creatures and environments, which become inseparable.

Throughout her career, she has shown how what appears to be an individual creature is always co-created. This kind of diffused symbiosis means that creatures never evolve, never change as individuals, but rather as unlikely concrescences in a perpetual exchange of roles, attributes, services, and so on. This feat is also accomplished through

---

1 Dismissal of the Gaia hypothesis is common in social science, perhaps more so than in the physical sciences. It is usually not argued for, but relied upon for the supposed obvious absurdity of the hypothesis. For example, Malm (2018), in critiquing Latour, takes it as a sign of the latter's weak arguments that he relies on Gaia's "discredited" idea. This is simply not true—the idea is not discredited; if anything, it is becoming more and more important.

the exchange of genetic material, a discovery that seriously questions the primacy of genes in what are called individuals. The view of life that Margulis championed is an enchanted one that cannot be abstracted from generative interactions; it is nothing but generative interactions.

The genesis of the idea of Gaia is important in order to understand how it develops into political theory. Stengers and Latour each have their particular versions of Gaia, and I will mostly rely on Stengers' conception. However, I want to first discuss the general contours that I think they nonetheless share and that can serve us well in laying a different kind of political foundation.

Gaia is an old name, so old in fact that she "is not a goddess properly speaking, but a force from the time before the gods" (Latour 2017, 81). As a *force*, she is portrayed by Hesiod as a "figure of violence, genesis, and trickery" (83), one that "emerges in great outpourings of blood, steam and terror" (81). According to Stengers, what Gaia retained of her old self was the idea of force, expressed as the irruption of processes within human life that are inherently indifferent to human life itself (see Stengers 2015, 44). It is also important to dwell on the concept of terror, which I will argue is shared among all kinds of creatures. Gaia terrorizes, a fact that is becoming clearer as moderns are relearning the sheer shock that the forces of nature can provoke. This kind of deep, near-debilitating fear is necessary for the survival of humans as much as owls, spiders, or bees. Sheltering from devastating forces is a necessity that is brought home by terror.

There are several aspects of this conceptualization of Gaia that Latour and Stengers take up. First, there is the idea that our designation of the world as abiotic, and the living as biotic, is wrong because the two are strictly inseparable. It bears noticing again that planetary science, of which Gaia is an offspring, is not the science of ecologists, but rather that of astronomers and geologists (Latour 2017, Lovelock 1995). In other words, Gaia as planet becomes strange and interesting when compared to other planets (as we saw Lovelock do) that—as far as we can tell—are indeed strictly abiotic. The Earth is not a lifeless planet because of the inseparable interaction between life and its conditions of existence, which are themselves nurtured by life. This is what makes the Earth interesting and special. Every major characteristic of the planet can be traced back to interactions of life and matter. The only exception is the geological makeup of the Earth, which is in fact the only aspect of our world that makes it comparable with other bodies in space *as* planets.

The other characteristic of Gaia that is of great importance is the stochastic nature of its particular processes. There is no necessity for Gaia to be the way that it is or to endure in the form in which we may observe it at any particular moment. This is also where Lovelock's conceptions are left behind and those of Latour and Stengers take over. Though it is true that the living have a decisive role in material affairs, this does not also mean that natural processes (formed, as we now know, through complex biotic-abiotic alliances) take sides. Here Latour and Stengers also seem to differ. For the former, it seems as if the self-interest of any particular being somehow enacts conditions that favor its own life. For Stengers, Gaia is the name of an intrusion first and foremost, which would imply that it is radically indifferent to the affairs of any particular being. It is only on aggregate that we may discern patterns that seem to favor one being over another, but from any embodied point of view Gaia appears as a violence that must be endured, a whimsical force that may or may not blow in the right direction.

These differences notwithstanding, there are some important consequences of thinking about the world in terms of a *living* world. This need not mean that the world itself is alive, which is an interpretation often given to Lovelock's Gaia, one that he himself has encouraged, though with much more nuance.[2] Instead, this simply means that we cannot conceive of a world within the terrestrial realm (so excluding other planets) that does not owe some of its fundamental characteristics to the living. If we conceptually strip away life from the Earth, it is no longer the planet that it is; it becomes a planet like any other, namely dominated entirely by abiotic processes. This, though it may at some point in the future become true, is for all intents and purposes (that is, from the point of view of any living creature) strict fantasy. The planet we live on is what it is because of the living.

This point is deceivingly simple, but it has tremendous consequences. The most important one is the realization that the figures of the globe

---

2   For Lovelock, the aliveness of the planet is related to an unintentional intelligence that can be inferred as a characteristic of Gaia as a superorganism. The planet's *active* self-regulation leads to the idea that it functions as an organism that has its own metabolism and states of homeostasis punctuated by disequilibrium. He therefore concludes that the Earth is alive "only in a physiological sense, and therefore the science of studying the planet should really be called geophysiology" (1995, 11).

and that of Gaia are strictly incompatible. Latour develops this point at length in *Facing Gaia* (2017), concluding that "[...] one can grasp nothing about the intrusion of Gaia [...] if one confuses it with the contemplation of a globe" (222). Why? Because the image of the globe mischaracterizes what is proper to Gaia in every conceivable way. To start with, the globe is a planet like every other, whereas Gaia is entirely special within what we so far know of planets. Thinking at the level of the biosphere also mischaracterizes the way in which the Earth has become what it is, namely through a radically contingent series of interactions that continue to change and to determine 'the global'. In other words, the global level of analysis, viewed through the concept of Gaia, is derivative of smaller-scale processes, and not the other way around.

Instead of a whole system, Gaia is a patchwork of processes that conspire to generate greater (and always temporary) effects. The best image for Gaia is not the sphere floating in space, as if it were *as a whole* that it became significant. The more appropriate image is, following Latour, that of the skin, perhaps the flesh, of a body. The sciences have shown that the space of life, and by extension the precise space that makes Gaia what it is, is extremely thin, a matter of mere kilometers extending from the mid-atmosphere to the subsoil.³ That is it. That is the where and the how of life, the area that Latour calls the critical zone (2017, 2020), both in the sense that it is critical for generating the qualities of life, and for the battle for particular ways of living.

Gaia as flesh carries with it a whole new political potential than that of the globe.⁴ "The Globe offers a geometric way, as it were, of representing the supreme arbiter that reigns over all conflicts—and that consequently depoliticizes them at once" (Latour 2017, 238). The totality of the globe all too easily slips into techno-managerial plans to save 'the biosphere', while radically ignoring the fact that the issue of salvation is always located on the surface of the flesh, in the everyday decisions

---

3 As argued in Chapter 2, the soil itself is currently seen in soil ecology as a skin.
4 I have argued extensively that descriptions of the world are fundamental for understanding possibilities for action and are therefore always tied to political projects. It is therefore also the case that describing Gaia at the level of the globe also has political potential, but of a kind that is inimical to the political theory I develop here. The political project associated with the globe leads directly to proposals such as geo-engineering that are willfully blind to the living processes that make up the planet. This blindness is a direct result of their level of analysis.

that contribute to its health. In other words, there is no question of holism in the thought of a living world, but always already of particular situations, defined territorially and dynamically (that is, without fixed borders), that intervene in very particular local configurations. This *is always the case*. The global does not obviate it, it simply hides it. As Timothy Mitchell has shown, the grand politics of carbon on a planetary scale is nothing outside of its multiple local instantiations and variations (2013). Talk of the global at all should almost never happen, except as the cautiously drawn sum of partially counted interactions.

Refusing the holism of the global opens up the radical diversity of lives. This gesture of refusal entails a whole constellation of concepts that accompany the obsession with totality and unity. For the present purposes, two others are important to signal out: the ideas of balance and harmony. These twin notions accompany big, global thinking; the distance required by such thinking makes it seem as if the whole is ordered in a particular kind of way, reaching towards equilibrium. This illusion is shattered by the thought of Gaia as flesh, which forces us to look at particular interactions within a particular time. There are no overarching norms besides whatever norms the participants collectively decide upon. This is why politics is crucial to Gaia, but expelled by the balanced globe. And this is why there is a profound need for political concepts that are rooted in disequilibrium and fleshy messiness.

Ecology itself, particularly in its applied branches, has been infected by the thought of equilibrium, but ecology is also where some partial ways of conceptualizing the flesh reside. William Drury, in *Chance and Change* (1998), argues that "nature works on the basis of one-on-one species interactions, variability, and chance" (1998, 1). What he calls "comfortable disorder [...] is what makes the natural world work". He presents a detailed naturalistic argument for why "chance and change are the rule, the future is as unpredictable to other organisms as it is to us, and natural disturbance is too frequent for equilibrium models to be useful" (7).

This takes the previously-sketched thought of Gaia as a thin margin of liveliness seriously, and does so from a strictly ecological, naturalistic perspective, through a series of field observations that reveal both how the mind (trained in a particular kind of way) imposes order on the world, and how the world resists such imposition. One way in which the imposition can be resisted is indeed through a focus on the lived experience of organisms, which in the concept of Gaia cannot be counted out as irrelevant but instead become the bedrock of any worldly conception. The way in which individual creatures behave is, to echo the perspectivism we saw in Chapter 2, both radically similar (they follow their interests in almost perfect ignorance of the future) and radically discontinuous (owing to differences in embodiment). Naturalist fieldwork is in this sense very close to perspectivism and multinaturalism and, inasmuch as it acknowledges this common pattern of thinking, it is also that which discovers a heightened level of stochasticity in the environing world.

The uncertainty of the world mirrors that of the individual creature. Drury says that "individual organisms cannot afford consistency", precisely because the world around them does not allow for it. It may even be that, because of the multiplicity of biotic-abiotic connections, the world and its living beings mutually destabilize each other, creating the "comfortable disequilibrium" that allows for temporary flourishing. They are forces in their own right that manage to maintain a working disequilibrium *because* they are at odds with each other.

Latour and Drury both stress the fact that, seen from the scale of experience, individual relations are not infinite. Drury spends a great deal of time showing how in any particular environment creatures only really interact with, and therefore care about, a very limited number of other creatures. This is important, and I will come back to it. Equally important though is the implication that, due to the constancy of change, there is always a margin, created by uncertainty, that allows creatures to adapt to new conditions and to create new subsistence relations. This is the sense in which the living cannot afford consistency.

From this point of view, the very consistent model of modern development is its own worst enemy, precisely because it forces environments to the preferences of a particular kind of creature. This is bound to catch up with it in time, precisely because of natural variability, which is further intensified by cumulative human activities. By uprooting itself from territorial matters, modernity condemns itself to a deadly consistency. Instead, the politics of the living must be grounded in inconsistency and change.

No single creature can have a complete view of the world, for three reasons. First, the world changes continuously, partly in response to the actions of creatures, and so it can never be frozen in a single state. Second, each creature has a limited sensory range, and can thus never adequately represent to itself the full spectrum of space. Third, creatures are interested in a limited number of things, but these are in turn not necessarily representative of the wider situation, nor indeed are they the most important constitutive elements of that situation, nor are they 'proxies' for other, unseen elements. So, creatures are liable to undermine their own maps of the world by stepping on landmines that they do not see, because they do not know of their existence.

Creatures are also routinely wrong about what they expect to find where. This is part and parcel of evolution, because not finding an expected food source, for example, jolts one out of complacency and forces them to expand their map. Whether descriptions are outright bad or merely good enough, depends on the actions that they make possible. In any given situation, descriptions draw the boundaries of what is possible, and tell participants how, where and to what end the territory can be used. From this perspective, evolution is not just a matter of genetic mutations that are positive enough to pass on to future generations. There is also an interaction between the representation of the world by creatures, its continuous modification by these and chance events, and the subsequent adaptation of organisms to their own interaction with the world.

The territory frustrates the expectations of the living and forces them to adapt. This applies to bacteria and fungi as much as to bears. Each creature makes the best of its environment, and does not move about blindly. It uses an impression of the territory, whether inherited or built from scratch, that allows it to move about in semi-meaningful ways, which themselves modify the possibility of future meaningful movements, in a kind of heuristic evolution. It is not that descriptions are always one step behind reality; reality itself—or the characteristics of voluminous space, if you will—is hugely determined by these partial creaturely movements that unknowingly, and sometimes willingly (but also always to some extent unknowingly), modify their territory according to the failures of their descriptive apparatus.

From an embodied perspective, the world is but a series of local and fragmented interactions that matter to the experiencing subject. Everything that falls outside of this experiential range is, strictly speaking, uninteresting. However, anything at all has the capacity to become interesting, inasmuch as conditions change to make it so. The Ecocene is just such a radical change of condition for humans, both allowing for and demanding a radical expansion of what matters to humans. Political thinking in the Ecocene cannot be holistic, but must focus on the particular interactions that particular beings enjoy and need. The catch is that humans should be acutely aware of their own ignorance, as there is a vast reservoir of unknown relations that may be crucial to us but about which we know nothing.

The centrality of ignorance amounts to a perpetual commitment to observation and study, to finding out exactly what the nature of our community is. Given, indeed, both chance and change, this is a never-ending task, and a fitting one, I think, for basic political practice. Creatures in the abstract may only be circumscribed by the relations that they experience, but politics in the Ecocene knows better than thinking that its own knowledge of 'the biosphere' is complete, or can ever be. Ignorance is a cousin of uncertainty, both sharing in the genealogy of change as the norm in natural processes. Adapting to the requirements of ignorance and change requires us to break with the certainties of modernity. This kind of radical break is happening, and will continue to happen.

The biological sciences, as well as the political ones, have grown accustomed to thinking in terms of individuals. This is currently undergoing a radical reshuffling. In biology, for example, the holobiont is steadily enriching our understanding of what makes an individual. The argument is that "neither humans, nor any other organism, can be regarded as individuals by anatomical criteria" (Gilbert et al. 2012, 327). The radical nature of this statement is easily glossed over, but it bears pointing out that anatomical criteria have traditionally been considered the most *solid* ones for identifying, and analyzing, individuals. Instead, the holobiont "has been introduced as the anatomical term that describes the *integrated organism* comprised of both host elements and persistent populations of symbionts" (328, emphasis added). Lynn Margulis did much to pave the way for this work. As she reminded us, only bacteria are individuals in any meaningful sense (2000).

Gilbert et al., as well as others (see for example Tauber 2017), demonstrate that any anatomical feature can only be accounted for as the common work of several different kinds of processes, all of them accomplished through cooperation. It is pointless to ask what the ultimate unit is, in an attempt to save some version of individualism.[5] There is nothing but collective processes, all the way down. This is as true for human cell permeability (regulated through microbial symbionts; Sariola and Gilbert 2020) as for plant nutrition (accomplished through mycorrhizal networks; see Sheldrake 2020). In other words, multiplicity, variability, internal and external relationality, and enduring forms of mutual cooperation seem to be the rule, rather than the exception, in the organization of life.

* * *

The holobiont complements the ideas of multiplicity and relationality explored in Chapter 2. The perspectivist conception of a fundamental self-difference internal to any particular being is a literal self-difference, an infinite multiplicity.[6] Alongside the ecological necessity of change and variability over time, we are well accustomed to taking the existence of internal multiplicity as a fact, albeit a boundless one: there is no boundary around the potential aggregative nature of what we call an individual. Multinaturalism, perspectivism, and ecological thinking together propose a richly textured reality of multiplicity, both in the abiotic and the biotic realms.

Distinguishing between these two realms is of course important, though for a project of mutualism it is secondary to pointing out their

---

[5] The ultimate argument for the actual existence of individuals would have to be genetic: at base, there are different kinds of organisms with their own genes that cooperate in specific kinds of ways. But this turns out to be false. "Genomes evolve in such a manner that they need their partners to achieve complex genetic integration. None of the three species in that symbiosis has a "complete" genome. It is the holobiont that does. We are not individuals by genetic criteria" (Gilbert et al. 2012, 330).

[6] It is not just perspectivism that overlaps in interesting ways with the idea of holobiont. Māori philosophy, for example, also has a view of the body that is similar to the multiplicity sketched here in important respects. As Salmond explains, "body parts are often spoken about as agents in their own right, alongside the person themselves—for example, [...] turn and look at me, you and your eyes. [...] The body was at once a micro-cosmos and a living community" (2017, 200). It stands to reason that, if the body is conceived of as a community, different parts of this community may express themselves in particular ways in different times, therefore imparting a form of agency on what, from a strictly individual perspective, appear as 'parts'. For more on Māori philosophy and its radically relational ontology, see Chapter 5.

interrelations. In other words, the question of their difference matters inasmuch as it reveals the mode of their sameness. For example, the biotic and abiotic conceived as infinite multiplicities differ in terms of intensity, that is to say in terms of the rate of change over time and the nature of their respective endurance through time. The abiotic and the biotic are like two streams moving according to different internal rhythms, but these rhythms are what they are because of their interrelations, not because of the internal coherence of 'the biotic' or 'the abiotic'.[7]

Both multinaturalism and ecology foreground the ideas of multiplicity and variability. From the point of view of a particular individual, what then becomes crucial is the potential availability of space for expressing their own kind of variability, given certain fluctuations in environment. The ecological idea of habitat redundancy is therefore crucial for a terrestrial politics because it is the condition of possibility for successful adaptation and change. In ecological science, the idea of habitat redundancy simply points out that a multiplicity of marsh habitats, for example, is important for any particular kind of marsh-feeding bird, because it is what ensures their capacity to adapt to environmental change. So, if conditions change here, they can move there. If there is nowhere to move, the necessity of change leads the particular beings under pressure into a dead-end.

But there is no reason to suppose that the idea of redundancy only applies to 'others', and not to humans as well. Inasmuch as the characteristics of multiplicity, variability and change define the world of the living as such, the need for redundant habitats also applies to humans. It is a popular belief that human beings are so adaptable that they have settled in all possible habitats. This is true, but it is also false, in the sense that this process of settlement, particularly under the guise of modernity, has resulted in a radical simplification of human habitats and their respective homogenization.[8] In effect, the expansion of human

---

[7] Distinguishing the biotic and abiotic on the basis of temporal intensity is itself problematic at the margins: thinking about millennial trees, for example, reveals how the borders of matter and the living are themselves porous. Peter Wohlleben, for example, speaks of his discovery of a tree stump that should have long ago disappeared, given its great age, but which was nonetheless alive through its root association with neighboring trees. Similarly, the oldest pine trees discovered stretch back multiple millennia, being alive though mostly being made up of petrified wood. See Wohlleben's popular *The Hidden Life of Trees*.

[8] See the parallels here with the discussion of space in Chapter 2.

habitation in all possible biomes has also led to the homogenization of these biomes and their respective impoverishment (in terms of interactions between participants in those spaces).

Redundancy of habitat is crucial for humans just as it is for all animals, but the modern mindset has made it increasingly hard to recognize this fact, or to recognize that it is not just a matter of quantity (how many spaces are available), but primarily of quality (the exact details of each potential habitat). By enlarging the human presence in a fundamentally similar way in many different kinds of environments (as the project of modern development has done), societies have begun to slowly cut the branch from under their own feet. Whatever future disturbance will occur (this is impossible to predict exactly in terms of content, but formally guaranteed) will, under conditions of simplification and habitat homogenization, be much more deadly than if there were qualitative redundancy.

Modern development has tried to muscle out environmental disturbance by literally hardening the environment. Dams, canals, barriers of all sorts, straight lines that are predictable, all of these features of the 'developed' landscape are meant to insure the gamble of uniformity. In the Ecocene, this kind of approach reaches its limit: it is not disturbance as such that is the news, but rather the kind of disturbance that makes our barriers obsolete. All of a sudden, the need for qualitative habitat redundancy has caught up with us.[9]

There are ways of renovating relationships between humans and all other inhabitants of worlds, such that the quality of potential habitats is ensured. Some of those ways will be presented in Chapters 4 and 7. The point I want to make here is that the ideas of multiplicity, variability, and redundancy are much more firmly grounded in ecology and,

---

9   One deadly aspect of homogenization is the quintessentially modern practice of paving. "Modern contemporary society has a new perfect tool for the complete destruction of soils: constructions. We are not speaking about construction of new houses and dwellings for still increasing numbers of population. We are speaking about one- or two-storied shopping centers, warehouses and administration buildings, roads, and airports. They occupy hundreds of thousands of square kilometers where the soil was dug out and replaced by concrete, pavement, and asphalt" (Kutílek and Nielsen 2015, 18). This process, basically synonymous with modern development, permanently annuls the generative properties of soil by replacing it with hard surfaces that are guaranteed to disrupt processes, such as hydrological circulation, that had ensured variability and redundancy. This will prove increasingly deadly.

dare I say, ontology than the dominant idea of 'diversity'.[10] Diversity as such (including biodiversity) rehashes, perhaps unwittingly, grand systems thinking, but misses the point of what makes for a rich natural community: it is not diversity—sheer number—as such, but rather the interplay of multiplicity, variability, and the redundancy of potential habitats.[11]

For humans as well as for other gregarious animals, the availability of different kinds of habitats is not only a survival necessity but is part and parcel of what may be called their quality of life.[12] Elsewhere (see Tănăsescu 2017), and in dialogue with the work of William Jordan on environmental restoration (re-encountered in Chapter 6), I have proposed that the redundancy of variable habitat (achieved through restoration) is directly relevant to the cultural richness of future human beings. Put simply, there are a handful of ways in which one can relate to parking lots, so if everything becomes a parking lot, the very possibility of cultural diversity is foreclosed. This is so because of the strict relation between ontological multiplicity and variability and its sublimation into cultural, expressive forms. But this may hold true for other animals as well. We can easily imagine that when elephants are confined to just one of their potential habitats, elephant cultures become much poorer too. The same is true for an incalculable number of different embodiments.

The physical simplification of an environment has long been used by colonizers as a great tool of subjugation, precisely because cultural resilience is so reliant on worldly multiplicity. The settlers wishing to subdue the Native Americans on the American plains managed to do so by reducing the number of buffalo. Settlers everywhere, from New Zealand to Australia to the Americas and Africa, as well as from the internal colonial projects of modern development within Europe itself,[13]

---

10 For a sustained critique of biodiversity, see Deliege and Neuteleers (2015), and Youatt (2008, 2015).

11 Much of the literature on biodiversity reduction, particularly as caused by 'invasive species', comes from the study of islands. However, nothing is an island except an island, and it is because of non-redundancy that islands are so precarious and amenable to violent shifts.

12 This is also true if we interpret quality of life as health. As Sariola and Gilbert (2020, 13) argue, diseases like asthma and phenomena like antimicrobial resistance are "expected consequences of lower resilience to perturbations".

13 Nation building in Europe itself has also applied the colonial recipe of simplification. The nation could only emerge as a homogenous category through the literal reduction of multiplicity, both in natural and cultural terms. The annexation of

have tended to homogenize landscapes, and this has always been crucial to colonial ambitions. Modernity in this sense is the ultimate colonizer, as it has been (and continues to be) extremely successful at simplifying habitats, particularly through the project of development. The contemporary dramatic decrease in sheer numbers of animal lives, often termed the sixth mass extinction, is a direct consequence of the modernist drive for reduction in complexity.[14]

Part of the difficulty of accepting the centrality of multiplicity and change is the dominance of the idea that each species has its own place of life, its own 'niche'. As Drury (1998, 157) reminds us, "rather than specializing on a narrow band of resources, each species occupies a diversity of habitats, and habitats themselves are conspicuously heterogenous. We must appreciate as well that during most of a species' history nearly all habitats differed greatly from what we see today, in part as a result of the impact of environmental events such as ice ages". The idea of a niche may have a particular circumscribed usefulness, but as a model for how the world works it is radically insufficient.

In principle, anything can live anywhere inasmuch as holobionts manage to make a living there. Unfortunately, the applied branches of ecology have been less than faithful to the insights of their own founding science, and instead have embraced discredited social scientific concepts to apply to the natural world. Conservation biology has therefore become one of the last places where one can use designations such as 'invasive', 'alien', or 'non-native species'.[15] It has also led to extreme efforts to keep

---

new territories by the nation state has more often than not gone hand-in-hand with engineering projects that 'tamed' natural variability and, by extension, population variability. Also see discussion of the Danube Delta in Chapter 2.

14   Simplification need not always take the form of an intentional project (though it often does—the best example is perhaps the worldwide drive to extinguish wetlands and render rivers predictable). There are many ways in which modern development, for example, simplifies habitats and is deadly to a staggering number of creatures, simply as a 'side-effect' of actions that are otherwise deemed necessary for human well-being. Think, for example, of the effect of lighting on ecological dynamics: artificial lighting is extremely disruptive to creatures adapted to the dark and is itself responsible for a good slice of the reduction in insect populations everywhere. Yet obviously in this case lighting is not employed in order to simplify habitats. Rather, lighting is understood narrowly as a benign intervention for human well-being, and all its other effects become invisible from the point of view of development.

15   It is significant that most of the literature on the pernicious effects of such invasive species comes from islands, which, as we have seen in footnote 11, are poor examples for the vast majority of habitats on earth.

habitats composed in a certain way, as if those were the only ways in which they could be composed, by natural law. Instead of focusing on the redundancy of potential habitats, conservation biology has all too often focused on a legislated form of diversity for habitats that effectively become islands. The belief that a certain arrangement of 'diversity' is the best possible one is pervasive and surprisingly stubborn, though it is thankfully increasingly challenged.

> An important portion of the order ascribed to landscapes is supplied by the perceptions of the human observer. Keystone species in vegetation made up of relatively few species attract attention and are called dominant or primary. [...] Some species are called rare, yet most species occur in relatively small numbers. And, for our own reasons, we call some species attractive and others weeds or pests (Drury 1998, 182)

The Ecocene can no longer afford this kind of fundamentally modernist thinking. Instead, heeding Latour's call, the Ecocene forces a coming-down-to-earth, whether violently abrupt or willfully sought out. It also forces a perpetual rethinking of the fixed concepts we use to understand the world, whether these be ossified criteria of belonging (native versus alien) or racing to find *the* thing that makes a situation work (keystones, niches, autochthons). On the other hand, thinking in terms of the planet, the globe, the grand system, is what stands in the way of our responses to planetary convulsions; radical localization and reterritorialization are needed, such that multiplicity and variability can be given adequate space to develop. A small politics of open-ended assemblies, defined simply in contextual and changeable terms, is what the dawn of ecology, the irruption of Gaia, demands.

* * *

From an embodied point of view (the only point of view available, in the final analysis) the characteristics of the world (volumetric multiplicity) and of the living (intense multiplicities) are also problems to solve. In other words, the interaction between creatures and the world consistently throws up the problem of survival, which must be actively sought out. Doing nothing literally leads to wilting away, because living is a constant process of readjustment to a constantly variable background. This means that each creature, whilst being directly interested in its own survival, also fundamentally shares in the universal problem of survival. In other words, each creature has an innate basis for approximating another's tribulations, inasmuch as they are similarly structured by the very fabric of a living world.

This is in part the insight that Descola and De Castro draw out of animism. As Peter Skafish explains it,

> the subject is confronted in its experience not with a reality where other beings are initially objects but rather by a seemingly limitless panoply of other subjects, whose specific identities are derived from but also concealed by their various kinds of bodies. That is, beings are experienced as subjects that are only different from humans in that they are clothed in strange, exotic bodies, and truly understanding these subjects (who they are, and what and how they think) therefore requires understanding their bodies (80)

But attempting to understand the body only works because of the fundamentally similar nature of being embodied, that is to say because of the similar demands that enduring through change presents to any embodied subject.

Rich Borden (2017), commenting on Whitehead's notion of process (as opposed to matter), argues that "what we take to be 'things' are actually more like 'events'; akin to standing waves that come and go over time, though they may appear to be permanent, they are variable, transitory concrescences". Being situated at the crest of such a standing wave—the embodied perspective—cannot but constantly present a challenge, one that is intuitively shared across embodiments. Even though bodies differ greatly, they also share a kind of fellowship, given by the relationship of their very embodiment to the dynamic volumetric spaces in which they live. In other words, all embodied creatures share, in light of being bodies, in some degree of constitutive vulnerability.

The notion of vulnerability is important for understanding what may act as an onto-normative grounds for imagining political communities. Following the discussion above, vulnerability is a feature of lively existence in the same way that multiplicity and variability are. In this sense, vulnerability cannot be construed as merely a lack, which has been the usual way of presenting it in political thinking. The vulnerable is not lacking something, but rather any being participates in the fact of vulnerability as an openness to change. This is what I call constitutive vulnerability, which is a power, the power to be changed and therefore to endure through change. Adaptability in general is not a willful process, but rather a blind search whose very condition is vulnerability, that is to say creaturely openness towards the tribulations of the world.

Vulnerability is too often associated with powerlessness of some kind, and therefore is investigated through either passivity (Harrison 2008 examining sleep, insomnia, and death) or harm (being vulnerable, in Butler's sense). I don't mean to deny those senses of the word. However, they do not exhaust the concept. An ecological view of vulnerability reveals it as the condition of possibility of change and successful adaptation. In this sense, the vulnerable are the more powerful because, in being open to new relationships, they can also survive changing environments. The idea of an ideal fit between organism and world (nativism) infects thinking to the point where it becomes hard to recognize that being slightly out-of-synch is what has allowed, and continues to allow, a multiplicity of forms of life to flourish. The opposite of vulnerability is not power or strength; it is rigidity.

In this ontological sense, the chances of creaturely endurance are directly proportional to how vulnerable the creature is, in the sense of how structurally open towards new possibilities that natural variability may offer. This sense of the term hails from the previous discussion and remains on a strictly ontological level. However, the description of creaturely existence as sharing in constitutive vulnerability offers a basis for an ethical (and therefore political) concept of vulnerability as denoting a structural similarity between beings that is crucial for understanding political practice in the Ecocene.[16]

We have already seen the particularly Amazonian, animist take on this concept. Now, I want to turn to another rich source that can help spell out the ways in which constitutive vulnerability imparts, on human beings, a duty to try to understand the position of the other. This duty is itself made possible by constitutive vulnerability. In other words, inasmuch as a fundamental kind of fellowship in the community of life can be conceptualized, it requires of human beings a vigilance as to the potential application of this kind of fellowship. This is closely related to the point about our vast ignorance as to how the worlds around

---

16 Ethics and politics are concerned with how to act based on what is. It is in this sense that descriptions of the world matter, greatly. How one characterizes what is has everything to do with how one may act.

us are composed. This ignorance, wedded to the fact of constitutive vulnerability, demands that humans be *a priori* open to (if not actively seeking) imaginative extensions of their creaturely fellowship. People regularly do this, and in fact it takes effort and sustained violence to stop people from identifying with landscape features and other lives in a fundamentally sympathetic way.[17]

The growing literature on care (for example Puig de la Bellacasa 2017; Martin, Myers, and Viseu 2015) is very important for the transition from constitutive to ethical vulnerability. But it is not about caring for one particular match between a kind of life and a kind of world, but rather caring for the very possibility of dynamic matches. Care responsive to constitutive vulnerability is about helping creatures endure *despite* the vicissitudes of life.[18] It is, in this sense, to enter into properly political community with a growing number of existents, inasmuch as there is concern for their ability to adapt, and therefore to change and survive. To care for one's child, for example, is not to stunt them in a perpetual childhood, but rather to help them adapt to changing conditions, both internal (given by self-multiplicity) and external (environmental).

I have characterized constitutive vulnerability as a fundamental openness towards the environing world. We have seen several theoretical strains that are already predicated on the ontological dimension of vulnerability, as the very basis for traveling in the direction of a different kind of embodiment. In this constitutive sense, vulnerability is a fundamental part of the ability to endure through time, by changing one's form in relation to the changing environment. Ethically, however, vulnerability tends towards powerlessness and passivity. Is there a sense in which the power of constitutive vulnerability can be extended to its ethical variant?

To find out, I want to turn to Cora Diamond, a philosopher who has produced some of the most evocative work on the moral significance of creatureliness, the feeling of fellowship with another animal, and the functioning of the moral imagination in the context of embodied life.

---

17 For a detailed engagement with the intuitive movement of the moral imagination through creaturely fellowship, see Crary (2002, 2007, 2016), Mulhall (2008), Diamond (1978, 1991, 2003), Gaita (2016), Cavell et al. (2009).

18 There are fruitful overlaps here with Haraway's notion of response-ability, that is to say, the ability to pay attention to and maintain dynamic assemblages. See Haraway's (2016) *Staying with the Trouble: Making Kin in the Chthulucene*.

Work on vulnerability has largely focused on human beings, in ways that are problematic for a wider political engagement with the Ecocene (as explored below). Diamond's work allows for a concept of vulnerability that is both constitutive in my sense (ontologically grounded), and normative in ways that are productive for wider political concerns.

Diamond has explored the work of the moral imagination in ways that go beyond the mere application of moral judgment,[19] and instead relies heavily on the feeling of fellowship that humans may share with an indefinite number of creatures. She has therefore taken literature as a medium through which the kinds of creaturely connections pertinent to the moral imagination are questioned. Following the arguments presented so far, we could also use ethology, ecology, and critical anthropology as inspiration for how the moral imagination may inhabit the skin of another.

In *The Importance of Being Human*, she argues that "through novels and stories, we are able to see how our pursuit of private ends may conflict with what we owe others; we come, through such literature, to care about the sufferings or the humiliation of a wider range of human beings" (Diamond 1991, 49). Though in this essay she is specifically concerned with the moral significance of the concept of the 'human', elsewhere she shows that the moral imagination functions similarly in relation to other creatures (for example, Diamond 1978).

In discussing a Walter de la Mare poem about a titmouse, Diamond pauses on the expression the poet uses to refer to the little bird as "a traveler between life and death" (Diamond 1978). The fact that the bird "has a life"[20] is not significant because it transmits biological knowledge. Having a life, in this sense, is not a biological fact; it acquires moral weight when understood as participating in the stimulation of a certain kind of fellowship with a creature that, despite vast differences in embodiment, nonetheless participates in the same fundamental process that renders all living things vulnerable.

---

19 For a Diamondian ethics developed specifically away from moral judgment, see Alice Crary (2007).

20 This expression of Diamond's is contrasted with the idea that having a life is a biological fact. As a biological fact, it is morally meaningless; it acquires moral weight, as it were, when understood as an expression that signals a certain kind of fellowship, allows the listener to contemplate the mystery of another's life, to be touched by someone else having a life to lead.

Through literature, Diamond tends to focus on vulnerability as the expression of an ability to suffer, though she is very critical of strict utilitarian interpretations of suffering as morally significant. Citing Rorty, she argues that literature may help us grasp "the kinds of suffering endured by people to whom we had previously not attended" (1991, 49), but there is no point in trying to quantify just how much suffering. Instead, the idea is that the sympathetic imagination can be made to resonate in the tone of another, that is to say that through literature (but not only literature) we may be able to understand the specific way in which another embodiment relates to the problem of surviving in a challenging environment.

To this end, she comments on Dicken's character Scrooge, who goes from a cruelty of spirit in relation to children to some form of mutual understanding. What changes Scrooge's attitude is not a utilitarian calculation of children's interests. Instead, he can only start to see the importance of other people having interests of their own when he acquires "a live sense of oneself as, with others, bound toward death, of others as one's 'fellow passengers to the grave'" (Diamond 1991, 49). This parallels the idea that imagination permits the embodiment of a titmouse via a similar idea of fellowship in the vicissitudes of life.

Scrooge becomes generous toward children only after he "is touched by human childhood, the vulnerability of children, the intensity of their hopes, the depths of their fears and pains, their pleasures in their play, their joy in following stories" (Diamond 1991, 42). What allows Scrooge to become available to the needs and interests of children is not the force of those needs themselves, but rather the whole state of living-as-child, which is characterized by mystery and vulnerability. In other words, it is a certain kind of moral imagination that Dickens, and Diamond, foreground as fundamentally important. Dickens "attempts to show us how an imaginative sense of the touchingness of childhood, tied to a sense of oneself as child, may be present in acts of humanity, and how its absence may also be felt in what we do and what we are capable of feeling" (Diamond 1991, 42). Having an imaginative sense of what it is like to be a child is discernible in the way we act toward children, with generosity, kindheartedness, and so on. Being callous toward children may reveal a lack of such imaginative bonding.

By paying close attention to how people may act *vis-à-vis* fellow creatures, we can discern the ways in which the moral imagination may be playing a role in connecting the constitutive vulnerability of embodiment to the ethics of dealing with one another. In Diamond's words, we may characterize actions "by the imaginative activity that enters them" (1991, 41), and this characterization becomes incredibly useful in renovating terrestrial relationships. In particular, it becomes important because it allows us to discern the ways in which imaginative activity always already suffuses multispecies relationships. The way in which people speak of particular trees, or the care that they take with the needs of their pets, the way that they may characterize landscapes as possessing certain powers, goes beyond mere metaphor and instead exemplifies how the moral imagination suffuses ways of speaking and acting.

Literature stimulates the moral imagination regardless of whether we are speaking of human or animal others, and what Diamond allows us to see is that it does so by engaging fundamental mechanisms that are embedded in how we live and speak. In literature, we use the criterion of imaginative identification as a marker of good representation of the characters: we say the author succeeded in representing the character well inasmuch as we can empathically imagine the character's particular subject-position. Stephen Mulhall, commenting on Diamond's use of Dickens, expresses the point of what the novelist is doing as an attempt "to attend to a child *as* a center of a distinctive view of the world, and so to attend to children in their own right" (2008, 8, italics in original). Similarly, what de la Mare's poem suggests is that a titmouse, by virtue of being a living subject, can (and perhaps should) be approached in a way that allows for an imaginative construction of *its* embodied position.[21]

Mulhall develops at length, in *The Wounded Animal*, what exactly it is that the sympathetic imagination relies upon, or rather what it is that is common to embodiment such that sympathetic representation can work. For both human and nonhuman animals, there are certain basic facts of embodiment—"they too are needy, dependent, subject to birth, sexuality, and death, vulnerable to pain and fear" (2008, 32)— that renders them constitutively vulnerable. The vulnerability of being embodied is not a matter of counting an exhaustive list of qualities one

---

21 There are obvious parallels between this view and the multinaturalism and perspectivism discussed in Chapter 2.

must share in order to be worthy of moral consideration, but rather itself the very basis of our ability to travel in the direction of another and to inhabit her position. Using J.M. Coetzee's Elizabeth Costello as an example, Mulhall argues that it is "the fellowship of mortal creatures that provides our means of access to nonhuman animal being" and that this access is fraught with "resistance, contradiction, impossibility". This is because "understanding any manifestation of animal life, of finite embodied experience, is a matter of deploying our imaginative capacity to be dead and alive at the same time, and risking the panic-stricken collapse of our whole edifice of knowledge" (47).

In other words, the moral imagination requires that we inhabit the distance between vulnerability as a power to change and therefore endure, and the creaturely resistance to change as potentially dangerous. From any individual point of view, openness is also a problem, because change is both necessary and fundamentally threatening. Staying roughly the same is somewhat preferable to changing and therefore ethical vulnerability appears as a problem, the problem of exposure. It is in this sense that Mulhall and Diamond focus the ethical concept of vulnerability on the fact of death and finitude more generally, but this need not mean that ethical vulnerability is a lack, or the inscription of harm. Rather, it is the negotiation of change caught between creaturely fidelity and wider processes of de- and recomposition.

Inhabiting the perspective of another, or trying to answer the call to understand another's embodiment entails deadly contradictions. Elizabeth Costello discusses the case of the people living against the backdrop of the Holocaust, who supposedly did not know what was going on, though surely anyone that used their human capacities even to a minimal degree did know what was going on. This knowing while not knowing is one instance of the suppression of the sympathetic imagination because of the personal difficulty that comes with heeding its call. But a similar contradiction, a kind of knowing and not knowing, is also characteristic of the proper use of moral imagination, which itself leads to suffering on behalf of the other, even if the other is not a subject in pain. There is a moment of death in leaving oneself behind in order to understand another, and a moment of unbearable contradiction in this flight from oneself only to inhabit a perspective as vulnerable—constitutively so—as one's own, and as incomplete and provisional.

There is, in other words, a grave difficulty in sustaining the call of the moral imagination.

According to the literature I have used, as exemplified through Diamond, Mulhall and Coetzee, there is no logical limit to the sympathetic imagination. This is a point made very clear by the critical anthropology explored earlier, and here we see a fruitful juxtaposition of ideas of diverse origins that coalesce towards a political ethics for the Ecocene. As Skafish argues, "at the moment of a global ecological crisis whose material conditions owe so much to Western metaphysical categories, it would be extremely tone deaf to continue to think that only better modern concepts are sufficient for thinking it, and that those of other peoples have already been converted into modern ones or are simply irrelevant to us" (2016, 72). Similarly, we may find on the margins of mainstream Western modern traditions the fragments of ways of thinking and doing that may allow for renovation and recomposition. Crucially, we may also find ways of forming alliances beyond the modern/non-modern distinction.

Today, a great variety of works, in philosophy, art, and science, are already sustaining the move away from strict hierarchies of species and towards creaturely assemblies united by moral imagination. In ending this chapter, I want to further specify the contours of vulnerability as a moral concept, as well as the overall importance that its relationship to constitutive vulnerability has for Ecocene politics.

* * *

So far in this chapter, I have tied creaturely multiplicity and self-difference to environmental multiplicity expressed as change. I have explored the opportunities and problems this ontology throws up and its political importance. As a possible bridge between the ontological and the field of action (politics), I have developed the concept of vulnerability as an onto-normative category that can stretch the moral imagination in ways that do not betray its ontological foundations.

Politics is bound to inhabit the space between processual change and the endurance of particular creatures through time. This space is well understood through the concept of vulnerability, in its double sense of constitutive (denoting the definitional openness that creatures must have in order to endure) and ethical (denoting the experience of change as a potential problem by individual creatures) vulnerability. In concluding this argument, I want to spend some time on the space between processual change and individual embodiment and endurance.

The growing awareness of the Anthropocene has been met with a growing literature on the end of the world. It has become weirdly commonplace to talk of the sixth great extinction and to accept, to some degree, the inevitability of an increasing and generalized loss. But the whole imaginary of 'the end' is fundamentally tied to just one sense of vulnerability, namely the ethical one: *this* particular thing is ending, and there is a level of desperation understandably felt at this loss. However, focusing too narrowly on the end misses the broader point of the necessary reframing of politics in-between the concern for individual beings and the ability to adapt to changing processes. This is why I choose to speak of decomposition and recomposition, rather than 'the end'. It is not in order to deny the idea of loss, which is absolutely implied in both the Anthropocene and the Ecocene, and to which we must respond, but rather to uncover the possibilities that arise when we accept the structuring role of ecological processes over and beyond particular ideas of belonging.

Vulnerability is pertinent to the Ecocene both as a condition, and as an ethical principle invoking the power of the moral imagination to inhabit the exposure of many different kinds of beings (the list is, crucially, endless). The Ecocene only increases this fundamental exposure because it is the irruption of processes over and beyond any single being. To focus too narrowly on beings appears a luxury of relative stasis, something no longer sustainable in times of profound and indefinite change. Yet to ignore beings for processes risks callousness. Furthermore, vulnerability is increasingly known through the vast apparatus of science. Whereas in the Holocene humans could rely on their intuition and direct senses for most of their labor, this is no longer the case; the pathogens affecting plants and animals alike, the changing weather patterns to which we are not adapted, all of these require an alliance between the micro-scale of the senses and the capacity of the sciences to generalize through the extensive deployment of immense sensory devices.

The concept of vulnerability that I have tied to the Ecocene is a tortured vulnerability, caught between the acceptance of—and the desire to protect oneself from—change. It undermines any idea of 'solving' the

Anthropocene. The significance of the new era is precisely that it cannot be solved, and it is as if we are waking up from a bad dream. As the general intensification of change threatens a growing list of attachments, politics is tasked with remaining within the undertow created by rapid transformations. The Ecocene is tragically caught between constitutive vulnerability and the capacity to live in another's skin and therefore experience its vicissitudes. It is useless to wish this condition away. Instead, the question is which political concepts can build on this new condition so that recomposition can accompany loss. Reciprocity, responsibility, and mutualism are such concepts, as I will argue in what follows. But these ideas do not deliver us from the necessity to endure within the permanent difficulty of the Ecocene. They may simply allow us to grow accustomed to the difficulty itself.

The possibility of renovating practices is a very real one, and it flows through exactly the same channels of expanding the moral imagination that have always been there. The way in which practices evolve in relation with the increasing knowledge we may have of the environing world is instructive. Currently, for example, a debate is simmering in the biological sciences on whether we can use the concept of pain for plants, or whether their ways of communicating and sensing the environment can warrant speak of their partaking in conscious activity. The point is not that, once we have decided the matter of whether or not plants feel pain, we are required to change practice. Rather, it is questioning itself that changes practices, inasmuch as it opens up relational possibilities that did not exist before.

Raimond Gaita, in exploring his own relationship with his dog, notes that "we do not think of behaving towards goldfish or insects in the way we behave towards our cats and dogs". He continues: "I suspect it is not their objective differences in themselves that matter to us so much as *the relations those features make possible for us*" (2016, 19, emphasis added). Indeed, it is not a matter of settling ethical disputes by invoking biological facts. Rather, the more we know about the multiplicities that lie behind appearances, the more likely it is that new kinds of relationships can be forged. Here, again, the anthropological record is highly instructive. There is no reason to believe that one cannot have relationships with goldfish similar to that which Gaita has with his dog. It is always a matter of what counts, and what counts is always already a hybrid of fact and value. In the Ecocene, what counts is both forever open to change (adding more) and inscribed within a wider program of perpetually rethinking membership in a community. The fact of vulnerability can become an important criterion of belonging.

The Ecocene tension between the desire to control processes such that our preferred creatures survive and the enabling of creatures themselves to use their exposure to their advantage is seen in very practical ways. In the next chapter I will show this idea in practice through the work of rewilders who introduce animals to environments from which they have previously disappeared. In doing this, they want the creatures to endure, but often to endure as they have been imagined. The creatures, on the other hand, always surprise us because they are encountering fundamentally new environments. A European Bison that became extinct in an area 300 years ago *cannot* be introduced to the same environment, and therefore will not be the same creature, whatever that might mean.

Focusing on processual change instead suggests a kind of suspension of expectation, and a certain tolerance for finitude, for mortality perhaps. It may be that caring for the conditions of life, like habitat redundancy, and therefore fighting against modern simplification, is a way of deploying vulnerability politically. It may be that we have to literally make space, and give up on strict notions of what should live where. This would allow for the possibility of caring, through a focus on process, for things unseen, unremarked, disliked, or even not yet existing.

This is an intergenerational care that takes time to cultivate because it does not, and cannot, control what should and should not be. It is not just a concern for the existence of future humans as such (this is not the intended sense of 'intergenerational' in this discussion). It is a series of interventions guided by the sympathetic imagination and the requirements for the tribulations of any life to endure. Intergenerational care in this sense is anti-individualist: it is not about my children, because what I may care about matters as a momentary concrescence in a process that cannot deliver, in the future, *what* I care about. It can only deliver the inheritance of caring itself. This is an intergenerational relay with the difficulty of the moral imagination, and an insistence on inhabiting and passing on that difficulty itself.

4. Renovative Practice

Enhancement and Ritualization through Restoration

One of the most pernicious effects of modern development has been the wide acceptance of the idea that people are bad for nature. We see this in too many forms to count, from the resurgence of Malthusian population panic, to the idea that people are inherently consumptive of the land. This is paradoxical, because the only thing that is empirically true is that modern development *itself* is inherently consumptive and ecologically destructive. 'People' is a hopelessly broad category that does not suggest any particular way of inhabiting the land. To think that 'people' are inherently bad for 'nature' is therefore to, perhaps unwittingly, buy into the dominance of modernity, as if there were no other ways for people to live, except consumptive ones.

An increasing amount of mobilization happens precisely around the idea that cultures need not be inherently consumptive but can also be regenerative. I prefer the term renovative—taken from the idea of renovation—as it expresses both the necessity of radical change, and the impossibility of returning to some idealized past. The Ecocene is forcing a renovation of multiple ways of inhabiting lands, moving away from modern notions that hamper cyclical rejuvenation, and towards mutually beneficial partnerships with a wide variety of beings.

There are several important aspects to this shift away from development and towards the renovation of ecological relationships. First is the recognition of the fact that human responsibility for human well-being cannot be separated from wider ecological processes or, in particular, ecological multiplicity. The simplification of the natural world is also a radical simplification of the human world, as well as an abortion of possible relationships, both now and in the future (see Chapter 6).

Second, people can be extremely beneficial to the land. In fact, countless ways of being in the world have benefitted a wide number of creatures and places and have made possible multiple ecological processes (see the discussion of soil in Intermezzo I). What we need to overcome is not our own embodiment as mammals with needs, but rather the structuring of these needs in inherently destructive terms. Third, each one of us has inherited a ghostly apparatus of practices that are not inherently committed to reproducing extractivist modernity. Rediscovering these practices, and their renovation through ritualization, is a crucial part of the work of building new infrastructures of reciprocity.

These highly abstract terms have an incredible power to act. From river restoration in the inner city to the reintroduction of lost species to diverse environments, responsibility, reciprocity, enhancement, and ritualization of land-based practices are already transforming communities. There is no need to invent practices out of nothing, as multiple communities are already experimenting with renovating their ecological relationships. None of them is perfect, and none transferable *as such* to other situations. Many of them fail. This is precisely where abstractions are crucial: they allow us to move experiences from one place to another, by transposing their meaning (or, better, their hermeneutic thrust) above and beyond their particular realization. They also allow us to keep the borders of any particular situation open, to never stop and decide that the job—however it may be defined—has been accomplished.

* * *

The history of nature conservation has been the history of setting aside land 'for nature'. This process has of course involved the displacement of human populations, as well as those of undesirable animals and plants. The idea of a space dedicated for nature alone has, in other words, come with a paradoxical amount of policing the naturalness of the spaces thus created. The national park model, pioneered in the United States in the nineteenth century, has been exported throughout the world, often along colonial lines and replicating colonial practices of exclusion and control.

Büscher and Fletcher (2020) usefully track the early history of conservation in tandem with the early history of capital accumulation. They write:

> conservation and capitalism have intrinsically co-produced each other, and hence the nature-culture dichotomy is foundational to both. This point can quite easily be illustrated by looking at historical evidence, in particular the earliest foundations of modern conservation that were laid in a swiftly industrializing Great Britain in the seventeenth and eighteenth centuries. As has been highlighted many times by different authors, it was during this time that the infamous enclosure movement not only established elite tracts of 'wild' lands mostly used for preservation and hunting but at the same time forced people out of rural subsistence and so aided in the formation of the labor reserves that industrial capitalism needed (72, italics in original)

There is now thankfully an ample literature dealing with the problems and contradictions of this history. What is of interest here, and what points us towards the idea of renovative practices, is the development in the last decades of forms of nature conservation that are consciously trying to get away from the loaded history of this practice. The extent to which they manage to do so, and the ways in which past histories are unconsciously inherited and reproduced, remains to be seen. But what is notable is the fervent experimentation that has been undeniable in the structuring of the idea of conservation, from the question of what there is to conserve, all the way to the many hows.

To begin with the what: it can no longer be taken for granted that nature conservation is about protecting a nature 'out there' from inherently consumptive humans. Many have already shown that areas of the natural world that had been relegated to 'pristine wilderness' have always had a history in common with people. The Amazon rainforest, for example, is rich in species of fruiting trees in part because they were planted, intentionally, by the considerable human populations that lived there before colonization. Similarly, the North American planes are the result of symbiotic relationships between humans and buffalo that occurred through the practice of wielding fire in constructive ways. The same story repeats itself, from African savannahs and tropical rainforests to the Australian outback. People have always been in intimate intercourse with the world around them, often in ways that have *enhanced* environments and helped other creatures thrive.

It would be misleading to portray this knowledge as universally accepted. It is not the case that nature conservation attempting to radically separate people and environments no longer exists. If anything, it is still a dominant practice, as well as a resurgent theory; a conservative backlash is happening, with some of the most prominent conservationists of the twentieth century proposing that, in the twenty-first century, 'we' should set half the earth aside for nature, leaving the other half for people (for example, Wilson 2016). This kind of proposal is an acceleration of what nature conservation was already doing, and leads it to its logical conclusion: a stark separation of humans and nature, which is assumed to be the only way of preserving the variety of life.

In *The Conservation Revolution* (2020), Büscher and Fletcher spend a great deal of time exploring the tensions and contradictions of these two waves of conservation, which they call "new conservation" and "neoprotectionism". They are particularly interested in how both of these ways of conceiving of conservation are still tied to varieties of modern development, and in particular to capitalist accumulation. It is true that, in practice, many new conservation projects, whether rooted in stark separation or in human-nature assemblages, uncritically accept the need to make nature profitable in order to conserve it. This, as they show, is highly problematic, because it ultimately fails to address the root cause of the Ecocene, namely the unsustainability of consumptive modes of development.

Whether consumptive development can only be 'capitalist' is a moot point. In my view, modernity need not be capitalist in order to be destructive, whereas for many others in the radical conservation debate it is capitalism as such that is the root cause of ecological crises, hence why they adopt the term Capitalocene for the present era. However that may be, the point remains that neoprotectionism upholds an untenable, radical distinction between humans and environments, while new conservationists too often embrace market mechanisms that end up eroding the very foundations of their goals. In other words, conservation theory has not yet managed to find radically alternative ways of enhancing, for the long term, human-inclusive spaces.

The ethos of new conservation, which is based on a rejection of this dualism, is steadily expanding and gaining ground. Its sites of experimentation are also multiplying, and offering pragmatic solutions to intractable seeming conflicts. New conservation increasingly resembles an extremely dynamic jumble of theories and practices that travel in multiple directions. Developing the non-dualist ethos in a staunchly anti-capitalist form, Büscher and Fletcher offer the concept of convivial conservation as a way forward. I will engage with this specifically below. Before that, I want to pause and take a closer look at some conservation practices that seem to be faithfully rooted in an embedded, non-dualist way of being in the world. I will now turn to the practice of ecological restoration.

* * *

Restoration in a classic sense means returning something to a previous state. In ecology, it has therefore meant the attempt to recreate a natural assemblage that has previously existed. The previous state of affairs that acts as a guide for the restoration goal is called a baseline: that to which one is trying return.

This technical meaning of restoration has been amply criticized for producing environments that are of less value than the original, as well as for inviting a moral hazard: the possibility that this kind of technique could let environmental perpetrators off the hook, inasmuch as they could always offer to restore an already damaged environment. These are not baseless concerns: environmental restoration of this kind is a routine part of industrial projects that promise to put everything back together again after the mining is done. The exact way in which the pre-mining and post-mining environment is the same remains to be experienced by communities, and is often no longer the responsibility of the perpetrator once the mining is complete.

The most extensively articulated critiques of restoration along these lines come from Robert Elliot and Eric Katz, who both argue that it is deeply problematic. The origin of land in nonhuman agency is, for Elliot (1982), a crucial part of its value. Restoration cannot but modify the origin story in ways that diminish natural value. Katz (1996, 2009, 2012) went further and claimed that restorations are always ethically problematic, because they perpetuate the dominating culture which brings about natural degradation to begin with. For both Elliot and Katz, the real danger of restoration is the promotion of moral hazard, the idea that we can destroy because we can later restore. As Basl expresses it, "the worry is that restoration, as opposed to preservation or conservation, will govern our decisions concerning natural areas" (2010, 137).

Baseline-specific restoration does imply a dominating imposition on the environment, but only because it relies on the modern dualism of nature and culture, essentializing both (one as valuable because it is free of humans, the other as inherently dominant). As Glenn Deliège points out, Elliot's "argumentation against the restoration thesis requires that we agree with a strong ontological dualism between nature and culture" (Deliège 2007, 138). This kind of dualism misses something crucial, namely the evolutionary story of humans within the environment. Quoting Marjorie Grene, Oelschlaeger argues that "only if we place ourselves [...] without blatant contradiction, within nature, only then can we save the concept of historicity from the self-destruction to which it seems so readily susceptible" (cited in Oelschlaeger 2007, 151). If we understand humans as intrinsic parts of the natural environment, then the task is to understand how human actions can be made to coincide with ethical membership in a natural community.

If lives and worlds are volumetric fittings in continual change, the very notion of the baseline becomes suspect. It is strictly impossible to return to the same state as before, and it is also questionable whether it would be desirable. Instead, there are other aspects with which restoration should concern itself, above and beyond the idea of returning the clock to some past hour and minute. It may be that what is worth restoring does not strictly have to do with the world as a space outside of human influence, nor does it have to do with humans as strictly civilized (outside of nature) creatures. Instead, restoration can migrate away from the modernity that has shackled it to techno-managerial solutions by fixing its gaze on to the very possibility of rich, enhancing *relations* between humans and worlds.

William Jordan III has gone as far as to argue that restoration has the potential to become a new paradigm for conservation and even for the environmental movement writ large, precisely inasmuch as it becomes concerned with renovating relationships. For Jordan, "preservation in the strict sense is impossible" (Jordan 2003, 14), which means that restoration in one form or another is unavoidable in an ethical interaction with the world. But what, exactly, is restoration in this sense?

Jordan points out that human membership in natural communities is as old as human communities themselves, and that restoration in his sense is just as old. "In a general sense, humans have been rehabilitating ecosystems altered or degraded by activities such as agriculture or tree cutting for millennia, through practices such as tree planting and the fallowing of land" (Jordan 2003, 12). To restore, then, is to relate to the land in a way that promotes the endurance of certain ecological processes and the self-conceptualization of humans as beneficial parts of the environment. This mutualism of the ecological relationship implies that restoration is a normative relation, that when humans relate to the environment as restorers, they at the same time can improve their moral lot by becoming beneficial members of a natural community.

The term 'restoration' can apply to this kind of activity aimed at resuscitating a way of relating precisely because mutually beneficial human-environment relations have been part of the history of human communities. What is in fact new is the idea that one can restore according to a strict baseline, and it is new because it is inseparable from a particularly modern way of seeing nature according to the operation of bifurcation described in Chapter 2.

My view of restoration supposes that humans are part of nature and therefore can participate in nature positively (Jordan 1990, Oelschlaeger 2007, Deliège 2007). Restoration need not be understood as replication, but rather as the continuation (or initiation) of a relationship with nature (always in the guise of a particular environment or landscape). The kind of relationship Jordan has in mind is one that he calls "ecological" (Jordan 1994, 18), and he means by that a relationship that is "mutually beneficial". Oelschlaeger, commenting on Leopold's land ethic, argues that "in acting upon the land we define ourselves ('writing' our signature)" (2007, 153). This is similar in important respects, because it opens up the possibility of nature benefiting from our influence, just as we benefit from what nature has to offer.

In this view humans can become members of natural communities, as opposed to mere users, which further implies that restoration projects need to first and foremost engage with the human part of a natural environment. This engagement itself holds the promise of actualizing the potential of membership. In other words, it is not restoration itself, as Elliot and Katz argued, that perpetuates the domination of the natural world, but rather an understanding of restoration "as something humans do to the environment" (Oelschlaeger 2007, 152; he calls this 'weak restoration'). The weak view of restoration is predicated on a techno-logical relation to the natural world that intrinsically separates humans from nature, making the former into agents deciding the fate of the latter. "A richer account of restoration should instead of reducing nature to the status of manipulable object, ensure that the natural space surrounding us transforms into a unique, meaningful place" (Deliège 2007, 137).

In the relational view of restoration, baselines no longer feature prominently. The issue of whether or not a baseline is to be followed at all is secondary to the idea of using restoration for the creation of meaningful human-nature relationships. So, in some cases it might be that a baseline is useful for building membership in the biotic community. The University of Wisconsin Arboretum in Madison, one of the first modern restoration projects, initiated when Aldo Leopold was at the University in the 1930s, is an example of a baseline restoration. But even there, the baseline is used as a *guide* for what is possible, and not as a replicable model. In other places, baseline restorations might be impossible, and then the existence of novel ecosystems (Hobbs et al. 2006, 2009) can in itself be seen as a possibility for creating meaningful relationships. It is, in the abstract, impossible to say what criteria may lead a project of restoration in any particular case. The point is, precisely, that such criteria do not exist above and beyond the renovation of a beneficial way of relating to the environing world.

This way of seeing restoration is radically freeing, and radically democratic. In fact, there is nothing that would be *a priori* excluded from its reach. This opinion is supported by practice. Consider the effort currently underway to restore the Bronx River, flowing through the city of New York, USA. For centuries, it has been used as an open sewer. Industrial pollution, household waste, and raw sewage were all routinely dumped in a river that crossed poor and minority parts of the city. The social dimension of the river's neglect is fairly clear and repeats the same pattern of environmental injustice apparent everywhere else. In 2005, the Bronx River Alliance started putting forward a vision for a restored river. This vision calls for the cleaning of the river's waters, the reintroduction of key species (for example, the oyster, which once thrived in the river, and which could also help in the cleaning of the water through biofiltration), and the creation of a park along the river's watershed.

These kinds of projects are long-term and committed affairs because the time of the intervention is adapted to the complex time of the natural community of which one is becoming a part. Just like relations with olive trees cannot be based on human lifespans, so too relations occasioned through the restoration of a river cannot be short-term. This initiative is based on local participation; through it, local residents take control of their own emancipation and create for themselves a cleaner, more enjoyable environment. Of course, in the process, the river itself becomes more ecologically sound. But the point I want to draw out of this example is in fact best summarized by a local participant in the cleanup operations (Jasmine Benitez) who was asked why she cares—why she shows up to clean the river every day. Her answer: "this is so important for me because this is home for me" (Al Jazeera 2013).

This participant's comments attest to the genealogical importance of restoration in this sense. Introducing the first oysters, cleaning up the garbage, removing debris, rewilding the banks, are all occasions for intermingling the fate of participants with that of the place. Fates become mutually determined, and in that sense a rich genealogical tapestry is being created where none existed before. Those that participate become local, inasmuch as they are now tied, through moments of reciprocal exchange, with the life of the place.

The blueprint for the restoration was drawn up using historical maps of the Bronx River that showed the extent of marshes and forests, now long gone (American Museum of Natural History 2012). This, then, would appear to be a baseline-specific restoration. But because the project is in the Bronx, a dense urban area, it is no longer feasible to use the maps as exact guidance for restoration. In other words, marshes will never cover their previous territory. Even if the overall marsh volume were reinstated, these marshes would still not be 'the same' marshes. In this context, the maps don't so much provide a baseline, as give guidance specific to the river. In other words, based on historical data we can ascertain what used to live in the river, and therefore we are in a better position to judge what could live there now, and what its impact might be. This is to say that the Bronx River restoration is a live example of a project that is only superficially tied to baselines.[1] What it is really

---

[1] The idea of a baseline appears to be most useful as a route into historical research about the environment in question. By choosing particular baselines, one is able to plot how the place has changed, and to determine how it could continue changing, given where and how it has been.

passionate about is restoring the relationship between the community and the river. It is about remaking a community.

The importance of ritual is undeniable in such a process of restoration. If what is aimed at is a renovated relationship with a meaningful place (a "legible landscape", to use Martin Drenthen's term;[2] see Drenthen 2009, 2011, 2018), then this goes through a series of ritualized steps that are themselves part of the creation of membership within a given locality. By 'ritual' I do not mean just the habitual repetition of a series of procedures, but rather that kind of habitual repetition that illuminates aspects of the world that are not directly tied to the acts being repeated. Concretely, the seeding of oysters in the river necessarily happens in a repetitive, scheduled way that has the outward trappings of a ritual. But what indeed makes it ritualistic is the wider context in which the introduction of oysters takes place, such that the repeated act of seeding becomes symbolic of, for example, social regeneration.

Similarly, the Madison Arboretum has been ritualizing the use of fire in the maintenance of a flourishing prairie locality. Cyclically, the prairie undergoes controlled burns because fire is part of that kind of environment. The burns are not just a technical matter to be implemented by specialists, but rather an occasion for participation in forging the genealogical links that will allow people to bequeath that place as inheritance, or to become conscious of the way in which they are holobionts traversed by infinite multiplicity. The repetition of the act of burning is not a mere habit, but rather a ritual; it gestures beyond itself, to the creation and perpetuation of meaningful and reciprocal relationships.

This same analysis can be applied to a project that at first sight may seem far removed from meaningfulness in this sense. The Dutch Oostvaardersplassen is an area of 'new nature' located on land claimed from the sea. It aims to reconstruct a Pleistocene landscape, complete

---

2   Drenthen himself borrows the term 'legible landscapes' from Willem van Toorn and deploys it in his hermeneutical analysis of the environment. He specifically adopts a Ricoeurian perspective, in which he explains that the legible landscape contains "fixed signs that are in need of interpretation, while the author of this text is absent" (2011, 134). The basic idea is that "landscapes contain signs which enable people to 'read' them as meaningful texts" (126). As a further development of this notion, Drenthen has also deployed the concept of a palimpsest (see Drenthen 2015), that is to say the creation of an object of experience through historical layering that is amenable to reading.

with proxy species for long-extinct ones: Heck cattle in place of the Aurochs, and the Konik horse instead of the wild European horse. This kind of restoration—or rewilding, as it is also increasingly called—did not happen where anyone lives and has very little connection to any past extant in living memory. However, the place generates an enormous amount of interest and debate every year in the Netherlands, particularly in relation to the issue of culling (or not) animals in the winter. Whatever one thinks of the Oostvaardersplassen, it is clearly being incorporated in networks of meaning for many people (for more information see Lorimer and Driessen 2014). Although the examples discussed are very different from each other, they all exemplify equally well how restoration in all of its guises always has to be understood in conjunction with the generation of meaning. Nature and culture are not opposites; without one, the other does not exist.

* * *

One of the ways in which people are changed by ritualistic interaction with the environing world is in becoming aware of the radical autonomy of that world. The idea that the environing world deserves to be left to its own devices straddles the border between the dualism of classical conservation and the radical potential of baseline-free restoration. On the face of it, making room for the autonomy of the natural world may imply the kind of separation that this book, and so many practices, are trying to think beyond. On the other hand, the self-willed nature of the world surely has a place in the Ecocene, the time when it is precisely the irruption of natural processes that re-dimensions humans. There is a sense in which renovating ecological relationships is always predicated on the capacity of the environing world to mend itself under the right circumstances. The role of humans becomes the creation and maintenance of such circumstances through ritualized practice. One way in which this is being attempted is through rewilding.

Rewilding is a relatively young concept and practice, though there is already significant debate and a complex and variegated history to recount (see *inter alia* Prior and Ward 2016, Tănăsescu 2017, Gammon 2018, 2019, Drenthen 2018, Jørgensen 2015). That is not what I want to do here, but rather I wish to zoom in on the way in which this concept can contribute to Ecocene politics, and the dangers that lie within. The project of rewilding started as a fairly classical baseline restoration focused on the return of ecological processes. It quickly became unmoored from baselines, in part because of their untenability and incoherence, and instead came to mean the practice of restoring ecological processes through the (re)introduction of particular animals (Prior and Ward 2016, Tănăsescu 2017).

The basic idea is simple and sound: worlds are what they are because of how they are composed. So, in areas where a great number of animals with a big influence on their world have disappeared, it stands to reason that returning these animals would also return certain processes that have subsided in their absence. For example, the return of the European bison to its former habitats also means the return of a different kind of habitat, namely one where the biggest land mammal in Europe is grazing and stomping and digging and otherwise living its outsized life. In ecology, these kinds of animals are called keystone species or, more popularly, ecosystem engineers.

Rewilding has latched onto the reintroduction of these engineers as a way of recreating rich ecological networks without the need—pronounced in classical conservation—to maintain nature in a particular form. In other words, let the bison do the work. In principle this is laudable and makes good sense as a step away from the management-intensive concern for what should live where, and in what form. But in practice it often becomes hard to distinguish between rewilding and the older conservation it is trying to supplant.

As early as the 1990s, well before rewilding achieved its current prominence, Drury had characterized much conservation work in this way:

> Enormous amounts of effort are invested in studying and managing ecosystems, even though the practitioners involved will usually confess when pressed that they cannot identify the boundaries or even the full composition of their 'object' of study. Underlying much of this work is a basic assumption that in the absence of humans, wilderness will itself evolve to produce a balanced harmony of best use, defined in terms of some set of tangibles such as primary productivity, biomass, or species diversity

Rewilding often appears to be covered by this kind of characterization, as if by introducing the right animals into the right places some sort of optimum would be achieved. The idea of stepping back and letting the animals do the work is routinely not implemented in practice, because of how that 'work' is thought of. The reintroduced animals are considered as having a task, which contradicts the spirit of experimentation that in theory accompanies their release.

What is missing is the idea of relational, hermeneutic connection that is fundamental for the renovation of ecological relationships. Rewilding projects have had no trouble becoming popular with enthusiasts, but they have been much slower in becoming radically participatory. In theory as well as in practice, they are agnostic as to the kind of radical democracy that necessarily grounds relational restoration. Perhaps this explains why rewilding has so quickly migrated to the mainstream of policy, abandoning some of the early substantive commitment to a *socio-ecological* approach. Increasingly, rewilding is presented as a solution to climate change, biodiversity loss, and so on, that is to say, as yet another techno-managerial tool that fixes problems generated by that very way of thinking and acting in the world. Rewilding appears to be the solution that will give back to nature, but that solution comes uncomfortably close to relegating half of the earth to wilderness.

Introducing animals and letting them determine their environments can therefore become another way of setting environments aside, even if they are now appreciated through the actions of certain creatures. But what happens when those animals move out of the area designated for rewilding? How, in the absence of reiterative interactions with this kind of project, are people going to accept the return of megafauna that their ancestors fought hard to extinguish?

Instead, we need to create diffuse infrastructures that support communities in restoring and, most importantly, in restoring cyclically, such that restoration becomes ritualized and engrained. There is no use restoring once, rather we need to constantly adapt, alongside environments and their creatures. It is in this sense that the idea of autonomy can be deceiving and can support exclusionary politics as long as people 'encroach'. Autonomy instead should be seen as the mystery that binds people and natural processes together, that life force that keeps on moving and that can be used in order to enhance communities. Alas, without natural autonomy there is no possibility of restoring anything! Autonomy is the capacity of natural processes to exceed human understanding and expectations, and to work of their own accord even though they may benefit from enlightened intervention.

Rewilding practice is by no means decidedly on one or the other side of the conservation debate. Instead, it is still finding its footing and evaluating its commitments, although it is increasingly co-opted by businesses in strategic partnerships. This is visible, for example, in the insistence of major rewilding organizations (such as Rewilding Europe) on ecotourism as some kind of miracle revenue generator for local communities. So far, the evidence that this kind of economic activity can actually serve a community is very scarce, and mostly consists of self-generated publicity around apparently successful businesses. But very little radically democratic work actually happens in specific projects such that local communities would not only be able to monetize certain aspects of their environment, but also be able to decide what to introduce where, and how to maintain their own livelihood within their environment. Fortunately, the need to design rewilding projects democratically is felt despite the organizational structures and funding mechanisms that render it increasingly difficult.

For example, in the Southern Carpathians, Romania, a rewilding project has, since 2014, introduced a number of European bison (also known as wisent) to an area where they had been locally extinct for centuries. Despite this long absence, toponyms and oral histories still recall their presence. Several elements of this project deserve highlighting, as it shows how a radically emplaced strategy can lead away from human—nature dualisms and towards conviviality.[3]

The very beginning of the project started with a public meeting between the rewilders and the mayor, open to any villager wishing to participate. It was within this forum (and not as a policy directive from above) that the very idea of reintroducing wisent to the communal lands of the village of Armeniș was brought up. After agreeing that wisent would be brought to the village lands, the project continued to operate on an open and participatory basis, recruiting local rangers and making a festival of subsequent reintroduction events. In other words, there was a conscious attempt to ritualize the reintroduction of the animals in order to forge genealogical links inclusive of both people and wisent.

---

3   I am grateful to Alexandru Bulacu and Adrian Hăgătiș for their generous guidance through this project.

The animals introduced to the surrounding Țarcu Mountains have themselves had to forge new cultural ties. In this setting, a complex relationship with humans was developed, and the herds were supported in their quest for a new kind of emplacement. I have documented this process in detail elsewhere (see Tănăsescu 2019), but here I just want to point out that the idea of autonomy also means being surprised by what partners in relationships may do. Many wisents did not behave as expected, and in fact the group as a whole has started to write their own history. As I wrote in the article detailing this case,

> trusting the wisents to find their own path in a new environment has given rise to unexpected behaviors. In the Țarcu mountains, herds have spent weeks at 1600 meters in the middle of winter. The wisents reintroduced in 2015 have changed their behavior so profoundly that they are almost impossible to get near: within three years, fed individuals have become so shy rangers can barely see them. Within the past two years, the only wisents that had problems (one died, the other is very interested in people) were two that came from an intensely managed breeding center. The rest are charting their course through new territory (Tănăsescu 2019, 105–106)

The fact of creatures surprising the human observer is actually routine. Without this kind of surprise and frustration of expectation we may not have had a natural historical approach to begin with. In the case of the wisent, an important element in their development of a new kind of culture is also the site of introduction. The disappearance of this animal from the European landscape (only twelve wisents had survived by the end of World War II) was the result of a long history of persecution, both in terms of habitat appropriation and hunting. It is therefore obvious that for a long time before their disappearance, their cultures were transformed by an antagonistic relationship with people. It is this history of antagonism that drove these animals to forests. Given a choice of territory, they would settle in prairie-like, or in any case more open, environments, just like their American cousins, the buffalo.

When that option disappeared, they became forest animals. There is still no possibility of them living outside forests today, even more so than centuries ago. We are still reintroducing wisent into a kind of exile, to the very places that they formerly used as refuge. And yet, the animals themselves have changed, and will continue to change, in relation to forest environments.

From the point of view of renovating genealogical links, this project seems very successful. However, this core feature of any renovative practice is often overlooked and effaced when reverting back to the standard grand narratives that regard rewilding as a universal solution. As we have seen, one increasingly important part of rewilding advocacy is that this kind of project can become economically important for local communities. The thrust of the argument is that rewilding can pay, mostly in the form of tourism revenues. This has the effect of neutering the politically radical core of the idea of ecological renovation. It is not about attracting tourism revenues, but rather about empowering communities to define their own membership within wider ecological communities, in such a way as to fundamentally question the role of the managerial state (and its subjugation to 'the economy') in structuring the multiplicity of their relations.

* * *

Restoring ecological relationships, whether under the guise of rewilding or anything else, is a process that will look different in different locations. Despite these differences, the ideas of contributing to mutually beneficial relationships, forging genealogical links, and engaging in reciprocal exchange, are common threads that can be seen in grassroots projects everywhere. Bram Büscher and Robert Fletcher have done a lot to push conservation away from the dualism of its early days and towards convivial forms, namely ones rooted in the kind of genealogical imbrication developed here. They have also been rightly insistent on the ways in which conviviality needs to resist appropriation by dominant forms of political economy.

In particular, they have positioned the concept of convivial conservation as fundamentally anti-capitalist. In their own words, "our conceptualization of conviviality is necessarily post-capitalist and non-dualist". In particular, they focus much attention on how conviviality must be combined with a sustained strategy for degrowth. Just like this book, the ideas they present are advanced as part of a broader coalition of rethinking and reinvention of practices, at all scales. Convivial conservation would then be part of a wider strategy of overcoming capitalist development and moving towards a world of stable or decreasing consumption that would leave much more room for the kinds of engagement that I argue for here.

Their contribution to the conservation debate seems to me one of the most important of the past several decades, precisely because it moves decisively beyond dualism. The insistence on post-capitalism is also welcome, inasmuch as it is understood as a commitment to political-economic critique. However, that commitment is wider than (post) capitalism itself, and should therefore reflect the fact that, even in a post-capitalist world, environmental destruction is eminently possible. This is not to deny the urgency of focusing on degrowth now, of calling out industrial culprits, or of stopping the runaway power of investment capitalism. All of these are necessary, even urgent, steps. But the exclusive focus on capitalism obscures the role of domination and Diamond's "deadness of spirit" (see next chapter) in producing human rupture from the environing world, as well as aiding in the radical simplification of nature. As the collective authors of *The Evolution Observatory* (2019)[4] put it, "why hasn't any revolution succeeded in rooting out the logic of domination itself" (40)?

This is not mere nitpicking; it strikes at the heart of a current theoretical rupture, nicely exemplified in *The Conservation Revolution*, between post-humanist critique and anti-capitalist commitments. Post-humanism seeks to understand the ways in which humanity as a concept has been decentered by the Anthropocene, while anti-capitalist critique has little patience for such decentering, worrying that this makes it hard to call culprits out and to engage in the class struggle that they see as necessary for the revolutionary moment. But this is, in many ways, a false dichotomy that distracts from the important points that both kinds of theorizing raise and ultimately have in common.

David Graeber serves as a good example of how radical theory can remain radical without becoming entrenched in a particular semi-dogmatic camp. He usefully reminds us that 'revolution' need not mean a cataclysmic moment (something that many leftists dream about), but rather can be an everyday practice (see Chapter 7 for an extended discussion). He also shows how organized political and economic power is less real than is usually presumed, and therefore also less stable; the everyday of most people's lives still goes on outside of formal power configurations, and therefore has tremendous potential. He was

---

4   'L'observatoire de l'évolution', in *Manifeste pour l'invention d'une nouvelle condition paysanne*. « [...] pourquoi aucune révolution n'a véritablement réussi a endiguer la logique de la domination ».

also extremely invested in showing how current forms of capitalism are inherently destructive and should therefore be opposed, but the opposition does not necessarily mean "taking over the state", and the destructiveness of capitalism is part of the tendency of power to dominate and be destructive. It is that tendency, as much as capitalism itself, that needs to be addressed.

That is precisely what post-humanism does. Decentering the human also means recontextualizing its power, and critiquing power as such, in all of its forms. The ethic of mutualism that is inherited from early anarchism and that has most significantly been developed in modern biology is precisely a radical challenge to placing power and domination center-stage in the conduct of life. Domination is neither the best, nor the only way of leading a human life, nor is it the evolutionary engine that social theory, enamored of power, snuck into early biology. It is true that in the present moment capitalist development is the most urgent form of domination that needs to be opposed, but it does not follow from this that with capitalism, domination will disappear.[5]

Convivial conservation, or my own conceptualization of restorative practices, needs to be situated within a wider political-economic context, but it also needs to be seen as a way of forging humans, and environments, that participate in mutual beneficence more so than in mutual domination. The post-humanist reliance on relations is a positive step towards this, as is the concept of conviviality and its critique of capitalist development. It is on that common basis that radical theory and practice can move forward, beyond stating one's commitment to anti-capitalism as such. We currently need all strategies to work towards a more mutualist world. But it remains the case that a mutualist state is still a state, and it will therefore be the small spaces of resistance that in the long term continue to fight for radical ecological democracy.

More than a hundred years ago Peter Kropotkin, writing about evolutionary theory, remarked that "the fittest are not the physically strongest, nor the cunningest, but those who learn to combine so as mutually to support each other, strong and weak alike, for the welfare

---

5   A similarly ethos of anti-domination and continuing experimentation is also present in the work of some ecologists and soil scientists. For example, Marc-André Selosse, in *L'Origine du Monde* (2021), writes: "no methodological revelation, no philosophy from another century will guide us" [...] One should not "consider any solution as eternal, and no state of affairs (especially past ones) as perfect" (440).

of the community" (1903, 2). This holds as much for political dynamics as it does for ecological ones: the fittest, and therefore the most resilient, are those that can adapt to change through mutual cooperation, and therefore by definition the units of political resilience are scaled down towards the local level. The power of the state has to be co-opted to support the resilience of these levels, and it therefore may be that it is supranational organizations that offer the best model for revolutionary, big-scale change, and not sates. Taking over the state may now mean dissolving it in favor of a direct, supra-national-to-local network of relations. Achieving this would mean fighting against the nativism that so often infects politics and opening up towards principles of common life based on reciprocal relations with the environing world. I now turn to these.

5. Ecopolitical Ethics, Part I

[handwritten: what kinds of action does an ontology make possible?]

Reciprocity

In the previous chapters, I started to sketch the ontological contours of a politics geared towards living, permanently, in the Ecocene. I also intimated that the importance of ontological description is in great part generated by the kinds of actions it makes possible. Though this account of the relationship between description and prescription risks being accused of committing the famous naturalistic fallacy (one cannot base ought on is), this is not so. Instead, I mean to draw attention to the features of description that are intrinsically tied to the mechanisms of power, and therefore to a great extent come to define prescription as well.[1] Now I want to shift towards developing two moral concepts that are crucial for a mutualist politics and that fit neatly within the ontological scaffolding already built: reciprocity, and responsibility (next chapter).

The idea of reciprocity is usually conceived of within a human-centered context, mainly because it is assumed that only humans can reciprocate, or that is to say, only human relationships can be built on the idea of mutual and commensurate exchange. It may be more easily accepted that certain kinds of animals reciprocate human actions, but reference to landscapes, rivers, plants, or apparently simpler animals as capable of reciprocity seems to have been largely regarded as nonsense in Western philosophical traditions. I suggest that this is so for two reasons: the relegation of anthropology to the margins of philosophical thought, and the dominance of recognition (whether implicitly or explicitly) in moral thought.

---

1   For a much more extensive treatment of the relationship between descriptions and prescriptions, based on a reading of Wittgenstein, see Cavell's *Must We Mean What We Say?* (2002). Also see my use of this discussion in Tănăsescu (2020).

This chapter argues that recognition is not the only, nor the best, way of conceiving of ethical relationships with environing worlds. To see this, we will have to take a serious look at philosophical traditions that center on reciprocity, and try to learn from them how this concept could work. I will also draw on the ontological foundations laid down earlier in order to build up the concept in ways that can facilitate a politics fit for the Ecocene.

* * *

Part of the poverty of thought on reciprocity comes from the assumption that this term applies first and foremost to material exchange. The paradigmatic model here would be the exchange of gifts between two or more people, where one act of gifting leads to a reciprocal return. At most, this model can be extended to acts as such, though they may not contain the exchange of something. Acts of kindness, for example, can be reciprocated.

These senses are there, to be sure, but they do not exhaust the ethics of reciprocity. In fact, they obscure the many different ways in which reciprocal exchange is mostly non-material, that is to say, it is involved in practices and acts that do not have an immediate material gain as a goal. Even more crucially, it is also involved in perception as such, explaining in part how the perception of worlds works. In other words, there are ontological elements to the concept of reciprocity, and these are what some philosophical traditions have seized upon in order to build infrastructures of reciprocity that structure human interchange with the world.

This is not a question of juxtaposing 'Indigenous' and 'Western' philosophies in a binary and often caricatured way that is inimical to the recomposition and renovation of diverse practices. Instead, I am interested in following the thread of a concept as it appears through multiple instantiations, and these are to be found wherever they have manifested, whether through 'Western' philosophers or 'Indigenous' ones. These particular terms quickly outlive their usefulness and become stereotypical portrayals.

Especially when speaking about indigeneity, it is impossible to escape the colonial history that relegated anything substantially different to this category, while being completely blind to continuity, similarity, or 'indigeneity' within colonial nations themselves. In other words, there is no such thing as 'Indigenous philosophy', except as a hopelessly general term that wishes to distinguish itself from Western modernity. But as Chakrabarty eloquently points out, modernity is not really Western anymore, if indeed it ever was. Instead, what is meant by modernity is a way of thinking that is predicated, as I have argued via Debaise in Chapter 2, on the bifurcation of nature. If this is all that modernity is (and, of course, its attendant projects of development that make no sense without the bifurcation of nature), then there are non-moderns in Paris and moderns in the Amazon.

The preceding sentence makes sense because of the fact that 'Paris' and the 'Amazon' have become placeholders. I hope, by the end of this argument, that this kind of sentence will make much less sense, as we will have become accustomed to thinking of details, differences and similarities to such an extent that 'Indigenous' and 'Western' can no longer apply to imagined geographies that flatten volumetric worlds. Instead of using this false juxtaposition between supposed enemies, I want to think about both what may be useful in the concept of indigeneity, and where the lure of modernity may reside. I will start here with the concept of indigeneity, leaving the lure of modernity for the next chapter.

There is a need to think through risky concepts even though they carry with them colonial histories that may perpetuate themselves. The risk must be met so that, with enough vigilance, key notions can turn a new page and mean something new, just as revolution shifted from meaning the return of the same to the irruption of the spectacularly new (Arendt 1963). Being indigenous has had, in colonial history, a stubborn and dangerous association with nativism. Instead, it can signify reciprocal relations between lands and their inhabitants, with no nativist criteria whatsoever. In that sense it can move from a racialized term, to one of political ethics.

This movement from one meaning to another is not arbitrary: the seeds of plasticity are internal to the term, or more precisely to the forms of life that it inhabits. It is through Indigenous practices that we see how racialized notions are not intrinsic to their lives, but rather hail from colonial legacies. It is from particular Indigenous people that we learn what makes them indigenous in their own eyes, namely genealogical relations to particular lands and particular communities of beings. But this is not a return to some mythical kernel that magically survived hundreds of years of colonialism. No, it is always about reinventing.

Nandita Sharma, in *Home Rule* (2020), shows persuasively how the concept of the indigenous native, as well as that of the migrant, are inseparable from the history of the passage from empires to nation states, a history largely coinciding with the core of colonial expansion. She argues that "those categorized as Indigenous-Natives were subject to a new imperial regime of 'protection', one that worked to enclose them within 'custom'" (23). The association of natives with some form of "harmony with nature" also owes its existence to the imperial creation of native reserves. This particular history of enclosure and the subsequent "protection" of native populations in designated areas has also been decisive in the history of nature conservation until today (see Chapters 2 and 4). In other words, how colonial power has thought about nature (as an 'out-there' to be protected) has everything to do with how it thought about Indigenous people (as people fundamentally belonging to nature, and therefore with no history).

The way in which colonial power perceived the relationship between people and different places is crucial for understanding the nativist undertones of indigeneity. Sharma shows how, in the case of the category of migrants, states conceptualized them as out of place, whereas the Indigenous natives were considered as in place. It makes sense to think about the importance of place in the creation of these categories, but I think that the suggestion that states perceived a tight fit between different kinds of populations and different places does not quite touch on why the notion of place is instrumental.

The idea of being out of place relies first and foremost on a concept of place. This is precisely what the migrant threatens, an idea of home, an abode, a place in other words that is already somebody else's. On the other hand, the idea of place is *not* that which allows states to literally create the categories of natives and migrants. The post-WWI shuffling of 'national' populations feeds the deceptive idea of place as employed by budding nation states. It is precisely not the determinacy and detailed context of particular places that counts. Instead, it is an empty idea of space, of flat and vacant (and therefore easily appropriable) territory, that the nation states are working with. In this sense the migrant is not out of place, but rather *unplaceable*, that is to say a figure that is radically spatialized, to such an extent that it cannot come down to earth and find a place.

It is the supposed native that is always already in place, though here again this is misleading: the native is *placeable*, not already in place, otherwise how could someone become native, and how could reservations that bear only tangential relationships with self-defined territories be constructed? At the base of the migrant—native dialectic that state power has depended on, as Sharma brilliantly shows, is a dialectic of space and place within which these categories operate. In this sense, native Indigenous individuals are seen as always already belonging to a place (an idea that thrives today in the notion of harmony with nature, for example), but this can only be so—from a nationalist perspective—because of the very possibility of being moved about in an abstract space in order to emplace a tangible space. What is sorely missing here is the multiplicity of places and the volumetric nature of space, which allows for the development of myriad relationships, relationships that have no connection whatsoever with racial categories or with forms of nativism. For indigeneity to be de-nationalized, in this sense, it has to break through the space—place dialectic of the state and instead insist on relationality itself as carrying the infinite work of emplacement. There is nothing but dynamic fitting, because there is no such thing as an unplaceable creature.

Sharma argues that ideas of Indigenous nativism are inseparable from those of autochthony, literally meaning someone who "sprung from the earth", that is to say who naturally belongs to a place (40). "Autochthons were defined not only as 'springing forth from the land' but also as *immobile subjects*. In being so closely associated with a place, Indigenous-Natives were natured" (41, emphasis added). The idea of immobility plays a key role in the construction of nativist indigeneity, and in the fencing off of radically different possibilities of being. In much Indigenous politics today, the unreflectively assimilated idea of Indigenous-Native insists on rootedness to a particular land. This does two things: it encourages fantasies of harmony, and it effaces the history of migration that defines *any* people. In other words, the idea of inherent rootedness sits very uneasily with actual human history.

Much of the history that Sharma explores can be denied power by thinking differently about what makes someone indigenous. There is an undeniable lure to the idea of belonging, and surely it is not *that* that needs to be denied or thrown out altogether. But are there ways of belonging, and in that sense of being indigenous, that can escape reproducing the racialized nativism that initially gives meaning to these terms? Can one belong without positing a migrant that, definitionally, does not? I think the answer is yes, particularly if we move away from state-level dynamics that perpetuate nativist tropes, and towards philosophical practices that remain fluid, multiple, and free from racialized categories.

Māori philosophy and practice are excellent sites for exploring the possibilities of being indigenous in non-nativist ways.[2] Instead of looking towards an idealized past that naturalizes people in place, Māori philosophies are rather concerned with recuperating pasts from the perspective of the relations they promise. They are also excellent philosophies for starting to explore the idea of reciprocity which, as I will argue, is at the core of a concept of belonging that is open, changeable, multiple, and fundamentally non-nativist.

* * *

Aotearoa or New Zealand is one of the last lands to be settled by people.[3] Until about 800 years ago, there were no *mammals* on those islands at all, because none had been able to reach them. The reason for this is quite simple, if one considers the location of Aotearoa in the middle of the biggest and most turbulent ocean in the world. The eventual settlement of the islands by people appears then all the more improbable. Polynesian navigators achieved this astounding feat by taking their navigational cues from the stars, winds, currents, birds and whales. When they finally saw, on the horizon, the long cloud formations that are indicative of land, they knew they had reached something interesting. The islands became known as Aotearoa: the long, white cloud.

The relatively recent settlement of these lands allows for a contemplation of the rapidity of cultural evolution. Māori became

---

2   Surely not the only philosophical tradition appropriate for this task. But one must start somewhere, especially so as to avoid speaking in generalities that would cover all 'Indigenous philosophy'.

3   What follows in this section is based on independent fieldwork carried out in New Zealand, as well as consultation of original sources and Māori scholarly work.

Māori[4] after that initial settlement, and constructed philosophical, legal, political and social traditions within a voluminous space that was completely different, in almost every way, from the Polynesian islands of their ancestors. In a very real sense Māori became native to Aotearoa in a relatively short period of time, and this can only appear surprising from the colonial vantage point of a strict relationship between places and people. If, on the other hand, we adopt the volumetric thinking developed in the first chapters of this book, we are in a position to appreciate the inventiveness and creativity of Māori philosophy without being incredulous about its relatively short history, and without essentializing it as a necessary expression of the land.

Between this first settlement and the European one started with Cook's expedition landing in 1769,[5] Māori developed a series of philosophical concepts that were instrumental to their making a home in a new land. In particular, Māori ontology developed in radically relational ways that explain the environing world in terms that embed human action within infrastructures of reciprocity. To be clear, this does not mean that Māori were "in harmony with nature", or that there is something about the racialized category of Māori that is somehow more in tune with the environment. The first mass extinction of New Zealand's megafauna followed Polynesian settlement, an outcome that was but the latest in a long history of extinctions triggered by human settlement. Instead of facile notions of ecologically benign natives, Māori philosophy develops ways of acting in the world that conceptualize human behavior as inherently ecological, that is to say as always already participating in wider processes that define the very nature of the human.[6] This offers much more solid foundations for thinking our way through the Ecocene.

One of the basic concepts of Māori philosophy is the idea of *hau*. This is the idea that things, as well as people, are traversed by animating

---

4   The name Māori does not accompany the first settlers of the islands, of course. It is a self-given name that post-dates European settlement. It simply means normal, ordinary, usual, and is the name that the first settlers of Aotearoa gave themselves once there were newcomers to distinguish themselves from.

5   This subsequent feat of navigational prowess is also in great part owed to Polynesian sailors. As documented in Salmond (2017), Tupaia—a Polynesian high priest and expert navigator—was the guide and interpreter of the expedition that eventually reached Aotearoa.

6   The nature of the human, in this sense, is as changeable as the surrounding ecology. An ecological and relational understanding therefore does not preclude the possibility of humans driving animals to extinction.

forces that account for their vitality and power. As Salmond explains, *hau* is "the wind of life that activates human and non-human networks alike, animated by reciprocal exchanges" (2017, 3). This should not be taken in the materialist, Cartesian sense of there being a ghost in the machine. Rather, *hau* denotes the observable fact that networks are birthed and sustained through exchange, such that participants themselves cannot be conceptualized outside of the relational forces that enliven them. I want to stress here the eminently empirical nature of this concept: it is based on observation, as opposed to being deduced from some higher metaphysics.[7] *Hau* is what Māori postulated to account for the empirical intermingling that generates liveliness in the world.

The idea of *hau* is in another sense taken literally when Māori greet by touching noses, therefore intermingling, through their breath, their *hau* (in the Māori language, the same word is used for both breath and this other concept).[8] This gesture of intermingling points towards the interpretation of *hau* as a relational feature, and not something that resides *within* things, conceived independently of their relations. In fact, Salmond presents *hau* as an ontological category, because in Māori cosmology it "emerged at the very beginning of the cosmos" (11). In other words, it is not a feature of human exchange, exemplified through the intermingling of breath, but rather a feature of the world as such. That is why humans participate in the exchange of *hau*, because it is what structures the volumes of the world as such.

To say that *hau* is an ontological category is to recognize the structuring role of exchange in all ecological processes. That Māori society comes to be predicated on ritualized exchanges (of gifts or insults, cohesion or fighting) is simply a result of the underlying structure of a world that cannot sustain itself outside of constant exchanges of energy, in one form or another. The Māori universe is not simply added to a world defined through exchanges, but rather is itself an expression of that world, a way of structuring it. Māori ontology is, as de Castro and Salmond insist, not a "world-view", but rather the description of "a world objectively from inside it" (Salmond 2017, 14). And this world is entirely structured through relationships.

---

7   This is what I have argued, through the work of Drury, is the vocation of ecological science.

8   There are obvious parallels here with the Latin *anima* or the Greek *pneuma*.

"The Māori universe is a gigantic kin, a genealogy" (in Salmond, 14). The term *whakapapa*, translated as genealogy, denotes the idea that people (and everything else) exist in dense networks of relations, such that "it is the relation itself [...] that is ontologically prior" (17). But crucially, these relationships are much more similar to the ecological ideas of change and impermanence than the fixed relations of hierarchical ontologies. From the point of view of any being, there is an unknowably vast network of relations that animate them, and this network can be selectively used, and is constantly changing. The participation of particular beings in ontological networks is neither elective (one cannot exist otherwise), nor necessary, in the sense that no single relationship supports, or nurtures, the whole. This is very important to recall when thinking about ideas of responsibility (developed in the next chapter).

The ontological commitments of *whakapapa* are made crystal clear in Māori oratorical arts. When speaking in a public capacity (for example in the *marae*, the community gathering house), the orator starts with a recitation of *whakapapa*, in order to situate themselves in the relational network that makes the event of the speech possible and ties all participants together (whether for the first or nth time). But a speaker need not have a fixed recitation that she can use indiscriminately; it is not as if I would be obliged to present myself as the son of my father on every occasion, something that in patriarchal societies, for example, would be a requirement. There are no such formal requirements of content, but only of form: the speaker starts with the greatest level of abstraction and zooms into her own being, defined through relations across scales. But what other beings, places, landscapes, and so on are called into genealogical relation is a question that the orator can decide based on the audience and the occasion of the speech.

Historically, this practice was used by Māori chiefs to extend or restrict networks of influence according to their political motivations. Because there are no patriarchal or matriarchal requirements, chiefs could use any branch of their extensive family tree to claim a genealogical connection with a distant ancestor, whether this took the form of a person, a mountain, a river, or something else. Salmond explains that "in Māori oratory, a speaker often begins by reciting the names of the main mountain, river and ancestor in their home territory, binding people together with land, ancestors, mountains and rivers as tangata whenua (people of the land)" (48).

Tangata whenua, or people of the land, is composed of *tangata* (people) and *whenua*, which means both land and placenta, an etymological clue that suggests the kinds of relations that this ontology allows. Local, or native, people are thus in light of the particular relations that they entertain with the land, and in light of the genealogy that they can selectively activate. It would be wrong to think that the idea of genealogy ties native claims to birth too strictly. Obviously, birth does play a role, but genealogical links are also often *built* through alliance, whether this be marriage or the exchange of particularly important gifts (material or not). What is more, genealogical lines intermingle at a distance, as the becoming-kin of relatives also affects my own genealogical relations. In other words, there is no prohibition in the Māori world of becoming native, inasmuch as one is willing to enter into constitutive genealogical relations with a vast network of things.[9]

One of the guiding principles of action within this relational universe is the idea of *utu*, or reciprocity. As already explored, this idea is implied in the *hau* of the world. Put differently, reciprocity is not a vectored relationship between two parties alone, but rather a *constant exchange* that is a logical necessity of the way the world works. Unlike in hierarchical ontologies, like the well-known Great Chain of Being (see Descola 2016), Māori reciprocity is radically equal, relying on "balanced exchange". This meant that whatever was received by someone had to be commensurately returned, whether in objects, partners in marriage, insults or compliments, favors or betrayals. Marcel Mauss famously developed the idea of reciprocity in relation to gifting. One of the central tenets there, something picked up and developed further by Derrida (1995), is the idea that the gift obliges the recipient in a way that is fundamentally unpayable, such that each successive return of the gift (each revolution) entrenches relationships further through incurring a profound debt (also see Chapter 7).

This sense of reciprocity is telling, though in no way fully commensurate with the ontological *utu* of Māori philosophy. Indeed,

---

9 Salmond argues precisely this point when saying that "for Māori at that time [of initial contact with Europeans], it was possible for a pakeha [white stranger] to become Māori—i.e. a normal, ordinary person, bound into the whakapapa networks by acts of friendship and alliance" (p.145). Rejoining Sharma, there are no migrants in the Māori universe.

gifting obliges the recipient to participate in the reciprocal infrastructure that the gift itself sets up. In this sense, one of the longest-standing (and still very much current) claims of Māori against European settlers is the latter's failure to reciprocate gifts (of land, access to resources, and so on) that Māori have offered in the past, always with the understanding of a commensurate return through the generations (*utu* never expires, as it were). But besides the obligation that gifting imparts on participants, *utu* also points towards the tantalizing idea that reciprocal exchange is not just about human relations, but rather structures worlds as such.

Reciprocity becomes a way of paying attention to and registering what counts, both in the ecological terms developed in Chapter 3 and in ethical terms, that is to say what is worthy of being treated with the respect inherent in paying attention. There is no *a priori* limit to this process, as it is rooted in a constitutive ignorance that is perpetually open to new assemblages. The intuition that *utu* is part and parcel of the structure of the world, that is to say that exchange is inseparable from the manifestation of the world, is not just part of Māori philosophy, though it is extensively developed there. As I will argue, it is also part of the margins of other philosophical traditions, as well as the indigenous (that is, land-based in genealogical ways) practices of diverse people, including in colonial nations.

The ontological level of reciprocity is ethically developed by Māori thinking in terms of commensurate and balanced exchange, that is to say an obligation to return the gifts that one receives, in whatever form. This kind of obligation can lead to both deep-seated concern for the well-being of the relationships in which one participates, as well as cycles of revenge for the commensurate return of insults and misfortune. However, there is no necessity to develop the ethics of reciprocity along the lines of *balanced* exchange, and in an ecological sense Māori philosophy itself does not do that: the idea of reciprocating insults, for instance, seems to be reserved for human relations; it is not as if Māori would be obliged to cut down a tree whose branch wounded someone. Instead, an ethics of reciprocity achieves three things: it embeds all creatures within the environing world in a fundamental way; it foregrounds human ignorance of the vastness of the networks that support all life, human included; and it foregrounds the necessity of paying attention to environing relations in order to increase the number of things that matter.[10]

Maria Puig de la Bellacasa (2017) approaches the kind of reciprocity that I have described using different sources and practices, namely the relations that constitute soils. Discussing the work of soil scientists, she shows how scientific practice itself is pregnant with the kind of insight structuring Māori philosophy. One of the ways in which this is the case is through the idea that humans are not only "an unbalanced irruption in soil's ecological cycles" (193). Instead, "notions of humans *being soil* thrive outside science". She further points to the indispensable fact that this "outside science" is a space inhabited by scientists themselves when they step away from their institutional roles as guardians of a bifurcated truth.

Thinking of humans as analogous to soil highlights their web-like interconnection, with a vast number of creatures making up precarious wholes. And it requires an exchange between soils and humans that erases the supposed boundaries between these constructed realms. In this context, reciprocity becomes "multilateral and collectively shared" (192), because upholding the exchanges that structure the world cannot be the work of any one individual, a concept whose relevance diminishes towards non-existence in this way of thinking.

Soil scientists are able to make many previously unknown relations matter. Puig de la Bellacasa gives the example of Elaine Ingham, a soil scientist also known as the Queen of Compost because of her hands-on work with communities. Simple devices of sampling, for example, become crucial in informing participants about easily unseen participants, and this expands the ways in which care can be extended to soils. But this care is not the same as a responsibility for the soil. It is an injunction to participate in the cycles that make and remake soils, in full consciousness of the fact that it is impossible to count all participants that matter. This is why, in discussing Māori philosophy, I insisted on the idea that reciprocation is a formal affair, concerned with perpetuating exchange itself. But it cannot control the composition of relations. It can

---

10 This latter injunction is to be understood on the background of a potentially infinite number of relations that are in constant flux. This, as I will argue, complicates greatly the idea of balance that often accompanies notions of reciprocity as well as particular strands of ecological thought.

only commit to ritualizing infrastructures of reciprocity that embed the necessity of exchange within everyday practices.

* * *

An onto-normative concept of reciprocity is not entirely foreign to Western philosophy. As the example of soil science shows, it is not foreign to current practices either. In strictly philosophical terms, one of its best expressions is to be found in the work of Merleau-Ponty. Its eco-ethical deployment has been significantly developed by David Abram. Here, I want to take stock of their particular contributions to a robust concept of reciprocity.

There are several ideas that Merleau-Ponty developed that are of direct relevance to the present discussion. First among these is the notion of the reversibility of perception. Simply put, this is the idea that perception makes no sense for the model of a subject perceiving a world. In that model, all of the power inherent in perception is on the side of the subject, "in the head" as it were, while the object is passive and therefore plays no constitutive role in the experience of perception. What Merleau-Ponty shows is that this is a truly strange idea, because it takes for granted the incredible accomplishment of perception, namely the embedding of the perceiving subject within an environing world.

Instead of thinking about perception (which is routinely biased towards the visual) as a vectored relation, it makes more sense to think about it as reversible: whoever is perceiving can only perceive inasmuch as they themselves are part of someone else's perceptual field. This is the idea of reversibility, that is to say that seeing presupposes being seen, smelling being smelled, touching being touched. So, every time I touch something, 'my touch' already involves the idea of being touched, of my own body being an object of perception. More profoundly, the reversibility of perception suggests that perceiving creatures are embedded in the world such that they are subjects and objects simultaneously. There is in perception a fundamental reciprocity between perceiving and being perceived.

"Looking and listening bring me into contact, respectively, with the outward surfaces and with the interior voluminosity of things [...]" (Abram 2012, 123). Acts of perception, in this model, are not acts in the intentional sense, but rather ways of participating in the world.

Perceptual participation comes with the embodied assumption of a voluminous and synaesthetic environing world, one that is only flattened by a failure to pay adequate attention. But in every smell, sound, and touch there resides the implication that what is perceived possesses an inscrutable depth formally similar to my own.

This idea greatly resembles the animism discussed earlier via the work of de Castro. Abram argues that "direct, prereflective perception is inherently synaesthetic, participatory, and animistic, disclosing the things and elements that surround us not as inert objects but as expressive subjects, entities, powers, potencies" (130). The interiority of creatures in general is met half-way by the idea of reversibility of perception, because if we suppose other beings are capable of perceiving us as an object, than we are already very close to considering their internal scaffolding as fundamentally similar to our own.[11] It is this fundamental similarity that also connects the formal reciprocity of perception to the ethical idea of reciprocal relations across milieus. Merleau-Ponty introduces a further notion that is able to deal with this complex back-and-forth of perception: instead of talking about objects and subjects, he speaks about the *flesh* of the world.

The choice of word here is very telling: the flesh, as I argued when discussing the concept of ecology in Chapter 3, already points towards the depth and aliveness of the environing world, a world that is inseparable in biotic and abiotic forms given that it is produced by their constant exchanges and interactions. On an ethical level, this opens up two related possibilities: that the environing world contains an infinite number of significant relations, and that the flesh of the world obliges human beings to pay attention in a way that may identify new relations that count. In other words, human beings may have a duty to pay attention to the environing world in such a way as to discover the multiplicity of relations that sustain them, and that they sustain, under conditions of constant (alas, increasing) change. It is this duty that works on the basis of ontological reciprocity.

Through these remarks I merely wish to draw attention to how Western philosophical traditions have not been entirely blind to the intuition that the world is defined by aliveness of a kind that is

---

11 This recalls both the discussion of multinaturalism, and of the concept of vulnerability developed in Chapter 3. There are also obvious similarities with the concept of *hau*.

vulnerable in the double sense developed earlier: it is always changing and fundamentally open, while being structured in ways similar to the interiority of being human.

This last point is made abundantly clear by Eduardo Kohn when recounting the advice he received from a travel companion to sleep in his hammock face-up, such that the jaguar may recognize him as a person, and not a thing: ""If [...] a jaguar sees you as a being capable of looking back—a self like himself, a *you*—he'll leave you alone. But if it should come to see you as prey—an *it*—you may well be dead meat" (1). This kind of insight is also at the root of much of the most creative ethological studies of the past decades, particularly those exploring primate worlds (structured, as it turns out, around moral and political considerations; see De Waal 2007). In fact, the sciences partly responsible for the bifurcation of nature are themselves starting to question the world in ways that betray a fundamental shift away from bifurcation.

What is interesting in Kohn's remark is the reversibility of the act of seeing, which means that the act itself doesn't just connect, but rather constitutes, the subjects through their involvement in the act. It is a matter of *seeing*, of paying attention in a certain kind of way, of extending Abram's unreflective, direct perception (which works through the flesh of the world) into a reflective future. It is this paying attention that constitutes subjects on all sides, and it is a paying attention that works through biological manifestations but is not limited, in important respects, to particular configurations of flesh. Plants may pay attention in this kind of way as well, for example, though they may do so in ways that are multiple, corresponding to their very communal way of assembling. If, instead of assuming bifurcation, we assume deep continuity and indeed reciprocity as the very fabric of the world, we may even be in a position to extend concepts such as politics in new and interesting ways: plant democracy, primate oligarchy. Rafi Youatt (2020) suggests as much in thinking about how, in light of reversibility, we may be able to apply political concepts to non-human worlds. This kind of paying attention simply means operating on the perceptually based assumption that the environing world is composed of an infinite variety of agents.

This leads Kohn to argue that "how other kinds of beings see us matters" (2013, 1). But who does it matter to, and what does it matter for? Following the idea of reversibility, it matters because it is a crucial part of the world, of a world, of any world. How other beings see us is part and parcel of the fabric of existence, and not knowing that part is like being in Plato's cave, ignorant of the colors that nonetheless permeate existence. This kind of ignorance, born out of not paying attention, has practical and political consequences, becoming a kind of self-fulfilling prophecy: we may end up acting in ways that ignore the liveliness of the world, and in so doing we end up impoverishing the world around us further. Cora Diamond uses D. H. Lawrence's discussion of men hunting gorillas to express the point that such actions as shooting baby apes in the arms of their mothers reveals a fundamental "deadness of spirit": they are based on deep ignorance as to the fundamentally reciprocal relations to which perception itself condemns us. Above and beyond any calculations of interest, we are obliged to decry this kind of deadness of spirit precisely because it does not pay attention to the fundamentally reciprocal structure of, in this case, being a human and being a gorilla.

* * *

Ethically speaking, the paradigmatic case of reciprocity, and of its debt that can never be repaid, is that of the giving of life. Every living thing is in this sense radically indebted; this kind of moral indebtedness may even be said to be part and parcel of the fabric of the world, given the necessity of birthing. The indebtedness of birth reveals the impossibility of *balanced* reciprocation. In fact, this impossibility has taken shape in many different social groups throughout history in the idea that one is primarily indebted to the land that sustains them.

In the discussion of Māori philosophy, I mentioned that the expression people of the land—*tangata whenua*—uses the same word for land that is also used for placenta. *Tangata whenua* are, then, the people who nurture through the umbilical cord,[12] as it were, and not necessarily native or racialized people. Those who participate in the life of the land

---

12 In Intermezzo I, I discussed land practices in Valle D'Itria, an area within the Murgia of Southern Italy. One of the important towns in that area is Locorotondo, which in Italian simply means "the round place", an innocuous description of the shape of the town. In the local dialect however, the town is called *U'Curdunn*, which means "the umbilical cord". These kinds of clues show the deep affinity of land-based cultures in a variety of locations.

in a way that benefits directly from its multiplicity of relations, are people of the land. But this participation also imparts a duty to explore the possibilities for reciprocal exchange, such that the vitality that is received from and through the land can be reciprocated through acts that enhance the vitality of the land itself.

The idea of balance sits uneasily within this kind of reciprocal exchange: there is no sense in which the gifts of the land can be commensurate with those of people, or vice versa. Instead, balance can be interpreted structurally, as the very functioning of reciprocal exchanges themselves, and not as quantifiable and strictly comparable in terms of amounts or kinds of gifts. The point, therefore, is neither to give back to the land *the same things it gives*, nor to give back in ways that would uphold a supposedly natural balance, but rather to simply be preoccupied with the idea (and its practical consequences) of giving back. What that may be is always context-dependent and works differently at different scales. The fundamental point is to simply understand the very being of humans as already involved in reciprocal relations that, when reflected upon, impart a duty to enhance the worlds around us. How to reciprocate is a question of logistical importance, and therefore one that is to be decided on in specific cases.

Belonging to (a) particular land(s) is about what one *does*, not who one is. There is no point in insisting on the primacy of *being* a native in the Ecocene; the point is to constitute ways of acting that bring one—anyone—into reciprocal relations with the land. That kind of mutually beneficial action is what may qualify the terms 'native' or 'local'. One belongs, then, inasmuch as she contributes to the well-being of the world that she inhabits. It goes without saying that one can (and routinely does) inhabit multiple worlds, and that this kind of belonging is always subject to change.

[marginalia: belonging]

Being indigenous can then approach the Māori meaning of genealogy, that is to say the capacity to act in a way that upholds genealogical relations to the land. Everyone can become indigenous everywhere, inasmuch as they enter the genealogical web of particular worlds via reciprocity. Re-learning ways of living and hybridization between worlds is crucial for all people in the Ecocene. Tāmati Kruger, a Tūhoe leader largely responsible for the legal recognition of Te Urewera, the ancestral home of his people, insists on the duty of Māori themselves to re-learn ways of being that respect the philosophical notions that we have explored. It is not as if the ethnic category of Tūhoe comes with preset instructions as to how to act in the world; what being Tūhoe gives is a privileged access to particular lands, and to a particular line of inheritance that can be a guide for future living arrangements.

Reciprocity as a generalized impulse has never entirely disappeared anywhere where modernity has grown thick. What has happened, in the modern world, is that the infrastructures of reciprocity have been buried. That is what needs rebuilding, so that this most fundamental impulse can be expressed again (at all levels, and among non-human entities and processes themselves). It is not enough to "raise awareness", because the intrinsic nature of reciprocity is clear enough, and still visible in the ways in which people talk about valued natural objects (for example, how farmers speak of olive trees; see Intermezzo I). The political task is to build up its infrastructures, such that enhancement of the environing world is possible at all levels.

I have argued that reciprocity, built on the foundations explored earlier in this book, can be renovated as a political and ethical concept able to guide socio-political arrangements in the Ecocene. Now, I want to turn to a complementary notion that can work alongside reciprocity in spelling out an ecopolitical ethic: responsibility.

6. Ecopolitical Ethics, Part II

Responsibility

The concept of responsibility is usually seen as commensurate with capacity; in other words, only those capable of engaging in particular kinds of harm can be held responsible. But one also needs to have the capacity to *be* responsible, that is to say that the object of responsibility needs to be commensurate with the subject's powers.

These broad outlines have changed tremendously at the dawn of the Ecocene: both capacity for destruction and capacity for responsibility have transformed fundamentally. Here, I want to take stock of this transformation and propose that the most constructive meaning for responsibility going forward is within the mutualist framework that I have been building. As part of this argument, I will claim that responsibility is best understood in inter-human relations, and that it is through those that the responsibility for the environing world comes to have much needed purchase. Whereas in the chapter on reciprocity I argued that reciprocal relations are best understood in interspecific terms (humans and places and other creatures), here I want to present responsibility as fundamentally intra-specific. Together, these two notions can draw the contours of an ecopolitical ethics fit for the Ecocene, the appropriate scaffolding of a mutualist politics.

The idea that the human world may be responsible for the non-human one did not start with discussion of the Anthropocene, but rather with the nuclear age. The technological development initiated by German scientists and followed through by the United States and the Soviet Union led to the advent of the nuclear bomb, an event that immediately resonated within philosophical and social thought as a fundamental expansion of responsibility. In other words, before humans were able to destroy the natural world wholesale, they were not responsible for it.

This argument was amply developed by Hans Jonas, whose thought on the ethical implications of technological power has come to frame much of our understanding of responsibility. In his 1985 book *The Imperative of Responsibility: In Search of an Ethics for the Technological Age*, as well as the 1984 article 'Ontological Grounding of a Political Ethics', he developed a future-oriented ethics that could deal with what he perceived to be the disproportionate technological power of humans over the world.

His main point of departure was that technology radically increased the future horizon that present decisions need to reckon with. He argued that previous ethics was concerned with the future inasmuch as it was foreseeable, perhaps going as far as one's own children (Jonas 1985, 12–17). This was not a shortcoming of those ethical outlooks, but rather a response to the capacities of those times, when it was obvious that human nature would essentially stay the same, and that non-human nature would always essentially be an inexhaustible and fundamentally independent realm.[1]

These axes that ethics depended on were radically changed by technology. Indeed, we live in a time when all living creatures are potentially affected by human decisions. What constitutes a human or an animal can no longer be taken for granted, as it increasingly becomes the subject of technological tinkering. Similarly, nature can no longer plausibly be conceived as an infinite other, and therefore comes under the focus of present decisions in an unprecedented way.[2] Thinking of nature as wholly other is unfit for dealing with modern, technological capacities, and is itself a view of nature filtered through these capacities. Modern technology both posits nature as an object of alterity, and is incapable of regulating its relation to this foreign object. Under these

---

[1] From the perspectives developed in this book, it is quite obvious that the notions of human and non-human nature are deeply problematic. However, Jonas used them, and so I reproduce them here as such for the purposes of recreating his argument.

[2] The idea that pre-modern conceptions of nature regarded nature as inexhaustible is contradicted by anthropological studies (for example Berkes 2012, Anderson 1996, Turner 1981). What this body of work suggests is that in a-modern societies a sense of the limits of nature is crucial and, partly because of its importance, internalized and transmitted through ritual. Jonas is partly guilty of underestimating the ways in which pre-modern societies had conceptualized nature as limited, and I think this was for two reasons. First, his reference for pre-modern is the philosophy of European antiquity. Second, and related to the first, what he means by a conception of limitless nature only applies to a conception of the world as such.

conditions, ethics desperately needs to take into account the possibility of an indefinite future for human and non-human nature.

This starting-point led Jonas to look for an ethical perspective that could cope with the pressure that technology has placed on our horizons of action. He did not wish the development of technology away, realizing that it would be futile, but rather attempted to meet it head on. This is not to say that he did not see room for wiser technological progress. The point, rather, is that technology is to be reckoned with whatever its manifestations. Though technology, when understood as a tool use, is a primary interface between us and non-human nature, techno-logos as it has developed in modernity lacks the guiding principles of mere tool use; it instrumentalizes and objectifies for its own sake—"the juggernaut moves on relentlessly" (Jonas 1979, 35)—which is also why it has written within itself the possibility of utter destruction. Another way to express this is that scientific progress in the guise of technological development makes it imperative that there be norms, though it itself erodes all norms (Jonas 1985, 52).

Jonas is not nearly as careful as he should be in identifying which humans are responsible and which are not. He also tends to generalize from a Western, modern history of technological development to 'humanity' as such, in the same way that the concept of the Anthropocene does. However, what I want to extract from his work is the double point of the normlessness of technological development, as well as the way in which this normlessness extends responsibility towards the existence of future humans. But if that is the case, then it also extends responsibility towards the existence of the environing world as such. It would seem that, inasmuch as the natural world also risks annihilation, there is nothing to stop us from applying the concept of responsibility as commensurate with capacity to the natural world as well.

In fact, I have argued throughout that a-modern modes of human-environment relationality are not ethically steeped in responsibility, but rather in reciprocity. In the case of Māori philosophy, for example, the idea of guardianship was traditionally applied to supernatural spirits, not to humans, precisely because humans were not seen as having the capacity to *be* responsible for something that in fact sustained human life. Instead, humans had a duty to reciprocate such that their own role in the local ecology was upheld. As Stengers (2015, 45) writes in relation to the concept of Gaia, "if she was honored in the past it was as the fearsome one, as she who was addressed by peasants, who knew that humans depend on something much greater than them, something that tolerates them, but with a tolerance that is not to be abused".

The idea that long-term responsibility is attached to a particular form of technological power needs a lot more qualification than Jonas himself was prepared to provide. Crucially, we need to understand the differential distribution of that power, as well as the difference between the aggregate effect of many humans' actions and the individualization of responsibility. In the case of nature conservation, for example, Büscher and Fletcher show how many of the restrictions that come with preservationist policies are directed at immediate users of an environment (that is, local populations), as they are thought to be the ones that are directly responsible. However, the ultimate drivers of accelerated change and biodiversity loss are more likely to be the elite donors to environmental organizations, and urban citizens that consume orders of magnitude more than many locals around conservation areas.

Similarly, many of the actions that non-privileged people take to better their own lives do have an aggregate effect on the environing world. Take illumination as an example;[3] it is fairly universally sought out because of its undeniable benefits to human lives. However, it is also deadly to nocturnal insects, and incredibly disruptive to their own kinds of life. But it would be absurd to pin insect populations' decline on rural communities now installing electricity. The overwhelming majority of the historical impact on insect populations is still due to the relentless development of the West. This process has had to do with much more than illumination, but also with pollution and the overall cementification of the environment required by ever-increasing modes of consumption. This is to say that identifying a general concept of responsibility that is commensurate with technological capacity does not warrant the individualization of blame. In fact, it requires that we be careful in apportioning responsibility in light of both historical and actual capacity.

On the opposite end, this argument does not imply that there are actors that are *fully* responsible. We are only ever talking about degrees, though admittedly there is a very wide scale to cover. But the truly

---

3 The same would hold for home refrigeration, or basic sanitation.

frightening thing about the normlessness of technological power is precisely that nobody controls it. There is no single actor that could wield that formidable power according to his will, though not for lack of trying. Technological annihilation of the kind that Jonas envisioned is much more likely to be a mistake than the result of an action pursued by a particular individual.

The idea that technology, applied outside of guiding norms, can be totally destructive, is most immediately exemplified by the nuclear threat. However, beyond the spectacular nature of that threat, all sorts of creatures, humans included, are much more likely to drown in trash than be blown up. In other words, technological deployment today is coupled with the idea of modern development in such a way as to have become a veritable aggregate juggernaut, endlessly churning out things. It is this churning that is most destructive of environing worlds, as it transforms what is found in nature into cheap and valueless stuff, a diffuse apparatus that makes variegated resources privately profitable while draining their significance and value. Here, there is no human responsibility as such. Production and consumption of goods has become entangled in extremely complex networks that support countless human lives. The point is rather that the normless application of technology in the twenty-first century can hardly carry the idea that 'humans' are capable of being responsible for 'nature'.

* * *

Under the standard account best exemplified by Jonas, it would seem that technological capacity gives a blanket responsibility to 'humanity' for the perpetuation of the natural (and human) world. But this is a remnant of modernist ways of thinking that tend towards unstable universalisms. As I have argued, there is no 'humanity' as such that wields technological power, though that does not mean that there aren't many different kinds of humans who do have an outsized influence on the fate of worlds, both near and remote. However, it would be a mistake to think—as the Anthropocene discourse does—that because of the theoretical power of technology we are warranted to say that humans are now in charge. The devastating conundrum of the Ecocene comes precisely from the tension between an unevenly distributed power of destruction and the structural incapacity of humans to *direct* natural worlds. Humans are not in charge; they are merely using inherited powers predicated upon the bifurcation of nature in wholly irresponsible ways.

This has many impoverishing effects, for human as well as non-human worlds. For example, Andre Gorz has characterized the impoverishment of human worlds in direct relation to the increasing production of "goods" within capitalism. "A richer life", he writes, "is not only compatible with the production of fewer goods, it demands it" (1980, 28). In fact, rich and poor are relative terms—relative to each other—such that the elimination of one logically entails the elimination of the other. To be destitute, he explains, is the condition of not having enough. To be poor is to be denied that which already exists as surplus production. The infinite production of mostly useless commodities that characterizes contemporary capitalism is not only destructive of countless environments (through both production and consumption), but also generative of human suffering on an increasing scale.

In the so-called affluent world, there is such a tremendous abundance of unnecessary objects that the persistence of poverty can only be explained through the logic of capitalism itself. "Poverty is created and maintained, that is to say *produced and reproduced*, at the very pace at which the level of aggregate consumption rises" (28–29, italics in original). At the same time, the relationship between this highly unequal world and actual destitution is perverse in two ways. On the one hand, part of the destitution of large populations is directly related to the affluence of others. And the recipe for solving destitution inevitably leads to levels of consumption that inherently cause ecological and social misery. Achieving poverty through surplus consumption seems the only available option.

There is yet another way in which the powers of infinite destruction have morphed into consumerism and modern development, draining human practices of the meaning that had sustained them for generations. The creation of endless products happens at a time when aggregate wealth far exceeds the needs of *all* people. This means that working for a wage has become a wholly artificial way of apportioning goods. Logically, more and more people have to pretend to be working by becoming professionals of all sorts, a process that David Graeber (2018) has called the creation of "bullshit jobs". And one of their most perverse effects is the generalized de-skilling of countless people.

Ivan Illich has been instrumental in identifying and characterizing this ill. At its most succinct, it is the phenomenon whereby "the professional power of experts [...] eviscerates personal competence" (1978, 86). The disappearance of crafts and their replacement with mass production, as well as the delegitimation of a whole series of daily interventions for the maintenance of health, both personal and communal (understood ecologically), are part and parcel of what modern development requires. Tellingly, every society that is up for development goes through the same process of de-skilling, which is equivalent to the (temporary) loss of the capacity to interact with the environment in a relatively generative and meaningful way.

The power of technology, coupled with modern development, creates different kinds of responsibility for different people, but it cannot create a responsibility as such, especially in relation to the environment, because its capacity to eat everything up is not correlated with the ability to control the complexity and direction of wider ecological processes. The power of destruction that developed societies wield may seem total, colonizing everything and every mind. This is indeed the feat it continuously tries to accomplish, but the great effort that goes into maintaining and expanding modern development is indicative of the perpetual resistance it encounters. Even within a consumerist, de-skilled, seemingly barren landscape, people and creatures continue to misbehave.

To get a better handle on how the concept of responsibility can navigate the conundrums thrown up by the Ecocene, I need to return to how the environing world actually features in human lives, beyond the blindness that modern technology may occasion (alas, require) in human users. "Environmental hermeneutics focuses on the fact that environments matter to people [...], because environments embody [...] [normative] contexts" (Drenthen 2013, 17). From the hermeneutical point of view, nature is a text to be read (Clingerman 2009); indeed, it is the ultimate text, because it is at the same time the grounds of our being, the region (Heidegger 1966) within which reading and meaning can happen. The normative context that Drenthen refers to simply means that the natural environment is the necessary background for the existence of human meaning and values.

This is even apparent in the notion of nature that purports to be furthest removed from human meaning: wilderness. As many have shown (Oelschlaeger 1991; Cronon 1995; Schama 1995; Vicenzotti and Trepl 2009; Kirchoff et al. 2013), "what is constitutive of wilderness are not the specific biophysical properties of an area but rather the specific meanings ascribed to it according to cultural patterns of interpretation" (Kirchoff and Vicenzotti 2014, 444). It is possible to catalog the meanings of wilderness through the ages, because "this interpretation of wilderness as not being a complex of ecosystems, but a meaningful arrangement of symbolic objects, renders visible the multitude of diachronic and synchronic meanings of wild nature: the way wilderness is viewed, characterized and valued is subject to change over time" (Kirchoff and Vicenzotti 2014, 445). Said differently, even the ostensibly most removed concepts of nature play a hermeneutical role in human lives (see the discussion of Descartes in Chapter 2). The same holds true for near and very specific environments, such as a park that one may visit regularly and its birds.

The general meaningfulness of the environing world has been amply recognized throughout the history of the human species; its oblivion may only be a part of the modern project of bifurcation. However that may be, it remains the case that human well-being and flourishing is inseparable from the state of the natural world. So even though technological power is unevenly distributed and not really controlled by anyone in particular (though, again, there are degrees of control that have to be taken into account), the impoverishing effect that it has on the natural world is not only relegated to nature; it always also affects human communities.

Many in the field of political ecology have looked at issues of environmental justice and have amply demonstrated the link between environmental destruction and socio-economic deprivation, often along racialized lines. This is well established, and goes together with the widespread illusion (among elites, but not exclusively) that there is a way to safeguard against ecological impoverishment. The privileged, the argument goes, are always able to escape the worst effects of environmental ills. This may be true, but only to some degree: the most privileged suffer *less* than the disadvantaged and even then, only in the most visible ways. It is undeniable that living next to a steel plant affects the health of the neighboring people much more drastically than that of the ultimate consumers of the steel produced there.

But it is also the case that the privileged classes have created for themselves a world so removed from ecological processes that it is impoverished nonetheless.[4] One of the clearest expressions of the destabilizing effects that this kind of luxury impoverishment has is the increasing prevalence of mental illness in the developed world. Being ripped out of the reciprocal relations that our very bodily perception requires leaves marks that need constant healing. It is no surprise that some of the most soothing therapies for a range of afflictions involve nature retreats and/or the companionship of (domestic) animals. In a very real sense, the world of privilege is increasingly unlivable.

The illusion that one can be insulated from wider environmental ills is perhaps most clearly approaching its end when we consider the now generalized level of toxicity. Whereas pollution in minority neighborhoods makes the headlines on and off, the fact that microplastics are now to be found in streams at the base of glaciers alarms many more people. Walling oneself off has reached its logical limit. Perhaps the supposed winners of development will get some consolation from living in relatively less toxic environments; or perhaps they will realize that living outside of reciprocal bonds is necessarily harmful. But the choice should not be between a devasted, polluted hellscape and a manicured, walled-off environment of privileged depression.

Once the link between human and environmental well-being is front and center, we can start appreciating how there is no need to pin the fate of 'nature' to the responsibility of 'humanity'. Instead, it suffices to establish that humans are responsible for the well-being of fellow humans (and here there is a much better fit between capacity and responsibility) in order to articulate an ethic that *necessarily* passes through environmental flourishing. Some people are responsible for the poverty of others, in all of its senses; this is a responsibility that can be met. But it cannot be met outside of an approach that first recognizes the importance of ecological processes as a very condition of possibility

---

4   The effects of climate change are starting to seem quite democratic; the original expectations about supposed positive effects of climate change in rich countries (growing wine in Belgium, water availability in Russia, drilling in the Arctic) are proving to be wishful thinking. Droughts, hurricanes, floods, heatwaves are appearing in an unpredictable fashion and seem increasingly indiscriminate in their geographical preferences, though obviously affecting different populations differently. Considered from the point of view of chance, change, and locality, this should not be surprising at all.

for a rich life. At this point in time, and for the foreseeable future, responsibility passes through the concept of ecological restoration.

I have already argued that the concept of restoration is best understood as targeting mutually beneficial ecological relationships, rather than a particular previous state (a baseline). In any circumstance, what can be restored will be up for debate; the point here is that the responsibility that people have towards the well-being of their fellow humans obliges them to consider the concept of restoration. The Ecocene requires that particularly those in positions of power and privilege (and therefore in positions of causing greater harm) work towards enhancing the natural world and human relations to it. In the most general sense, this means not only ensuring that there is a world for future generations (Jonas' position), but also, perhaps especially, that there is a world of multiplicity for a multiplicity of future humans. And the best way to work towards that is through the ecological idea of redundancy.

The practice of conservation in a world of modern development has increasingly focused on the specialness of protected areas: an area being the most biodiverse, the most unique, and so on, is a frequent rationale for conservation.[5] Without denying the unique features of each and every environment, the insistence on uniqueness also encourages the homogenization that is a hallmark of modern development. We are heading towards a world where most of the available space is a sacrificial zone for the accumulation of capital, while the rest is a carefully curated bestiary of "the miracles of the natural world". Instead, this book has argued that we need to start thinking about embeddedness more thoroughly, such that it becomes possible to see the homogenization of spaces as the greatest danger to the multiplicity of worlds (human and otherwise), and their survival.

Instead of focusing on the uniqueness of what is left over, it is more radical to focus on restoring environments *everywhere*, such that *every* human being is part and parcel of a greater natural community in which

---

5   As intimated in Chapter 4, the history of walling places off as conservation reserves is also tied to the creation of poverty and destitution. This is partly because classical conservation is not based on the kind of idea of restoration that I am advocating, but on a radical separation of humans and wild nature. Humans are then interpreted as 'the species', though in practice it is always better-off humans that benefit from leisurely activities in conservation areas, and more marginalized humans that are excluded from using them in reciprocal ways.

they ritualistically participate. And just as in the history of species one of the greatest insurers against disaster is the redundancy of habitat, so too in human history will the redundancy of habitat be key to human flourishing. It is drastically insufficient to save one marsh here and there; instead, the future capacity of humans to lead meaningful lives depends on the responsibility of present generations to restore countless marshes, such that they become, yet again, redundant.

This also applies in urban settings, where most people increasingly live. There is no reason to suppose that the urban environment needs to be uniformly paved over and therefore deprived of countless interactions. In fact, the intuition that diverse environments are needed for human flourishing is already on display in the universally distributed difference between rich and poor neighborhoods in terms of the 'green space' that they have. In virtually every urban setting one could think of there is a stark difference in terms of the permeability of the ground, the availability of natural spaces for leisure, the amount of pollution, the density of population and car traffic, and so on, distributed according to class and socio-economic status. Evidently, people rich and poor know that their well-being depends on their direct environment.

But the manicured environment of wealthy suburbia, though relatively healthier for people, is also stifling in its poverty. It is the opposite of a rich space; it is uniform, dogmatic in what lives where, phobic with respect to any kind of creature that does not have a pre-approval to exist. Its obsession with control leads to environmental pollution through the wide use of pesticides and the creation of lawn monocultures lacking in life. It would be a mistake to take those impoverished green spaces as the standards to be sought in restoring urban environments in general; it would risk instrumentalizing restoration in an 'ecological service' way and missing its point altogether. The point of urban restoration, just like restoration elsewhere, is to embed people within their immediate environment in reciprocal ways. Suburban lawns are generally speaking not an environment of reciprocation, but one that often relies on precarious labor to maintain the illusion of 'nature'.

Ecological restoration has become increasingly mainstream in the last decade. It is now routinely proposed as a simple way of mitigating climate change through the carbon sequestration that restored environments can provide. The implication here is precisely that, without these measures, there will be a radically impoverished world left for future generations. But this insight is endangered by the very grand scale and managerial view of restoration as a technical solution. It is not enough to restore flagship environments and enclose them away from people. Instead, I am advocating a diffuse politics of restoration at all scales, such that mutually beneficial ecological relationships can in themselves become a way of life, as opposed to a technical solution for a problem that keeps being generated. It is not about restoring some patch of mangrove, but rather about restructuring human lives such that they contribute more than they take away from whatever environment they happen to live in.

Ecological restoration needs to be deployed in the service of rebuilding networks of *ordinary* environments, not in the service of saving the special through technical interventions. The task is to recreate environmental conditions that allow for generalized flourishing, and the truly daunting thing is the number of practices and beliefs that need to change in order for that to be the case. Some possible practices are in fact simple but stifled by techno-managerial thinking. For example, many restoration initiatives, whether we are talking about recreating prairies or restoring the meanders of an urban river, depend on relatively straightforward techniques. These are often broken down into a hierarchical chain of command that is led by professionals and executed by (poorly) paid labor of a mechanized and repetitive kind. The kind of network involved in hands-on interventions recalls Illich's idea of deskilling, where the capacity of interacting with the surrounding world in skillful and careful ways is simplified, professionalized, and largely inaccessible.

In Chapter 3 I talked about the Queen of Compost, through the work of de la Bellacasa. Restoring relationships with soil is there presented as a low-tech, ordinary affair that people can *easily* engage in. The skills that they learn are applicable to a variety of situations that cannot be authoritatively counted. For example, practices such as composting with worms in the city hold great potential. Having worms as companions, and reciprocating their stubborn efforts at creating soil by feeding them what would otherwise be refuse, transforms relationships with the idea of garbage as well: it is no longer waste, but worm food. Learning to become soil is about everyday, even banal, practices that invest creatures in one another, and that consequently enrich countless lives.

Ecologists have started taking the social dimension of restoration much more seriously, though the ways in which it is pursued is still hobbled by a view of restoration as an expert-driven affair that is really concerned with biodiversity above all. It is telling that what should be routine involvement in ritualized restoration is always conceived of as a "social" addition that is often a nuisance, something that increasingly needs to be formally done. For example, the restoration of Medlock River (near Manchester, UK) was achieved without the local people knowing it was being done at all. They all appreciated the resulting ability to walk through an interesting area, but their appreciation was limited by the very process of restoration, which was only really driven by the species assemblies of the river itself (De Bell et al. 2020). Humans became mere users, in a similar way to being a user of one's lawn. It is evidently preferable to restore a river than plant a lawn, but at the level of embedding people within their immediate environments, the result is similar.

Options are available. Many are already engaged in renovating their own ecological relations in ways that provide inspiration. Chapter 4 presented the case of the longest-standing restoration project, started by Aldo Leopold at the University of Madison, Wisconsin, and aimed at the resuscitation of prairies and their natural fire regime. This case gets close to the idea of infrastructures of reciprocity, where certain grooves of practice are carved out such that reciprocation becomes commonplace through its ritualization. This is possible in all sorts of environments because its only requirements are interactive, and do not have to do with a final form at all.

A last example: in the city of Brussels, there are many nests made by the common swift (D'Hoop 2022). Finding wildlife in cities is in fact common around the world, but most city dwellers are either not aware of it or see it as a nuisance. The increasing renovation of buildings in Brussels is threatening the nesting grounds of swifts, and a local organization is proposing tours for residents, as well as engaging with mayors and urban planners in order to include the swifts within daily experiences. This is not an expert-driven affair; the organizers and the participants are people that are re-learning kinds of skills, and manners of paying attention. Renovating one's house becomes a way of noticing what had been previously invisible, of gifting something to the swifts who bring the sounds of spring year after year. Making these kinds of practices the norm is not a logistical or technical problem. All that is needed is a manner of thinking that allows for them.

***

The idea that human responsibility towards fellow humans passes through the enhancement of the natural world may easily be seen to go hand in hand with concepts of guardianship or stewardship over nature. Here I want to challenge that assumption and show further how responsibility cannot logically extend to the natural world as such, but rather needs to pass through inter-specific relations. Simply and hyperbolically put, humans cannot be responsible for nature as such.

There are models of interaction that do not need to rely on the figure of humanity saving nature. The idea that the Anthropocene requires that humans become guardians of the planet is but the latest continuation of modernist thought. From the point of view of deep multiplicity and embeddedness that this book has presented, the idea of guardianship is suspect also on account of its sidestepping structural human ignorance. This kind of fundamental ignorance is fully present in the best scientific practices, as well as in many locally based traditions. The illusion of control only comes from the refraction of this ignorance through the bifurcation of nature that is foundational of modernist thinking. It is also exacerbated through the normless application of technology, which makes it seem as if humans are capable of manipulating worlds at will.

Māori philosophies are relational, where the identity of individuals is simply a knot in a series of relationships extending in space and time, forward and backward. This is reflected in Māori art as much as cosmological stories and philosophies. Relationships with ancestors are powerfully important and, like in so many other philosophies worldwide, animals and plants, the land and the sea, can themselves be ancestors. This means that one can enter into relations with these natural entities, and human life is simply the traveling node in which all sorts of life-forms interact. The sign of a good relation is reciprocity, the mutual exchange of gifts.

This kind of relational thinking is not alien to 'Western' philosophies either. Anne Salmond, in *Tears of Rangi* (2017), shows how the very first Europeans to arrive in New Zealand were, in part, themselves steeped in relational Enlightenment science, though by far the dominant philosophy of the time (late-eighteenth century) was the Great Chain of Being: the idea that the universe was ordered on a string of increasing (or decreasing, depending which way you looked at it) importance, with God at the top and the rest of creation strung on hierarchically. The meeting of these worlds, the Great Chain and the relational one of the Māori, is still productively shooting sparks today. Though we can easily sneer at hierarchical thinking, it is so insidiously embedded that it is far from extinct.

The interaction of different ontological worlds has never stopped producing interesting hybrids. Lately, the domain of law—so dominated by Western philosophy in settler states—has started to be productively intertwined with Māori *tikanga* (ways, laws, customs). For example, the ancestral home of Tūhoe, Te Urewera, as well as the Whanganui River, received the status of legal entity (in 2014 and 2017, respectively). The legal status that was granted to the Whanganui River and Te Urewera is but a node in a process of hybridization that began with Captain Cook, in 1769.

Since then, the various Māori descent lines have lost the use of much of their ancestral land at the hands of European settlers. The Whanganui *iwi*, the tribes inhabiting the Whanganui lands, and Tūhoe, the inhabitants of Te Urewera, sought to obtain ownership of their respective lands by challenging the Crown in court for having breached the founding treaty of New Zealand, the Treaty of Waitangi (signed by many but not all chiefs in 1840). The *iwi* (tribes) claimed that they had never given the Crown exclusive rights to their lands. Predictably, the NZ government resisted granting *iwi* ownership and, instead, it was granted to the land itself: hence, the Whanganui River and Te Urewera are now legal persons with ownership of themselves.

A useful way of conceptualizing alternative views of the kind of responsibility imparted by the Ecocene is precisely by attending to these kinds of locally based thinking. However, attention to the details of each case is easily traded for generalities. For example, it is a commonplace of environmental thought to suppose that indigenous practices are steeped in guardianship.[6] This assumption runs so deeply that even when indigenous cultures themselves do not use the concept

---

6   See my critique of harmony with nature narratives in Tănăsescu (2015, 2020, 2022).

'guardian', coverage of what they do still insists on using it! When in 2017 the Whanganui River was inaugurated as a legal person in New Zealand law, almost universally the Whanganui *iwi* were described as the guardians of the river. A closer look at what the law actually says, in the context of a deeply relational Māori philosophy, suggests much more tantalizing and promising alternatives.

The Whanganui River, as a legal person, needs to be represented in the legal and political processes in which it can now participate. This representation is the task of a board created especially for this purpose, as the law mandates. The composition of the board is half members of Whanganui *iwi*, and half members of the state government. So already at the level of board composition, this is completely different from the Whanganui *iwi* being sole guardians of the river. Instead, the board is a political construction that mandates dialogue between parties with traditionally different ontological and epistemological claims. The commitment to dialogue across deep and often painful divides is itself worth pointing out.

Does this mean that *the board* is guardian of the river? The 2017 law nowhere describes it as such. Instead, the board is referred to as the river's "human face", and this is following Māori philosophical commitments. If the NZ government had had the upper hand in defining the role of the board, they may as well have defined it as one of guardianship. Instead, given the deep Māori involvement in the negotiations leading up to the law, the board became quite simply a human face of a non-human entity. This is not because Māori do not have a concept akin to guardianship. In fact, the term *kaitiakitanga* is often translated as guardianship, but in the Māori universe the *kaitiaki* (the guardians) are almost never humans, but rather *taniwha*, or supernatural spirits, such as sharks or stingrays, that guide the integrity of a place (see Salmond 2017). In other words, the figure of the human is too fragile for the weight of responsibility that being *kaitiaki* would place.

What people *can* do is speak in legal and political terms after consultation with non-human beings. In this sense the river, which is anything but mute in Māori philosophy, can only speak with a *human voice* through actually embodied humans. Who those humans may be remains at the level of local political practice, but in more general terms the ability of humans is mostly that of interpreting what a fundamentally independent being is saying, and not that of directing the river's life. It would be a mistake to think that this is because the Whanganui River is pristine, untouched, unpolluted, and so on. Quite the contrary. As Geoff Park (1995) and other NZ scholars have shown, and as *iwi* members themselves know, the Whanganui is deeply anthropic. But no amount of pollution and transformation can take away from the fundamental independence and autonomy of the processes that are called a river.

The idea of guardianship is very seductive, being somewhat flattering, and painting a picture of responsible humans taking care of the world. It is also, in this account, deeply steeped in Great Chain of Being thinking. How could humans take care of nature without having the knowledge and the power to do so? The point of Māori philosophies, as well as other relational ones, is precisely that humans are not above the natural order, so in that sense guardianship or stewardship become logical impossibilities. In fact, humans are always in debt to natural beings, trying to assuage their power through behavioral tricks (prohibitions, offerings, and so on). More people everywhere are likely to rediscover the awesome powers that overwhelm human agency, now that we have entered the Ecocene: the era of increasingly erratic natural agency barging into the polis.

Parallels between Indigenous philosophies and the idea of guardianship may be well-meaning, but ultimately wrong-headed. Māori philosophies challenge that easy identification, showing it to be a continuation of hierarchical thinking. The relational mode that is present in alternative ways of being and thinking is exemplified through *whakapapa*, or genealogy, encountered in Chapter 5. The natural entity that one may claim as an ancestor is not under the guardianship of the person, but exactly the other way around: the natural entity is what nestles the person and gives them meaning and identity. This relationship, much closer to ecological science, is what must be expressed and lived. Guardians of the Anthropocene not only does not come close to it, but it points us in the wrong direction.

Denying the possibility of meaningful guardianship does not deny the possibility of acting in ways that enhance the environing world, quite the contrary. Not placing oneself in the position of guardian also comes with the freedom to *be* responsible in a commensurate way, that is to say to act in ways that do bear on the capacity to be responsible.

In genealogical terms, the greatest responsibility of present humans is towards the future possibility of descendants, what Hans Jonas expressed as the responsibility for the very existence of future generations.

In this sense, genealogical links to the land make one responsible for the future existence of multiple generations, which in turn commits present generations to perpetual enhancement of the environment. Human impact on a river's health is more often than not guided by stupidity and short-termism, not by some master plan that would control what the river does. This is so even in societies that have managed to control their waters to a staggering effect, such as the Netherlands. But in the Ecocene, water is re-establishing its agential power, and the Netherlands, a top-down water management regime if ever there was one, is being forced to change its water policy from control to "living with the river". Of course, this does not imply that it is done in the restorative way argued for here; one can try to "live with the river" in fundamentally managerial ways, as a smarter measure of control that outwits the Ecocene. This kind of doubling down side-steps the important opportunities our new era gives for recreating relationships, as opposed to regimes of power and control.

In any given circumstance, humans can participate within larger natural processes by lending their voice to them in increasingly diverse fora.[7] But to think that humans can be guardians of nature, directing it according to their will and anticipating all possible deviations from this will, is a dangerous illusion. The challenge of the Ecocene is to re-dimension humans appropriately, that is to say in such a way as to accord responsibility for what can actually be achieved. We need to re-establish the bonds of responsibility that bind humans together, and through these reawaken ourselves to the active worlds around us and speak for them when needed. Instead of some blanket managerial solution, we need a multiplicity of practices reflective of the multiplicity of worlds. There is no endgame that these practices need to correspond to, no utopian state to be achieved, but rather only internal requirements of mutual enhancement.

Modernity has never managed to entirely stomp out the human intuition that the natural world is greater, more independent, and more mysterious than we may think. The Ecocene is rapidly reinstating the

---

7   See last chapter for more examples of this.

central role of this intuition. In many different settings—the Māori philosophical and practical context as much as the ancestral memory of environmental co-creation in many European contexts[8]—the connection with the past is as important as the responsibility for future generations. The Māori discussion is again telling: the idea of genealogy is a way of relating to ancestors as much as to the land. In fact, ancestors are seen through the land, as their own practices are inherited by present generations, and therefore to a great extent set the stage for what is possible. "Māori walk back into the future", as a Māori aphorism says (in Kawharu 2010, 222). Or, as Sir James Henare puts it, "when I look at these landscapes, I see my ancestors walking back to me" (in Kawharu 2010, 228).

This kind of walking backwards can be expressed as a specific kind of genealogical awareness that is nonetheless widely distributed. We are inheritors of our own ecological ignorance as much as of relational strategies that can be recuperated. The placenames (toponyms) we interact with on a daily basis bear traces of ancestral knowledge that can be reinvigorated, literally given the vigor to live again (see Tănăsescu and Constantinescu 2018, 2020, Tănăsescu 2019). The ghosts in the cemetery of practices are our ancestors; we already speak to them when visiting actual cemeteries or when we commemorate the past. It may be time that we ask them different questions.

* * *

There is nothing easy in being responsible for the wellbeing of another, or in responding to the environing world in partial and always imperfect ways. Yet basic aspects of moral life are unthinkable without this kind of difficulty, as I have shown through the work of Cora Diamond. Moral action always fails, can never approximate enough, frustrates continuously, demands the impossible. The sympathetic imagination therefore moves in a universe of impossibility, which makes the moral stance one of endurance, of refusing to exit what is always uncomfortable.

Thinking of morality this way forbids one from supposing that the work of living with tragedy in the Ecocene is easy, or even bearable. It will rip the flesh, but the alternatives will always be worse. And yet,

---

8   See, for example, Squartiti (2013) for a history of human co-determination with chestnut trees in medieval Italy.

for a time, and perhaps for a long time still, many have been fooled into thinking that the difficulty of reality, in Diamond's expression, can be evicted from its structuring place in human life. The attraction of modern development trades on this kind of liberating promise.

Critiques of modernity assume that it is enough to point out the many ways in which it severs crucial ties with the environing world in order to fatally weaken its very lure. Sadly, this is not so: no amount of "consciousness raising" will re-enchant the environing world and its material processes. The real challenge is to build a politics that gives back more than it takes, which under circumstances of free capitalist consumption is logically impossible. The irruption of Gaia will likely strengthen both the resolve of building gated, air-conditioned communities, and that of renovating reciprocal relations with the world. That will be the great political battle of the future. But it would be a mistake to think that the project of modernity, because it is so morally bankrupt and so clearly suicidal, is also already dead. As Büscher and Fletcher suggest, modernity is moribund, but some of the greatest strength is wielded precisely at the moment when the gravest wounds are being felt.

Andreas Malm argues that "one is led to the prediction that the higher the temperatures, the more conclusive the science, the more radical the required measures of mitigation, *the more confident and belligerent the denialism of the winners will be*" (2018, 134, emphasis in original). He is specifically concerned with climate change and its denial, but this observation could well apply to all kinds of ecological crises looming on the horizon. The point is that it is naïve to think that the ones considering themselves the winners of modern development will give up their lifestyles without a fight. It would be equally naïve to think that their allies will only come from the same social class (something that Marxists often tend to think). The lure of modernity is stronger than that, fooling all sorts of people into thinking that they, too, can float above the ground.

It has seldom been appreciated just how much enchantment there can be in *alienation* from the surrounding world. Driving a big vehicle, wearing protective gear, living in air-conditioned spaces, trades on the illusion of overcoming vulnerability, a powerful feeling. Modernity, in this light, and particularly through the project of development from which it has become inseparable, appears as a kind of immortality cult. The ethics of this cult is the 'deadness of fiber' that Lawrence (quoted in Diamond) talks about, the idea that you can shoot a baby gorilla in its mother's arms and suffer no consequences, because you are beyond the level of a mere creature, therefore need not participate in the fellowship that having a life imparts. The promotion of this kind of deadness of fiber is key to understanding modernity's appeal, its ease if you will, and the appeal of consumerism as the latest face of modern development. It is also crucial in order to understand that *many* will defend modern development to its last breath, precisely so as to save the immortality illusion. Hardly anything has ever been so powerful as secular immortality.

Modernity (particularly of the capitalist kind) is also highly invidious, and therefore keeps those in positions of deprivation hoping to one day be on top, freeing themselves from the difficulty of being responsible for the wellbeing of their neighbors. A lot of political discontent comes from the perceived betrayal of that promise of power, not from the inherent destructiveness of churning out indefinite trash. The idea of material development allows the winners of the process to partake in the immense power and magic of transforming nature's stuff into humans' stuff and exempts them from caring about those that remain in the negatively vulnerable position of 'closer to nature'. Those in disadvantaged positions often object to their not being able to also take flight from the world, as the neoliberal state and openly authoritarian ones both promise.

Invidiousness goes together with shame, the feeling that failure to partake in the project of becoming modern is a kind of sin, a sign of backwardness. Modern progress is routinely connected with the desire to be perceived as modern, to "be in the twenty-first century". This partly results from the seeming inevitability of progression towards development. Consumption becomes not only normalized, but expected, a crucial part of what legitimizes the status quo. Often, delivering consumption is the only thing that legitimizes it.

The attraction of the modern consumptive apparatus is directly related to the bifurcation of nature that is the stamp of modernity. Every time a mountaintop is removed, an ocean depth drilled, the special significance of a place to its creaturely ensemble is assaulted and often driven into extinction, as if to confirm the notion of the world as devoid of any inherent hermeneutical resistance. Consumer goods are a conjuring trick, a propaganda for bifurcation, which shows its power through the seemingly infinite capacity to transform matter into anything at all, precisely because it is treated as devoid of any inherent qualities. But the sciences behind this infinite production know all too well that matter is not dumb, as it is only by working with inherent qualities that it can achieve the production of goods that are then inscribed into the consumer ethos of a disenchanted world.

What many critics of modern, capitalist development fail to consider is the affective alliances that this form of development has already built across social divisions. The idea that anyone can be freed from matter-of-fact bonds of responsibility is powerful because the impulse to cheat your fellow humans, to dominate if in the appropriate position, has always been part of human affairs; it is not a product of capitalism itself. What is a product of capitalist development is the universalization of this freedom from responsibility. Inasmuch as one is permitted, alas encouraged, to ignore the earthly constraints of vulnerability that connect all the living, many will be fooled into doing just that. Instead of infrastructures of reciprocity sustaining responsibility, we have infrastructures of consumption generating callousness.

Alternatives are needed, ones that define the good life not in terms of increased consumption and the achievement of some kind of illusory immortality, but rather as the reciprocal networks of relations in which one is embedded and that generate joy as much as always-precarious protection from life's vicissitudes. Thankfully, side by side with the Great Acceleration, there are an increasing number of alternative worlds being built. Part of my claim is that these are implicitly predicated on versions of mutualism, understood not only as holding between people but rather as a structuring concept for relationships with and within the environing world, combining reciprocation and commensurate responsibility. I shall now attend further to the characteristics of mutualism understood among the living, as well as some of the many ways in which it is already being acted out.

INTERMEZZO II
Loss and Recomposition, Part II

Genealogies of Place

Sealed within narrow ways of thinking, we fail to grasp just how much richness still remains in worlds otherwise flattened by hegemonic development. In the most ordinary occurrences, there may be the glimmer of a different world; in the slightest gesture performed with natural conviction, there may be the shards of a radical vision. Ideas, conventionally described as being conceived by a mind, often conceive of us, find us and take us along to show worlds that without their own light, remained obscured by darkness. Ideas make us.

Seen this way, places that we encounter, whether familiar or strange, dimly understood or profoundly researched, are always pregnant with possibility. The gestation period is infinite, the time of delivery always unknown. As experiencing subjects, as always traversed by the multiplicity of being, we may catch a glimpse of what lays underneath the supposedly obvious. It suffices to pay attention, to ask, to listen, and to allow oneself to be taken in by a sympathetic imagination that is shared. The relationship between decomposition and recomposition is always there, always dynamic. It has never been any other way: the meaning of places constantly shifts, their partial decomposition providing the ideatic and practical compost for something new, yet related, to emerge.

Before modern development achieved an unprecedented flattening of worlds, the change of meaning from generation to generation, the transformation of places according to the whims of natural rhythms, was a matter of fact. The illusion of control over the world that modernity has so ably promoted veils this fact and makes it hard to recuperate the central insight of loss and rebuilding: what is always recuperated is the relation itself, not some romantic past that does nothing to challenge—and to decompose—modern ways of composing. An ethic of nativist bliss is anathema to the relational modes that one always discovers when digging through the concrete.

Places, all places really, are a living archive. As such, places hold powers that dictate, to a large extent, how they are to be approached and treated. The more we learn about the archival material of which places are built, the more we can read the landscape and find ourselves transformed, as we do in reading good literature. Being in a place that reveals its archive is very much akin to reading a novel: one is able to inhabit possible worlds, see their light and smell their scents, and one is able to feel the sadness of loss and the gratitude of endurance. Just like with literature, one can infinitely re-read, and each time it is different, the archive inexhaustible.

Returning to Auckland from having visited Waitangi, the place where the Treaty of Waitangi, the foundational document of New Zealand, was debated and signed in 1840, I stopped to visit Tāne Mahuta, a *kauri* tree in Waipoua forest that is believed to be the largest tree in the country. A representative of Te Roroa, the local *iwi*, stood nearby and chatted with curious travelers. He always spoke of the tree using either the personal pronoun, or one of his twelve names, given to Tāne Mahuta for good deeds he had done for local people throughout his life. It is estimated that he is around 2000 years old, which means that he was already very old when the first Polynesian navigators arrived in Aotearoa.

Back then, when Tāne was only 1000 years old, there was no Waipoua Forest, but a vast subtropical *kauri* forest that the newcomers slowly learned to live with and within. Today, he stands as testimony to what has disappeared, felled by the saws of settlers in pursuit of timber and pastures. Those past relationships that made Tāne can only be intuited; the relationships that made Tāne before Māori became Māori were surely a subject of local intuition before white settlers arrived. The representative of Te Roroa, contemplating the *kauri* that his ancestors named twelve different times, is testimony to the enduring significance of these beings, the uncanny survival of an embodied demigod that had, for a very brief period in history, become just timber.

For Māori each place has a force of its own, and human conduct has to take this into account. Geoff Park (1995, 164) explains it thus:

Before contact with the missionaries of the 19th century Māori believed their physical health and wellbeing were achieved in two principal ways. One was by maintaining the mauri of their places—the life force by which their natural elements cohere. The other was by lifelong observance of the laws of tapu [sacredness, forbidden, taboo]. Rites and rituals broke down the barriers between people and other species, allowed people to flow spiritually into nature and for nature's rhythms to permeate their own being. A host of daily tasks depended on conscious connection, both to benefit nature and limit human excesses.

Ritualized interaction with the environment allowed for the change inherent in natural processes to be incorporated as health, as the kind of vulnerability that makes one and that sustains sensitivity towards the *mauri* of places.

This way of being in the world meant that one observed the specific sacredness of particular places, like ones where giant trees grew (*kauri* is but one of many different giants in New Zealand). Rituals ensured that everyone respected the specificity of places. In order to suppress Māori and their philosophical ways it was therefore necessary to interrupt—to decompose speedily—their profound readings of places. Like elsewhere, white settlers had the correct intuition that you cannot control a people without changing their land. The beginnings of modernity themselves harbor the interrelation of people and places, albeit it negatively; this is a molecular residue of modernity within modernity itself, something that may as well become an auto-immune disorder, a kind of self-sabotage in order to return to this founding intuition as a positive project.

The early missionaries, in acquiring land and converting Māori to Christianity, had to physically destroy the *tapu*, the sacredness, of a place. They could not transform the ritualized interaction with the environment by wishing it away, or by converting people to abstract ideas. They had to intervene materially, because that is the level of interaction that sustains a certain way of life. Park recounts how, in the Mōkau Region, missionaries would perform their own rituals around sacred trees in order to drive their spirit out. The rituals were concluded by setting the tree ablaze, in what must have been a spectacular show of force on the side of the Christian God.

This spectacular force of destruction that makes the impossible real is a recurrent theme within modernity; it repeats itself wherever development takes over, going as it must through the process of driving out the special significance of places and things. In Puglia, olive trees—the giants of that territory—were mostly imagined as immortal and therefore acquired extraordinary significance. Olive time was first shaken by the project of development that increasingly transformed them into cogs in a productive machine, multiplying their numbers to the point of near insignificance. Only the 'monumental' trees are seen as special within a sea of monocultural monotony.

The appearance of *Xylella*, the bacterium that has killed millions of olive trees in just a matter of years, has accomplished the radical desacralization that development has always sought. Pathogens may seem to come from nowhere, as if they are mere bad luck. In some sense they are just a matter of luck because they are part of the chance and change that defines the natural world. But in another sense, their actions can only be as good as the conditions that sustain them; monocultures of purely economic significance are an ideal habitat for a creature that simply pursues its own way of life. Inscribed within the story of that place, *Xylella* concludes its history of decomposition by doing the unthinkable: *killing* the eternal olive tree. In the beginning of the outbreak, most people did not follow the official advice of uprooting sick trees because they could not *believe* that they could die. Nothing in their experience attested to that possibility. Now, a landscape of scorched trees makes the impossible real. As Janos Chialá has documented in painfully evocative fashion, dried trees are burning every summer, driving their *mauri* into extinction, the *tapu* of the land finally exorcised.

We tend to forget just how much *work* goes into desacralizing the world. We pass through strip malls and highways littered with industrial debris—the sacrificial zones of global capital—without realizing the effort that went into the sacrifice, and the repeated nature of the assault, from priests burning trees to loggers felling the remainder to ranchers grazing pasture to developers and bulldozers and cement. The placeless world that global consumer societies create and promote, the uniformity of shops, production, storage, transportation, requires an enormous amount of work against the special significance of so many places. Each iteration drives out the spirit that people recognize in a place, with the Christian priest driving out *tapu* as much as the developer drives out the significance of the pastoral landscape, the monoculture unraveling the story of generational inheritance.

The flat world created over the past several hundred years is rooted in the specific agenda of neutralizing the inherent importance that people discover in natural environments. In so doing, it also neutralizes the people that are part of a place's archive, the people that cannot conceive of themselves outside of an intimate relationship to a place. In this sense, the world of global capital is inimical to the possibility of humans living in a rich and significant natural environment. Under the conditions of global capital, we can only hope for classic nature conservation, predicated on the artificial exclusion of people from a world otherwise teeming with networks of significance.

The ways in which people have inhabited places, all over the world, is infinitely varied yet retains a commonality with the deep relationship between human groups and natural environments. Park describes the Mōkau River in 1852, on the cusp of its most momentous transformation, as

> an ecological mosaic. Supporting cultivations and community forests, both rich in useful species, it contrasted dramatically with the European idea of conservation which was to set aside large wilderness free of human interference, or keep remnant patches in a monocultural expanse of crops and plantations. Little of the Mōkau was left unexploited. Its people didn't act with any particular ecological nobility: they did whatever they had to do to feed themselves and their families. [...] And as the river landscape filled with history, it filled with emotion.

The emotion that past habitation has left behind is still legible in the landscape, inasmuch as the markers of legibility are left standing; some of those markers are people themselves, some the paper archives that document a passing. What remains true is that you cannot have healthy people is a sick land.[1]

Tāne Mahuta has witnessed, and recorded within his fibrous flesh, the events of natural history that make up a landscape. Today, he and his peers are fighting *kauri* dieback disease, a deadly pathogen spread through soil and spread by the hiking boots of well-meaning travelers. To protect him and the forest from the disease, wooden trails have been built that literally separate human feet from the forest floor. Once again, social distancing *avant la lettre*. The planks used in their construction

---

1 This idea was developed by Janos Chialá during a lecture series on *Xylella* at the University of California, Berkeley, in October 2021.

likely come from some logging plantation that long ago replaced rich forest. One can no longer touch the *kauri* or walk up to them. The landscape is adding another layer to its archive, one telling the story of a globalized species carrying around disease, as it has done for thousands of years, and continuing to separate itself from the landscape, as it has done for hundreds of years. Reading the landscape, in Tāne's shadow, filled me with sadness at the tremendous loss of history, and gratitude for the resilience of life. A young representative of Te Roroa is learning, from his elders and in their language, Tāne Mahuta's twelve names. Generations from now, he might have received a thirteenth name, or he might have been lost forever, as the majority of his peers before him.

Similarly, *Xylella* did not only arrive, but it has also been created before it even arrived, its arrival meticulously prepared. The social distancing for trees that is still the official response in order to save what is left similarly interrupts relationships older than memory; one can no longer touch an uprooted, burned tree. And yet, in pockets that are easy to miss, people are fighting to keep their heritage alive, by lovingly tending to sick trees that may yet endure the bacterial assault. In the face of tragedy—the likely repeated dying of a tree that is being repeatedly kept alive—some people persist. The possibility of tragedy does not condemn them to apathy, it condemns them to perpetual action. It denies rest. But the stubbornness to go on in the face of almost inevitable loss itself puts in motion new communities of practice that can rise up from the destruction of the old. Once the carefully tended olive tree dies, that loving knowledge of the surrounding environment can migrate to other creatures, other relationships, other means of recomposition.

The movements of history take as much as they give, and in this fragile hour we must do more than possible to give back a portion of the enormous amount we have already taken. One place to start is in learning to read landscapes, re-sacralizing and insisting on adding to their archive, leaving the signs of legibility for the readers of tomorrow to be transformed, humbled, re-situated, by the story of this place. The genealogical links that always tie people to places are hurting, and this pain is now felt through the forces that tear these links apart. But the brute fact of human life is made by its genealogical imbrication with the environing world, the fact that humans themselves are places, and can never be extinguished. It is there that the commitment to restoration will always reside.

7. Mutualism

A Philosophical and Political Orientation

I have presented different descriptions of what it means to be embedded within a given environment, always on the assumption that these kinds of descriptive experiments open up political possibilities. These possibilities are not absent otherwise, they always exist to some extent; but they are devoid of the vitality that naming breathes into them.

In this chapter I want to offer one more description of a concept that may succeed in threading together a common pattern that has been implied throughout the argument. I have no interest in tying a firm knot that would commit me, or anyone else, to a defensive stance, preventing the possibility of untying it. I have talked about the relationship between creatures and space, and how a voluminous description of both, without collapsing their differences, allows ecological thinking. Vulnerability marks the passage from an ontological to an ethical political ecology, one that re-dimensions humans by rooting them in the impossible necessity of reciprocity and responsibility. These thoughts were occasioned by experiments already underway and by situations that inspire, or at least have inspired me by undoing and reshuffling my own misplaced concreteness. These were situations that drew on, and further teased out, to borrow and modify a phrase from Isabelle Stengers (2015), the possibility of "conscientious objectors" to modern development.[1]

All of these stances share a fundamental intuition of the important and often overlooked role that mutual beneficence plays in natural phenomena. Mutualism is a simple name, but one with the power to connect the ontological and the ethical and breed commitment to the stubbornness of living in the Ecocene. The concept of mutualism is

---

1   The original phrase is "conscientious objectors to economic growth".

not new, but perhaps has been resuscitated. As Deleuze and Guattari wrote, "ideas do not die. Not that they survive simply as archaisms. [...] Their application and status, even their form and content, may change; yet they retain something essential throughout the process, across the displacement, in the distribution of a new domain" (1988, 235). Mutualism has indeed had multiple histories of prominence and obscurity. The part that stays roughly the same is the conviction that mutual beneficence plays a structuring role in the world.

The idea that mutually beneficial relationships are extremely important for life in general has had several histories that, if considered together, offer a chance to deploy the concept once again. I have in mind two particular strands of mutualist thinking: the biological and ecological sciences that have, for the past two centuries, been dominated by an internal tension between competition and mutualism, and the anarchist tradition of social and political philosophy.

Let's start with biology, as it will allow us to connect the imagination and understanding of creaturely life to the politics that is necessarily rooted there. But if ideas have a life of their own, traveling in surprising and unpredictable ways, there is no point in presenting them chronologically. I'll therefore start by walking backwards.

* * *

It is impossible to consider the history and practices of biology and ecology without thinking about evolution. Lynn Margulis decidedly moved the study of evolution away from a near obsession with competition and towards at least more sustained curiosity in the myriad ways in which life is only possible because of cooperation, as well as the ways in which it is free, to some extent, to pursue paths that themselves condition future evolution (also see Chapter 3). As we will see later, she was neither the first to do so, nor the last, but rather a bright node of renovation of an idea that is probably as old as natural history itself. This is not a romantic view that denies the many different struggles inherent in life.[2] Anything that is alive will struggle, definitionally, but the conditions of its liveliness are never assured by competition only.

---

2   Margulis championed what she called a "symbiotic" view of life. Symbiosis refers to parasitism as well as mutualism, and in the biological sciences these are both implied when using the term. For the political purposes of this argument, I focus

Instead, each creaturely life is only possible because of (often unknown) generative connections that benefit a wide range of participants.

The general idea that life is fundamentally cooperative has become refracted in many different ways throughout the natural sciences. In immunology, for example, Gilbert, Sapp and Tauber (2012) have championed the concept of the holobiont, already encountered in Chapter 3 (also see Thomas Pradeu's *The Limits of the Self* (2009), and Tauber 2017). Margulis traces the idea of "holons" to the work of Arthur Koestler, who observed the common phenomenon of smaller beings coexisting in larger forms ("holarchy"; Margulis and Sagan 2000, 9). The holons then are "not merely parts" but "wholes that also function as parts".

The holobiont does not deny the ways in which boundaries are formative of precarious individuality, but rather stresses the differences that make individuals separable to begin with. And those differences are never autonomously generated, but rather are always the result of dense relational networks. From this perspective, the relation between two human individuals becomes infinitely more interesting and more complex inasmuch as it becomes a relationship between two porous networks. As such, actions between holobionts are open to continuous reassessment as to who stands to benefit: microbes, gut bacteria, fungi, and so on.

Individual creatures are only ever individual inasmuch as that concept serves a purpose in forming relationships. For example, the relationship a person may have with a particular tree is only superficially the relationship between two individuals, but this does not mean that pointing out 'the tree' in question is a mistake. Instead, what the designation 'that tree' may make possible is itself influenced by the deeper knowledge of the differences that make the apparent individuality of the tree possible. Simard (2016, 2018) has shown how, for example, mycorrhizal networks are fundamental to the thriving of trees, to such an extent that making a stark distinction between roots and fungi is itself problematic and only useful inasmuch as it makes further probing possible (also see Sheldrake 2000). As Margulis and Sagan argue, "independence is a political, not a scientific, term" (2000,

---

on mutualism, but it should be understood that it is only one part of symbiotic relations.

20). And yet an ecologically congruous politics cannot afford a dogmatic concept of independence either.

Mutualism in one way or another operates through the holobiont, making relatively stable appearances possible. The biological sciences are producing incredibly exciting evidence for the vast interconnections that define the living world. As I have argued throughout, human ignorance is in an important sense structural, as nobody can consider the vastness of relationships that populate the environing world. But no-one needs to; that is why we need infrastructures of reciprocity built through political processes committed to the living world, such that ignorance becomes an openness towards populating the world with further agents, rather than a blindfold.

Biology is moving in the direction of a mutualist theory of life, from the formation of the tiniest creatures all the way up to the surface of the planet itself, the critical zone of life that cannot exist outside of myriad mutually beneficial relations. At the limit, it has also started to show the porosity of "biotic" and "abiotic" processes. Not only has "more and more inert matter, over time, [...] come to life" (25), but distinctions between, for example, minerals and animals are not as stable as one may think: over fifty minerals have been identified that are *only* produced in living organisms (29). These kinds of discoveries do not take anything away from the difference between tectonic movements and human embodiment, but they do plot a thick network that ties these together in ways that allow for much more interesting, and politically salient, questions.

Even before the sophisticated and vital instruments of modern biology could reveal the *extent* of mutual intermingling that is itself a feature of life, field observations pointed in the same direction. A particularly good observer, though often forgotten because of his ecologically congruent politics, was Peter Kropotkin.

The common root of mutualist thinking in both biology and political thought is nowhere better exemplified than in his 1902 book, *Mutual Aid: A Factor of Evolution*.[3] It is one of the widest reaching systematizations

---

[3] In strictly historical terms, the ideas of Proudhon are much more closely related to the concept of mutualism in anarchist theory. There, it is mostly developed as an economic theory, a strand of theory that continues today (see Carson 2007). However, Proudhon's theories are much less suited, in my view, to reinvention

to date of the role of mutualism across scales. The deep challenge that this work posed to social Darwinism has still not fully been answered, and the subsequent separation of political and biological thought, after its horrible fusions in the twentieth century, has yet to be mended in a satisfactory way. Kropotkin's main thesis is that what he calls mutual aid is "a feature of the greatest importance for the maintenance of life" (4). His argument is crafted against both the biological view, inspired by a selective reading of Darwin, that competition is the main driver of evolution, and the political view, obviously related to this, that normalized authoritarian forms of power because of their supposed naturalness.

Besides this main thesis, Kropotkin makes a series of insightful observations that have been strikingly uninfluential so far. One of the first things that surprises the contemporary reader of this text is how much of Kropotkin's descriptions of animal lives (which are much better than his decidedly dated descriptions of early human life) are expressed in what today appears as radical language. He routinely speaks of animal societies, he imputes various levels of consciousness to animals unproblematically, he speaks matter-of-factly about animal morality, and he generally describes animal behavior as structurally, necessarily intelligent. In the twenty-first century, using this kind of language has

---

for the Ecocene. His narrow focus on economics is one particular obstacle, as is his (and his followers') failure to see the environing world as itself possessed of various agents that labor in their own fashion. Not that Kropotkin theorized labor as applicable to non-human beings, but his development of the concept of mutual aid opens up towards such expansion and is therefore a much better ancestor than Proudhon's mutuality can be.

Besides Proudhon himself, many radicals of the nineteenth century operated fully within the bifurcation of nature. For example, in an 1867 discussion on the social ownership of soil, Cesar de Paepe argued that "the soil is not the product of anyone's labor, and the reciprocity of exchange is not applicable to it". This forecloses the possibility of the kind of concept of reciprocity discussed in Chapter 5, and definitionally restricts mutual beneficence to human-to-human relations. Kropotkin did not himself overcome these difficulties, *per se*, but his conception is much more open to reappropriation.

Finally, the idea of mutualism as coming out of Proudhon's work is intrinsically tied to individualism. This is also true for Kropotkin's concept of mutual aid, but the latter's forays into biology allows a renovation of mutualism that is open to the biological uncertainties attached to the concept of the individual. Taking all of these points together, it becomes clear that I am not proposing a historical exegesis that would *clarify* the meaning of mutualism, but rather reinventing a term within a conceptual constellation that takes decisive steps away from exegesis.

been the subject of serious effort on the part of courageous researchers. It is as if Kropotkin's inheritance skipped a century, more or less. It may be worth thinking about why Kropotkin's language appears so new today, even though it was inscribed within biological thinking in this extremely formative period of its history. The (temporary) hegemonic success of hierarchical and machinist views of life snuffed out a rich source of inspiration that never disenchanted the environing world to begin with.

Another revealing feature of Kropotkin's text is his treatment of nature, also very similar to the postmodern nuance which seeks to go beyond the bifurcation typical of modernity. Kropotkin's nature is not only suffused with intelligence, as in the animist philosophies explored earlier, but also sketched as a violent background. His 1902 book starts with a beautiful description of the irruption of Gaia within creaturely worlds, spelling recurrent disasters (which Drury also talks about) for untold numbers of individuals in ways that seem cruel and arbitrary. However, as Darwin also showed, these processes of recurrent destruction are "the natural checks to over-multiplication" and, as Drury shows, are already taken into account by the living through the widespread overproduction of young. This nature is neither the dumb, flat space of modernity, nor the romanticized version that was routinely opposed to modern conceptions in Kropotkin's time.

The arguments of *Mutual Aid* are mostly developed along a series of observations of the way in which life actually organizes itself. According to Kropotkin, it makes sense that competition would be a rare occurrence, rather than the engine of evolution, because of the obvious advantages that cooperation imparts to all participants. He makes the brilliant point that, when arduous competition does occur, the individuals undergoing it are left so debilitated by it that *"no progressive evolution of the species can be based upon such periods of keen competition"* (italics in original, 5). From this, he postulates mutual aid as an engine of evolution, on both empirical and logical grounds. Or, as Margulis and Sagan express it, "life is free to act and has played an unexpectedly large part in its own evolution" (4). This relative freedom often expresses itself in cooperative fashion.

Mutual aid can be thought of as applying, to some extent, to all living creatures. The thought would be that some form of mutualism helps many kinds of creatures further evolve. Turning it upside down, the idea of evolution presupposes mutualism, more or less across the board. Kropotkin only discusses the kinds of creatures for which there was evidence of mutualism during his time. Since then, the evidence has grown tremendously, and we can now postulate mutual aid as a principle of evolution much more broadly than he could have. It seems to hold in plants as well as animals, something that Kropotkin could only have guessed (see Simand's *Finding the Mother Tree* 2021).

Despite its roots in the early history of biology, mutualism never really left the fringes, and this is partly because of its political associations. It is as opposed to statist authority as it is to the primacy of competition in evolution, and this common antipathy towards authority and inter-specific as well as intra-specific strife made it incompatible with what turned out to be the victorious ideologies of the twentieth century. Mutualism as anti-statist and broadly anti-capitalist made it difficult for the work of its nineteenth-century proponents to be amply adopted. This marginalization testifies to the successful deployment of modern bifurcation through the modern nation state, which has perpetually suppressed anti-individualist and anti-competitive views of life and modes of living.

For both the biologist and the anarchist of the mid- to late-nineteenth century, mutualism is a feature of the living that is occasioned by the irruption of the elemental world and its destructive force, that is to say it is a feature that *allows* evolution despite the vicissitudes to which natural processes subject individuals. Mutualist relationships are therefore as old as the living world itself. Strictly speaking, then, anarchism is also part of the mechanisms of the living. If ecological processes are understood as stochastic affairs, then they are not subject to overarching systems that direct their functioning. The change in evolutionary processes and the shifting alliances of countless creatures need not be structured according to pre-determined patterns, which implies that mutualist relationships change all the time. There is no such thing as a final and forever decided mode of mutual interaction. Thinking this way presents a radical challenge to politics wedded to relative statis achieved through control, as well as competition-driven evolution, where competition would precisely be an overarching principle. Mutualism is in the fiber of interactions, not a strict natural law.

From the specific meaning of mutual aid in evolutionary theory we can move towards a wider concept that considers the ways in which the human animal practices mutualism both among its kind and in wider networks of living creatures. Anthropology is evidently a rich resource here. As David Graeber suggests, at the end of his book *Fragments of an Anarchist Anthropology* (2004), anthropologists "have tools at [their] fingertips that could be of enormous importance for human freedom". What he means is that anthropological studies have already been documenting the richness of human social-ecological organization, and partly because of that they can be read as containing important ideas about how societies endure or perish, thrive or descend into oppression.

What he has in mind as standards for thriving or resilience are not the usual fixations on monuments and kingly glory. Instead, he asks us to think about just how unlikely priestly and kingly casts are, given the vast experience of human beings with governing their own affairs in a collective fashion. The anthropological record overwhelmingly supports this thesis, as most human societies everywhere have developed along roughly egalitarian lines. Graeber is no idealist; he is quite explicit about the ways in which human life is always preoccupied by existential problems that egalitarianism cannot wish away. Instead, his account gives proper consideration to the processes through which human societies change, as well as embedding (albeit implicitly) the idea of mutualism within the matter-of-fact way in which most humans interact. He argues that "[...] anarchist social relations and non-alienated forms of action are all around us. And this is critical because it already shows that anarchism is, already, and has always been, one of the main bases for human interaction. We self-organize and engage in mutual aid all the time. We always have". What makes modernity distinct, in this reading, is the radical way in which it exiles people from what have always been bonds of reciprocity and responsibility.

Anarchism as practice is not a universal solution that would embed mutual beneficence within politics; it can become a dogmatic ideology like any other, foreclosing the possibility of new alliances. It often veers towards individualism of a kind that is anathema to the ideas developed in this book. It is no surprise then that libertarianism perpetually haunts it. Thinking sideways and engaging in small theory, insisting on the level at which situations happen, does not mean that anything that does not happen at that level can be ignored or opposed as such. In this sense, anarchism is not so much a goal to reach, another utopian end, as a continued fidelity to an operation of always challenging power relations, wherever they appear.

Anarchist political theory is a good bridge for mutualism precisely because of this commitment. At its best, it is rooted in the intuition that power always hides ties that cannot be predicated on power differentials alone, and that it is those instances of resistance that hold the most political potential. Anarchism is therefore a difficult practical problem, and it is precisely because of this that it cannot afford to be dogmatic. Anarchism and ecology work well together, and the idea of mutualism challenges the dominance of competition in both fields. Thinking ecologically and thinking anarchically by definition require a similar kind of situatedness, or what I have referred to in relation to ecology as its constant pull towards the terrestrial. Planetary managerial thinking will likely never disappear. But it can be perpetually challenged and brought to bear on specific situations, where it will inevitably be transformed.

The kind of mutualism that I have selectively extracted should not be applied to human relationships only. This is why Kropotkin is a great guide here, showing just how many different kinds of creatures also rely, structurally, on the practice of mutual beneficence. My argument is that mutualism can be a name for a political ethic that cannot decide, *a priori*, on a complete list of benefitted parties. Even if we choose to think about human relations only, the ways in which the biological sciences have themselves taken up their own radical nineteenth-century precursors makes it impossible to think about isolated individuals. Margulis' symbiotic view of life is both crucial to biology and—like mutualist ideas before hers—holds political potential that emphasizes the necessity of sustaining mutualism through infrastructures of reciprocity.

* * *

Mutualism has always implied spaces of multiplicity. This is not simply because mutually beneficial relations presuppose several participants. The multiplicity in question is part of the ontological and ethical underpinnings of the concept, as made clear by their respective histories. It makes no sense to speak of a principle of mutual aid in biology without also conceiving of the living world as one of voluminous depth, as I argued in Chapter 2. We cannot relegate mutualist relations, for example, to a curiosity that exists under special circumstances. No, if mutual aid is indeed thought of as an engine of the perpetuation and enhancement of life, then it is more akin to a rule, not an exception. And this is why an ecologically grounded political ethic needs to take this concept into account, as it is inescapable in the context of the ontological commitments developed here.

Some version or another of mutualism seeps into practices that do not self-consciously or explicitly adhere to it. In Chapter 4 I spoke about rewilding as a practice that tries to enhance ecological processes through the reintroduction of certain creatures to certain spaces. If we look at these practices from the perspective of enhancing the number and variety of relations between humans and their environments, it becomes obvious that they in fact pursue a project of mutual beneficence. The point is to have both the reintroduced creatures and the humans that participate be transformed, beneficially, by new kinds of interactions. These relationships are not limited to, for example, humans and wisents. No, the point is to encourage a vast number of relationships that had disappeared, or laid dormant, in the absence of human—wisent interactions.

The kinds of things that rewilders think about are the relationships that the wisent metabolism makes possible, from enhancing soil communities to extending the possibilities of life for countless insects and birds. All of these features become part of the human world, especially if humans participate actively in sustaining these renovated interactions. Yet rewilding practice seldom thinks of itself as a politics of mutualism, and therefore misses the point of what it *could* be doing that would be much more transformative for the humans involved.

As I have already suggested, one way in which an explicitly mutualist restoration could work differently is by insisting on intervening in ordinary environments. Renovating the commonplace relations that make up the daily lives of millions is not what ecological restoration usually contemplates, but there is no reason why it could not do so. My wager is that the preference for 'spectacular' environments comes out of the separation of the sciences, including the ecological ones, from a more widely conceived human meaning. Practitioners dealing with restoration think of themselves as specialists in technical interventions that relate to certain species, or certain processes. Their disciplinary training needs to be unlearned in order for them to see that, *in their own practice*, what drives their efforts is the pursuit of a network of mutual beneficence. In this, they are no different from any other human being that flourishes under conditions of environmental abundance and wilts with the impoverishment of the surrounding world.

Breaking out of its technical shell, restoration understood as a mutualist practice can be applied to any environment. Freed from baselines and therefore free to adapt to situations, it can work from relations with worms and bacteria transforming soil to relations with threatened species in the last remaining enclaves of their lives. I am not denying the importance of saving tigers and protecting their world. But saving tigers is ultimately useless without also addressing the underlying impoverishment of the world. Biologists and ecologists may have a hard time recognizing that their practices can become radically democratic and diffuse. And yet they must do so.

Just like field ecologists return to their study site time and again, sometimes for an entire lifetime, so too can everyone be incorporated into ritualized practices that repeatedly, and endlessly, commit to observing and enhancing the surrounding world. This is of course hard. But it can become easier, inasmuch as restorative practices are conceived of and built within infrastructures of reciprocity.

What is an infrastructure in this sense? One way to think about it is by looking at what infrastructures do: they allow movement to flow in directions that, outside of the infrastructural conditioning of space and time, would be *difficult*. One can travel from point A to point B on a rutted dirt road, but that kind of travel is slow and laborious, implying a space of volumetric resistance. A highway, by contrast, allows for smooth, featureless, frictionless travel, and therefore makes possible exchanges and events that would be very unlikely, even impossible, without it. The dirt road is infrastructural too, and so is a path, and each allows for specific kinds of things. There is no life without some infrastructure that makes up, to a great extent, specific ways for that life to have a life-form.

So, one of the main reasons for building infrastructures is to make it relatively easy to move about. This is not just a physical, literal moving, but also crucial for flows of power, energy, capital, nutrients, waste, and so on; flows in general. You could say that the flow of a river depends upon water building its own infrastructure, on the base that geology provides. The riverbed allows the river to flow, but it also allows all kinds of other processes to happen that would otherwise not exist, or would be much weaker. The natural world is dense with infrastructures, each particular process carving out its own or using those carved by others, often in tandem. The valleys that glaciers carve become the rivers whose nutrients feed the creatures that themselves carve the paths of their own movement—a continuous change in infrastructural possibilities.

As Marx knew, there is no edifice of power without a basic infrastructure that makes it possible. In today's consumer world, there is no consumerism as we know it without a vast network that makes it easy to fly a chicken from one part of the world to another in order for it to be plucked and returned. People do not do this because they find it to be a good idea in itself; they do it because, under current infrastructural conditions, it is the easiest thing to do (the cheapest, most efficient, quickest, and so on). Planting a lawn as opposed to using one's waste for the creation of rich soil around the house is easier, but not in any objective sense. If anything, letting fungi do the work is technically easier than riding a lawnmower every week, servicing it, fueling it, and generally incurring the expenses that it demands. Planting and maintaining a lawn is made easier by the infrastructural background that makes monoculture seeds more available than fungi, by planning permissions and neighborhood regulations that demand them, by immediate access to fuel, and so on.

Everything creatures do is made possible by some infrastructural network, and in the case of modern people these networks are built to make the most destructive behaviors easily attainable. The point of building infrastructures of reciprocity, as opposed to ones of consumption and control, is to make reciprocation one of the most straightforward ways of being. This is why ritualization is needed. Again, there are hardly any valid *a priori* logistical reasons as to why flying chickens around the world would be easier than raising one's own. Logistics is not a base category, but infrastructures are, because they create logistics.

Setting up and continuously fighting for infrastructures of reciprocity does not need pre-approval. It does not require a policy-driven approach, though it can surely benefit from policies that would more explicitly follow this kind of logic. The state apparatus that has transformed the infrastructural networks through which more and more people live into networks of consumptive destruction can be continuously challenged from below, even if enhancement through ritualized restoration were to become state policy. This is where the anarchist commitment to being vigilant whenever power differentials are normalized becomes crucial: the maintenance of infrastructures of reciprocity is always going to be primarily a local affair, and therefore will always largely function outside of the state's capacity to exercise control.

***

Mutualism need not have universalist tendencies: it is about specific relationships, inasmuch as relations always exist between specific terms. There is no meaning to something like "relating to the world", and therefore being "beneficial to the world", or saving it. This is crucial, as it implies that ontologically infinite multiplicity does not have to, and alas cannot, be translated into relations *to* multiplicity. Instead, the task is to understand under which sign specific relations must be developed in order to also stay true to the infinite multiplicity that permeates them. As the authors of *Manifesto for the Invention of a New Peasant Condition*[4] (2019) remarked, "inventing more desirable ways of living without waiting for a generalized social change. [...] this will be the work of those who have actually begun to break away from the most insidious forms of life" (40). And this always already implies the open-ended selection of the relationships that matter.

Many proposals and alternatives today implicitly engage this kind of conceptual apparatus. The kind of nature restoration William Jordan has proposed is rooted in the idea that people can be beneficial to the environment, and shows a practical commitment to an open-ended mutual beneficence. Restoring the prairies of the mid-West does not seek to recreate an era of supposed ideal conditions, but rather to recreate a relationship between people and lands that is predicated on the capacity to help each other. These practices are necessarily ritualistic, and the rituals that Jordan explores have to do with the cyclical gathering of

---

4 Published in French (2019) as *Manifeste pour l'invention d'une nouvelle condition paysanne*. The original quotation is: "[...] inventer de nouveaux modes de vie plus désirables, sans attendre un changement social généralisé. [...] ce sera l'œuvre de ceux et celles qui ont effectivement commencé à rompre avec les formes de vie dont on a le plus grand mal à se défaire".

people in order to engage, for example, in controlled burning of the prairie environment that is designed to help certain assemblages. Mutual beneficence can never be total (with the *whole* environment benefiting), but that is not the point. The idea is to consciously benefit a growing number of creaturely networks.

Similarly, the idea of commons as a mechanism of territorial governance is increasingly being reinvented, as its remnants are starting to grow in more and more places (see *inter alia* Gutwirth and Stengers 2016, Tanas and Gutwirth 2021, Bollier and Helfrich 2019). The commons are rediscovering land practices that treat the land as a good that cannot be legitimately appropriated by one owner, and that therefore is not subject to the whims of one. George Iordăchescu recounts how, in Northern Transylvania, the commons have survived centuries of enclosure and are currently fighting the fortress conservation model that is supposed to protect the diversity of life on their lands. Private buyers have consolidated enormous amounts of land that they plan to manage as conservation reserves (Iordăchescu 2019). This is the latest face of fortress conservation that, in its faithful merger with capital investment, mutates into private reserves supposedly serving the common good and inaugurating a new kind of consumption.[5]

Some rewilding projects have also embraced this model, which is inimical to everything that I have argued for so far. In Portugal, for example, Rewilding Europe works with wealthy owners to manage their private land according to 'rewilding principles', and the owners get a fantastic holiday retreat in return, plus the good conscience of saving the world. In the Transylvanian case, this kind of mutated conservation practice is the greatest threat to the commoners' way of life, and to their lands. The commoners, in their turn, are seen by the growing reserve as a grave threat to the natural world.

One need not look far to discover that commons have in fact had a tremendously important role in keeping lands both rich *and* useful for people for centuries, if not millennia. There is ample evidence for this. And one of the things that makes the commons work is the relationship that people develop with each other *through mutualist practices* that share both benefits and disadvantages. This does not only apply to land

---

5   Conservation has been a form of luxury consumption since its beginning, as reserves have always been enjoyed *as reserves* by relatively wealthy visitors.

practices, though here I am primarily interested in these, but works through any kind of social practice that pursues mutual benefits. Bollier and Helfrich give the example of a telecommunications company in Catalonia that set up Wi-Fi services through a network chartered as "free, open, and neutral" (25). The point of the network is to provide Internet services to anyone abiding by the network's values at the lowest possible price, and in a mutualist fashion that allows for free exchange of services and information without the overseeing eye of a communications monopoly. Crucially, it is *because* of the "mutualizing of costs and benefits" that the network can function in the most price-effective manner, marking a step away from dependence on money, "and therefore [on the] structural coercion of markets".

Bollier and Helfrich give many different examples, from homecare commons started by nurses resisting the increasingly marketized and alienated healthcare system in the Netherlands to community agriculture. But what they share is a commitment to a social process that ritualizes their interactions and generates knowledge primarily aimed at cultivating skills for mutual beneficence. The role of ritual is crucial, because it is through repeated, organized, and routine interaction that skills of togetherness are developed, as well as practical skills for creating lives outside the dominant modes of consumption and production. Another surprising example is the ritual of the hackathon, where hackers gather to solve difficult problems and learn from each other. In land-based practices, the members of an urban community garden getting together each weekend is a ritual, as is the regular transfer and creation of knowledge within communities dedicated to permaculture.

There is nothing romantic about this. I am not claiming that commons are perfect; nor are the restoration projects I have spoken about. These kinds of examples are not really examples, strictly speaking. Thinking of them as such is what may lead towards the charge of romanticism. They do not exemplify in that they are not models to be emulated. What they do give is an occasion for thinking of alternatives by picking out operations through which different kinds of infrastructures are set up, and different modes of mutual beneficence imperfectly pursued. It is crucial to notice the resilience of reciprocity and responsibility and think with others about how their implacable force can carve out its own grooves to enable them to flow more easily. In a sense, ritualizing practices simply allows suppressed reciprocity and responsibility to resurface.

There is no need for utopian solutions that depend on orthodox allegiance in order to deliver a better world. Instead, these and many other practices are ways of articulating an eclectic conceptual constellation that is increasingly being mobilized against modern development. It is counterproductive to nit-pick the faults and inconsistencies of each particular experiment. It is better to support their overlapping commitments, and to discern the kinds of life that are encouraged in each case, particularly through their interactions. This motley approach to revolutionary change does not have requirements of purity; one need not have the right utopian ideology in order to be considered as sharing "the right politics". Allies need only have partially overlapping commitments to the roles humans may play in ensuring a thriving living world. This seems like a tall order, but in practice it can take so many different forms that it would be a careless mistake to theoretically preclude most of them.

***

As I have argued throughout this book, reciprocity as a practice has never disappeared, but rather has been drastically marginalized through the disappearance of its social infrastructure. What I mean is that any social group, in order to practically express the reciprocity necessary for mutualist relations, builds and upholds conduits of thought and practice that make it relatively easier for people to engage with the environing world in a reciprocal way. Thinking back to the discussion of Māori philosophy, for example, it appears that in the pre-colonial Māori world, as far as we know, the entirety of social organization made reciprocal relations the most obvious ones for participants. It may be worth revisiting that world once more.

Inasmuch as status, for example, depended on the cultivation of relationships with wide genealogical networks inclusive of all sorts of creatures, it stands to reason that community leaders would have been those that were best at reproducing mutualist practices. Conversely, in a context of intense competition for infinite growth, predicated on the bifurcation of nature, it is *hard* to engage in mutualist practice, because the paths that would lead there have become clogged. How, then, can these vital infrastructures be restored?

An important ally of the practices already explored is indicated by one of the most famous treatments of Māori philosophies, in the work of Marcel Mauss. Mauss' work sought to show, through anthropological studies, the political possibilities inherent in human communities. In his 1925 (translated into English in 1954) book *The Gift*, he specifically attends to the possibilities for different exchange logics implied in the act of gifting, as well as in gifts themselves as objects imbued with particular powers. Above and beyond the anthropological debate generated by his work, I am interested in digging deeper into the idea of gifting as encompassing, already, a logic of reciprocity that escapes what we have grown accustomed to call 'the economy'. Instead, gifting is a practical embodiment of a deeper logic of reciprocity based in ontological commitments that modernity has never managed to fully exorcise.

Mauss' treatment of gifts in Māori society centers around the concepts of *taonga* and *hau*. We have already encountered the latter in Chapter 5, but here I want to extract the political possibilities that connect the work of reciprocity to a mutualist project, through its relation with *taonga*. As Amiria Henare explains (2007, 47), "Mauss argued that when a *taonga* or treasured possession is exchanged, it carries with it *hau*, 'the spirit of the gift', an animate force binding those involved in the transaction—persons and things—into a cycle of reciprocity", which obliges the recipient to return the gift in some form. Mauss interpreted *taonga* and *hau* as separate and separable concepts, attached as it were to separate ontological categories. But Henare, as well as other Māori scholars, have argued that this is a misrepresentation of Māori philosophy, which itself never makes the step from ontology to epistemology. As Henare argues, "according to Ranapiri, one *taonga* exchanged for another does not simply *carry* the *hau* of the gift, it *is* its *hau*, translated elsewhere by Best as 'the vital essence or life principle' (1900: 189). There is a precise identity, in other words, between thing and spirit, aspects which Mauss separated out in his analysis" (48).

The gifting of *taonga* obliges participants to enter into a perpetual relationship of reciprocity. The perpetuity of the relationship lies in the fact that the gift can never be repaid, precisely because of its identification with *hau*, that is to say with a spirit that has no equivalent but itself and that keeps on gathering force with each subsequent transaction. The signature of all those who had to do with the gift is etched within it, not as a matter of epistemological consideration (I know that so-and-so possessed this at some point), but rather as a matter of ontological augmentation (the gift itself becomes more endowed with *hau* the more it circulates).

Henare underlines that "the *hau* of the original gift lives on, requiring reciprocity through successive generations" (60). Taken together with the genealogical view of life explored in earlier chapters, this means that objects in the environing world that have been received as gifts are filled with the spirit of all ancestors (human and non-human) that have had something to do with them. Henare applies this logic to the founding Treaty of Waitangi and explains the current era of Māori claims for Crown breaches of the treaty through understanding the founding document as itself a precious *taonga*. The Crown has failed to reciprocate exchanges codified by that document.

The particular meaning of *taonga* and *hau* within a strictly Māori context is of interest in itself. However, I want to take the suggestion of an ontological reciprocity etched within gift exchange and extend it to other contexts as well. The first thing that is apparent is that gift exchange is not, in this account, strictly an economic activity. A gift is not necessarily a material good. Indeed, as suggested in Chapter 5, the ultimate gift is that of receiving life and of being embedded within forces that sustain one's life. This unpayable gift takes its most concrete form in relations of reciprocity with the land. The basic intuition of an unpayable debt towards the environing world is seen through routine expressions and practices in many different cultures, not least in Western ones. In the Southern Italian case of human—olive tree relations (see Intermezzo I), the olive tree itself can be considered a *taonga*, a gift that arrives striated with the actions and spirits of ancestors that live through it. The reciprocal relation to the tree is emblematic of a reciprocal relation to the past that has furnished one's present life.

This past-present dynamic is decidedly different from the modern one. The activation of the past in the present happens precisely inasmuch as the individual is engaged in relationships that generate the porous boundaries between present and past. Inheriting gifts (like olive trees, but also clean air, water, or rich soil) connects the present to the power of the past, a power that largely determines present possibilities;

reinvention and renovation are necessarily based on predecessors. Angelo, a fifth generation 'fornaio' in Puglia (caretaker of the oven—*forno*), emphasizes genealogy in how he presents himself, wearing on his sleeves the ancestral relationships to the land, to the oven, and to people, that make him who he is.[6] Tāme Iti, a Māori activist, emphasizes genealogy in how he presents himself, as it is the relations with ancestors and the mountains and the rivers and the land that make him who he is.[7] That core of indigeneity is not an exotic piece of anthropology, but is fundamental to who and what we are.

The modern cult of the individual, which by definition is poor in spirit (and therefore power), is inimical to genealogical relations of reciprocity. The individual is perfectly constructed for doing the work that capital accumulation and expansion demands. This is well documented through, for example, ethnographies of production (for the classic treatment, see Ong 1987), which show how inimical capitalist labor is to human beings. There is great violence involved in individualizing, the violence of cutting, slashing, stabbing at the dendrites that make up beings, the dendrites through which we all receive gifts that oblige us to reciprocate, indefinitely.

Angelo receives gifts from his clients, each according to what they consider his bread is worth. This is a good example of gifting surviving. The idea of equivalence here is that of goodness: "the things they bring

---

6   Interview with Angelo di Biccari available here: www.youtube.com/watch?v=pG8tcNKQsic. As the caretaker of a sixteenth-century oven, Angelo wants to encourage a general reskilling of people by teaching them how to make their own bread and other oven goods. He therefore does not work as a baker, but rather as a midwife for forgotten practices. Twice a week, he offers his own bread in exchange for other goods that, as he says, bear the signature of their maker (olive oil, fruits, cheese, eggs, wine, and so on). He explains that the partners in exchange must trust that what is exchanged is roughly equivalent not in economic value, but in quality and care. This, he says, is the first step towards a wider ethics of interaction that may apply to "the economy, social issues, banks, the internet" and so on.
    But one need not have an actual ancestral connection to a place and/or a craft in order to enter into this kind of generative relation. Genealogical links, as I have argued, are fundamentally open. For example, in Otranto, Puglia, a group of people that do not have a deep past connection to milling flour have opened the first communal mill in generations, pursuing ideas and practices similar to Angelo's. Through their actions, they add to the generative genealogy of that place. See http://ilmanifesto.it/il-mulino-di-comunita-utopia-tangibile/.
7   See, for example, https://interactives.stuff.co.nz/2020/11/tame-iti-50-years-of-news making/.

us need to be as good as the bread we give them. Good genuine products need to taste like the person offering them. They need a signature". The signature in Angelo's case is akin to the *hau* of Māori *taonga*, that is to say a power of spirit that is not separate or separable from the object, but rather *is* the object.

Being rooted in a rich genealogical soil also implies that the body is itself a composite of inheritances. For Māori, different body parts have their own agency, and this is reflected in *te reo* Māori (the Māori language; see Salmond, Chapter 3). Though in Māori the intelligence of the body is etched in syntax, in other languages it is still visible through idioms. A baker going about her business and perfectly 'weighing' dough says "*ormai le mie mani sono abituate*" ("my hands are used to it by now"). It is not *her* that is used to it, but her hands, and everyone that has had similar experiences knows that to be true.[8] It is not metaphorical to say that the eyes see, the ears hear, and the hands do. It is metaphorical to say that *I* do those things. Experientially speaking, the body is a composite of intelligence, interacting with intelligent worlds.

The sense of human beings being deeply embedded in meaningful landscapes (Drenthen's legible, layered landscapes) can never be eradicated, because of its deep ontological underpinnings. The challenge, however, is not to have it survive in theory and pockets of practice and idiomatic expressions, but rather to build a politics of reciprocity with the environing world. In order to do that, all political scales are needed for the creation of infrastructures of reciprocity, conduits through which human communities can again enhance their environments, in an open-ended and endless project of mutual beneficence.

I stress again that the exchange of gifts in the sense developed here, and the reciprocity it expresses, is not simply an economic matter. In fact, much of the most radical literature on the need to fundamentally change economic practices (degrowth and the sufficiency movement are key among these) is itself a plea to de-center 'the economy' from the pursuit of a good life. One could even imagine 'the economy' as such disappearing, and instead inscribing exchange within meaningful relationships. However that may be, in the here and now there is much that can be done in order to renovate the conduits of reciprocity that sustain thriving lives. One of the most important ones, with which I

---

8   Also see Richard Sennett's *The Craftsman* (2008).

want to end this chapter, is the pursuit of ritual in interactions with the environment.

* * *

Throughout this book, I have referred to the practice of ecological restoration (as well as its latest variant, rewilding) as a potential illustration of how a mutualist politics may look in practice. This is not to say that the practice of restoration *is* mutualist, by definition. It is to say that it has great potential to be so in the senses that I have developed. I want to now turn to restoration, and the politics of nature conservation more widely, one last time in order to think about what ritualization may mean in practice, and how infrastructures of reciprocity may be created.

I have argued extensively that nature restoration today must be about restoring relationships with the land. The same holds for the practice of nature conservation, which has arguably always been about promoting certain relationships (between urban dwellers and 'wilderness', for example) at the expense of others. The salient question today is what these relationships may be, how best to achieve them, and who has the right to be involved. According to the account presented so far, the kinds of relationships to be pursued may be called mutualist, that is to say relationships that benefit all involved participants. In the context of ecological restoration, the benefits for people are not only (perhaps not even primarily) about material gains, but rather the creation of meaning through engaging the environing world in a beneficial way. Jordan, in presenting the history of ecological restoration, talks about a supposed moment of "discovery of the value of this work [restoration] for the people involved as a distinctive way of engaging nature" (Jordan and Lubick 2011, 177).

No such moment need exist as a historically identifiable event; instead, it is a way of expressing the idea that ecological restoration has mutated, throughout its history, from a science of control (recreating, through technical means, what people want) to one of engagement. This implies that restoration is a science that is open to ecological variation and unknowns, inasmuch as the *process* of restoring is one that strives to benefit, in multiple kinds of ways, all those involved. Andrew Light has stressed the politics of this kind of restoration as having the enormous potential to be radically democratic. "At its best", he argues, "ecological restoration preserves the democratic ideal that public participation in a public activity increases the value of that activity" (in Jordan and Lubick 2011, 178). In Light's account, the democratic potential of restoration is expressed through the involvement of those affected. This means, for him, the active involvement of local communities, but there is no reason to suppose that only human communities have the right to be active participants. In restoration projects that involve the reintroduction of animals, for example, the latter also become active participants in the construction of new relationships.

The historical tendency to exclude those living closest to conservation spaces is still dominant today, though critique of it has never been stronger. The power of exclusion still haunts practices that try to be novel, like rewilding. In my fieldwork with rewilding projects, I have often come across the belief, on the part of rewilding practitioners, that locals were not enlightened enough to know their own interest in protecting the environment. This kind of mentality is a direct inheritance from the colonial history of conservation, and one way to overcome it is by designing rewilding projects to be *entirely* co-created, including the initial definition of their goals.

This is not easy, far from it. Idealizing the willingness of locals to "participate" is a mistake. What exactly does it mean to participate, who is it for, whose responsibility is it to do so and under which conditions? These questions cannot be conclusively answered, as if a formula of participation could be summoned, but one way through the thicket they imply is to realize that part of the problem is how we think about participation. Usually, the idea is that a project whose outline is more or less already settled is 'opened up' to locals who are now free to jump in and, at best, have some input. This is of course insufficient, and it is not the only reason why local people may rebel against conservation goals. Another reason is the facile idea that locals are always *a community*, when in fact every human life plays out within a network of friendship and animosity akin to quicksand. Or rather, approaching conservation as a project to be achieved by courting "local communities" misses the point in two ways: conservation suffers when thought about as a project to be achieved, and it is impossible to acquire allies from a notion—the local community—that is highly unstable.

These reasons combined mean that conservationists are generally content to identify representatives of the community and assume that through the partial participation of these people all will be pacified, and that the social goals will have been achieved. This is naïve and counterproductive, because whoever the representatives are, they are surely not unanimously seen as such, given that local power struggles logically exist. And whatever the project goals may be are not in fact drawn up after the lengthy and equal participation *of the conservationists* within the local environment. In one article on rewilding in the Danube Delta, I documented how one of the more salient wishes of many people from a particular village was the creation of a paved road to facilitate transport to and from the biggest town. Connection with this town was crucial in winter when the water was frequently frozen and therefore the river unusable for navigation. A new road would reduce the time needed to reach the town and would also reduce fuel consumption considerably: an infrastructural redoubling that would connect the towns year-round.

Building roads was not on the rewilding agenda. On the face of it, of course not. But then again, why not? *What* is the rewilding agenda such that it cannot accommodate this kind of wish? If that agenda would be more akin to what I have described as an underlying potential—the encouragement of mutual beneficence through ritualized restoration—then there is no reason to *a priori* exclude anything at all. Democratizing restoration is not about using the pre-existing channels of democratic practice, including elected representatives and power hierarchies, but setting up alternative modes that rely on deep familiarity with the situation within which reciprocity and responsibility necessarily work.

Under the dominant conservation regime, local inhabitants feel the exclusionary practices and the gaze that relegates them to perpetual nuisances. Their own ecological knowledge remains unused, and they are subject to the individualism of modern capitalist societies that reward consumption. Their own inheritance of ritualized practices, often all but gone, remains below the surface. In the context of the Danube Delta, for example, there is a strong memory of past rituals around commons such as reed beds and fishing grounds. Expeditions to pursue these goods were collective affairs that honed skills and built knowledge of the environing world. Today, the channels that these past practices have hewn are still visible in the many essentially instructive conversations that follow inquiries into these goods. One may ask almost anything about reeds and the conversation quickly steers towards their past as a commons, how best to harvest them, what season is appropriate for doing that, and so on.

Part of what has relegated these once ordinary rituals to an increasingly unapproachable past is the monetization of the goods around which they were articulated. Reeds are now harvested through concessions given to companies. From a classic conservation perspective, reeds are not to be touched at all, and this forecloses the possibility of ritualizing beneficial use. In other words, a democratic politics of restoration/conservation/rewilding approaches what Büscher and Fletcher call convivial conservation, that is to say a conservation model that is first and foremost concerned with equality among participants and fundamentally disposed *against* the dominant political economy. Conservation's current obsession with ecotourism is a good example of how conservationists fail to use existing, dormant practices by swallowing wholesale the idea that monetization is necessary. Conservation should not aim to monetize every last bit of the environment, but rather to create relationships that no longer see monetization as necessary.[9]

Ecotourism is but the latest manifestation of the search for the exotic. It is dependent on the duality of general impoverishment and an enclave system of splendid wilderness populated by natives doing 'native things'. It is also a tremendous driver of consumption. The Danube Delta has been promoted, by rewilders and conservationists as well, as a fantastic ecological destination. The assumption is that tourism can supplant resource use in those places deemed worthy of protection. Simply put, the local who can drive a tourist around to photograph birds will give up fishing threatened species because this is an alternative income.

This seldom works. In the context of a culture of consumption, there is no reason to suppose that a local resident wishing to attain the level of

---

9   For example, by fighting to return now commodified goods to an economy of use and exchange outside of formal economic institutions. Reeds are again a good example: under market conditions, they have become the most expensive building material for locals themselves to use, though villages are surrounded by reed beds. The Danube Delta has the largest contiguous reed beds in the world, but they cannot be used in a non-monetized way. Their monetization has also led to the radical de-skilling of local people, who no longer know how to use them as their ancestors did. This terrain is ripe for restoration.

consumption of his guests will not drive a boat *and* fish. In the Danube Delta, this is exactly what is happening. What is more, the tourist comes to the region with a preconceived idea—promoted through ecotourism itself—of what the local lifestyle is like, and therefore accelerates consumption. Fishing is now necessary in order to feed tourists what they think locals eat. There are not enough fish in the Delta to feed all the tourists, so restaurants serve Norwegian roe and Canadian fish as local varieties. Then there are the increased emissions from transport (flying all of the tourists in) or the necessary extra plumbing, water facilities, heating, and so on. The village that 'benefits' from ecotourism has now been modernized, perfectly integrated into a network of consumption that brings the alienation tourists are trying to escape into the homes of their hosts.

Travelers had always visited the Delta. But they were not tourists, a category that is inseparable from commodification. Ivan (2007) documents how, before mass tourism, the people of Sfântu Gheorghe would host guests that would often become their friends. Money was not seen as an important measure of exchange, and instead gifts in kind were common. The existing culture of hospitality worked. People had always had a spare guest room, usually the biggest and most decorated room of the house, just in case someone came by. That kind of hospitality was radically transformed by tourism because the infrastructure it required was not adequate for the flow of people paying for a predetermined service. Instead of the guest room, which has disappeared, the village is sprawling with 'guest houses', mini hotels made to feed the tourist flow.

Answering the question of how to move away from conservation's dead-ends and counterproductive proposals is not easy, but we can think about it by linking the practices of restoration/conservation /rewilding with ritualization. If we accept that the most important political contributions that these practices can make have to do with the creation of mutually beneficial relationships that allow for widespread meaningfulness, then it becomes quite clear that one way to achieve this is through the ritual practice of renewal of such relationships. It is through infinite reiteration that relationships are constructed, and the meaningfulness embedded in such repetition is fundamentally linked to the creation of rituals that mark the repetition itself as meaningful. This is not a new idea, but merely one that—like so many that go against the modernist grain—have fared poorly. Jordan remarks with respect to many societies that "rituals [...] shape, renew, and transmit the intellectual, emotional, and spiritual software that defines the relationship between the land and the people who inhabit it" (Jordan and Lubick 2011, 178). Or as Bollier and Helfrich put it, "rituals tend to work best when they are woven into ordinary daily life and are not treated as something separate and unusual" (105). Ritualization cannot be a project; it can only be a process.

In practice, this will take more forms than can be imagined. But the general outlines stay roughly the same, namely the repetitive engagement, in communal settings, with aspects of the environment that, through such engagement, are underlined as meaningful; this supports the creation of infrastructures of reciprocity. This kind of meaningfulness is often enhanced and passed on through the development of skills that the ritual requires. Earlier I spoke about the pride that one feels in reiteratively placing oysters in a formerly polluted urban river, or the respect that locals have for European bison partly because they participate in their release (a festive occasion). Through these practices, people learn about the surrounding world, populating it with many more creatures and processes that had formerly been invisible.

Restoration as a ritualized practice that aims to create meaningful relationships of mutual beneficence has no territorial boundaries; it can happen everywhere. Politically, this idea must migrate across scales, such that support depends on what practices achieve in a comprehensively restorative sense, and not on arbitrary indicators of success (like how many trees have been planted). Ultimately, one has to insist on the idea that human beings can, alas *must*, play a crucial and perpetual role in the enhancement of the environing world. The best possible answer to the Ecocene would be the inauguration of a perpetual age of restoration. This book has tried to pick up threads that may otherwise have remained disconnected in order to emphasize the need for this approach. Mutualist futures are possible; they have begun, through the systematic renovation of the forgotten inheritance that ties everyone fundamentally to their world. As unlikely as it may seem, we may yet collectively find ways not only to live through the Ecocene, but to thrive.

Outro

I was born in a totalitarian regime, the utopian dream turned inside-out, entrails masquerading as skin. My parents, out of the same kind of folly that makes some "conscientious objectors to economic growth" today (Stengers 2015), raised me for a world that did not exist. They thought and acted as if they were in a different world. Not that they were unaware of the dramatic situation that objectively surrounded them. But they saw no point in capitulating to it.

Many, though perhaps not most, of the people I knew then had the same kind of madness. All of them were very young when they were forcefully modernized in the service of a great ideal. They had grown up knowing nothing else, forbidden from accessing anything different that may have put their own situation in perspective. The world around them was in many senses natural, had the air of inevitability that any system must have if it is to endure. The status quo may be disliked, even hated, but it must appear inevitable.

The developed world of today seems just as inevitable in its consumptive apparatus. We can barely imagine a future that will not be one of parasitism, both inter and intra-specific. Increasingly, we cannot imagine a future without tragic loss. Though ostensibly very different, the consumer capitalism of today and the totalitarianism of the twentieth century are similarly stifling to the imagination; both ensure a decomposition of the surrounding world in tandem with a psychic and moral decomposition of the human.

Looking back at ancestors we may yet recuperate the resolve that some found, the freedom that came from refusing to dream the present away in favor of the lucidity of their historic loss. It is that lucidity that forced them to live in the shadow of the present, in a world that could create the possibility of joy. They were not perfect. They pretended and lied like everyone had to, they survived, martyrdom was rare. But they also subverted and fought against the inevitability of their future in their daily lives, in the small gestures and sideways steps that put them out of synch. They often acted as if no-one was in a luckier position than them.

Many of my parents' generation insisted on thinking freely, on having a conscience, on being fair. They did that from within a world where those kinds of commitments could be deadly. Their folly would not have been rendered useless by the indefinite continuation of totalitarianism. If anything, that indefinite continuation would have made it even more imperative that they endured in their hopeless obstinance. Hopeless they were. Their refrain after the revolution that concluded the regime was "we never thought it would end". They truly didn't. And yet they were stubborn, not only in the absence of a horizon, but because of it. That kind of stubbornness is the stubbornness of life, betting on that which it cannot hope for, because that is the only way to live.

Bibliography

Abram, D. (2012). *The Spell of the Sensuous: Perception and Language in a More-Than-Human World*. New York: Vintage.

Al Jazeera English (2013). *Earthrise: Bronx River Revival*. 10 October, https://www.youtube.com/watch?v=4zbuEM_ZzCA.

American Museum of Natural History (2012). *Science Bulletins: Bronx River Restoration*. 6 June, https://www.youtube.com/watch?v=tCClu3iTYIU.

Anderson, E. N. (1996). *Ecologies of the Heart: Emotion, Belief, and the Environment*. Oxford: Oxford University Press on Demand.

Arendt, H. (1963). *On Revolution*. New York: Viking Press.

Basl, J. (2010). Restitutive Restoration: New Motivations for Ecological Restoration. *Environmental Ethics*, 32(2), 135–147, https://doi.org/10.5840/enviroethics201032216.

Bates, V., Hickman, C., Manchester, H., Prior, J., and Singer, S. (2020). Beyond Landscape's Visible Realm: Recorded Sound, Nature, and Wellbeing. *Health & Place*, 61, 102271, https://doi.org/10.1016/j.healthplace.2019.102271.

Berkes, F. (2012). *Sacred Ecology*. New York: Routledge.

Bollier, D., and Helfrich, S. (2019). *Free, Fair, and Alive: The Insurgent Power of the Commons*. Gabriola Island, BC: New Society Publishers.

Borden, R. J. (2017). Gregory Bateson's Search for "Patterns Which Connect" Ecology and Mind. *Human Ecology Review*, 23(2), 87–96, https://doi.org/10.22459/HER.23.02.2017.09.

Braidotti, R. (2019). *Posthuman Knowledge*. Cambridge: Polity Press.

Buscher, B., and Fletcher, R. (2020). *The Conservation Revolution: Radical Ideas for Saving Nature Beyond the Anthropocene*. New York: Verso Trade.

Calabrese, G., Perrino, E. V., Ladisa, G., Aly, A., Solomon, M. T., Mazdaric, S., Benedetti, A., and Ceglie, F. G. (2015). Short-Term Effects of Different Soil Management Practices on Biodiversity and Soil Quality of Mediterranean Ancient Olive Orchards. *Organic Agriculture*, 5(3), 209–223.

Callon, M., Lascoumes, P., and Barthe, Y. (2011). *Acting in an Uncertain World: An Essay on Technical Democracy*. Cambridge, MA: MIT Press.

Carson, K. A. (2007). *Studies in Mutualist Political Economy*. Charleston, SC: BookSurge.

Cavell, S. (2002). *Must We Mean What We Say?: A Book of Essays*. Cambridge: Cambridge University Press.

Cavell, S., Diamond, C., McDowell, J., and Hacking, I. (2009). *Philosophy and Animal Life*. New York: Columbia University Press.

Chakrabarty, D. (2009). *Provincializing Europe*. Princeton, NJ: Princeton University Press.

Chakrabarty, D. (2018). *The Crises of Civilization: Exploring Global and Planetary Histories*. Oxford: Oxford University Press.

Clingerman, F. (2009). Reading the Book of Nature: A Hermeneutical Account of Nature for Philosophical Theology. *Worldviews: Global Religions, Culture, and Ecology*, 13(1), 72–91, https://doi.org/10.3390/rel11040205.

Constantinescu, Ș., and Tănăsescu, M. (2018). Simplifying a Deltaic Labyrinth: Anthropogenic Imprint on River Deltas. *Revista de Geomorfologie*, 20(1), 66–78, https://doi.org/10.21094/rg.2018.023.

Crary, A., and Read, R. (Eds). (2000). *The New Wittgenstein*. London and New York: Routledge.

Crary, A. (2016). *Inside Ethics*. Cambridge, MA: Harvard University Press.

Crary, A. (2007). *Beyond Moral Judgment*. Cambridge, MA: Harvard University Press.

Cronon, W. (1995). 'The Trouble with Wilderness; or, Getting Back to the Wrong Nature', in: Cronon, W. (ed.), *Uncommon Ground*, 69–90. New York: Norton.

De Bell, S., Graham, H., and White, P. C. (2020). Evaluating Dual Ecological and Well-Being Benefits from an Urban Restoration Project. *Sustainability*, 12(2), 695, https://doi.org/10.3390/su12020695.

De Castro, E. V. (2015). *Cannibal Metaphysics*. Minneapolis: University of Minnesota Press.

De Castro, E. V. (2019). Exchanging Perspectives: The Transformation of Objects into Subjects in Amerindian Ontologies. *Common Knowledge*, 25(1–3), 21–42, https://doi.org/10.1215/0961754X-10-3-463.

de la Bellacasa, M. P. (2017). *Matters of Care: Speculative Ethics in More Than Human Worlds* (Vol. 41). Minneapolis: University of Minnesota Press.

de la Cadena, M. (2015). *Earth Beings*. Durham, NC: Duke University Press.

de la Cadena, M., and Blaser, M. (Eds) (2018). *A World of Many Worlds*. Durham, NC: Duke University Press.

de Waal, F. (2007). *Chimpanzee Politics: Power and Sex among Apes*. Baltimore: Johns Hopkins University Press.

Debaise, D. (2017a). *Nature as Event*. Durham, NC: Duke University Press.

Debaise, D. (2017b). *Speculative Empiricism*. Edinburgh: Edinburgh University Press.

Deleuze, G., and Guattari, F. (1988). *A Thousand Plateaus: Capitalism and Schizophrenia*. London: Bloomsbury Publishing.

Deliège, G., and Neuteleers, S. (2015). Should Biodiversity Be Useful? Scope and Limits of Ecosystem Services as an Argument for Biodiversity Conservation. *Environmental Values*, 24(2), 165–182.

Deliège, G. (2007). Toward a Richer Account of Restorative Practices. *Environmental Philosophy*, 4(1/2), 135–147.

Descola, P. (2013). *Beyond Nature and Culture*. Chicago: University of Chicago Press.

Descola, P. (2014). Modes of Being and Forms of Predication. *Hau: Journal of Ethnographic Theory*, 4(1), 271–280.

D'Hoop, A. (2022). Crossing Worlds in Buildings: Caring for Brussels' Swifts. *Humanimalia*. Forthcoming.

Diamond, C. (1978). Eating Meat and Eating People. *Philosophy*, 53(206), 465–479.

Diamond, C. (1991). The Importance of Being Human. *Royal Institute of Philosophy Supplements*, 29, 35–62, https://doi.org/10.1017/S135824610000744X.

Diamond, C. (2003). The Difficulty of Reality and the Difficulty of Philosophy. *Partial Answers: Journal of Literature and the History of Ideas*, 1(2), 1–26, https://doi.org/10.1353/pan.0.0090.

Driessen, C. (2020). 'Descartes Was Here', in: AMO and Koolhaas, R. (eds), *Countryside, a Report*. Köln: Taschen.

Drenthen, M. (2009). Ecological Restoration and Place Attachment: Emplacing Non-Places? *Environmental Values*, 18(3), 285–312, https://doi.org/10.3197/096327109X12474739376451.

Drenthen, M. (2011). 'Reading Ourselves through the Land: Landscape Hermeneutics and Ethics of Place', in: Clingerman, F. and Dixon, M. H. (eds), *Placing Nature on the Borders of Religion, Philosophy and Ethics*, 123–139. London and New York: Routledge.

Drenthen, M. (2013). 'New Nature Narratives. Landscape Hermeneutics and Environmental Ethics', in: Clingerman, F., Treanor, B., Drenthen, M., and Utsler, D. (eds). (2013). *Interpreting Nature: The Emerging Field of Environmental Hermeneutics*, 225–241. New York: Fordham University Press.

Drenthen, M. (2015). 'Layered Landscapes, Conflicting Narratives, and Environmental Art', in: Hourdequin, M. and Havlick, D. G. (eds), *Restoring*

Layered Landscapes: History, Ecology, and Culture, 239–262. Oxford: Oxford University Press.

Drenthen, M. (2018). Rewilding in Layered Landscapes as a Challenge to Place Identity. *Environmental Values*, 27(4), 405–425, https://doi.org/10.3197/0963 27118X15251686827732.

Drury Jr, W. H. (1998). *Chance and Change: Ecology for Conservationists*. Berkeley: University of California Press.

Elliot, R. (1982). Faking Nature. *Inquiry*, 25(1), 81–93.

Emmett, R. S., and Nye, D. E. (2017). *The Environmental Humanities: A Critical Introduction*. Cambridge, MA: MIT Press.

Gaita, R. (2016). *The Philosopher's Dog*. London and New York: Routledge.

Gallagher, M. (2015). Field Recording and the Sounding of Spaces. *Environment and Planning D: Society and Space*, 33(3), 560–576, https://doi.org/10.1177/0263775815594310.

Gallagher, M. (2016). Sound as Affect: Difference, Power and Spatiality. *Emotion, Space and Society*, 20, 42–48, https://doi.org/10.1016/j.emospa.2016.02.004.

Gallagher, M., and Prior, J. (2014). Sonic Geographies: Exploring Phonographic Methods. *Progress in Human Geography*, 38(2), 267–284, https://doi.org/10.1177/0309132513481014.

Gallagher, M., Kanngieser, A. and Prior, J., (2016). Listening Geographies: Landscape, Affect and Geotechnologies. *Progress in Human Geography*, 41(5), 618–637, https://doi.org/10.1177/0309132516652952.

Galt, A. H. (1986). Social class in a Mid-Eighteenth-Century Apulian Town: Indications from the Catasto Onciario. *Ethnohistory*, 419–447, https://doi.org/10.2307/482041.

Galt, A. H. (1991). *Far from the Church Bells: Settlement and Society in an Apulian Town*. Cambridge: Cambridge University Press.

Gammon, A. R. (2018). The Many Meanings of Rewilding: An Introduction and the Case for a Broad Conceptualisation. *Environmental Values*, 27(4), 331–350, https://doi.org/10.3197/096327118X15251686827705.

Gammon, A. R. (2019). 'The Unsettled Places of Rewilding', in: *Interdisciplinary Unsettlings of Place and Space*, 251–264. Singapore: Springer.

Gatti, F. (2019). What Is the Worth of an Olive Tree? Political Ontology and Epistemic Conflicts in the Case of *Xylella fastidiosa* epidemic in Apulia, Southern Italy. Unpublished Master's thesis, International Institute of Social Studies, The Hague.

Gilbert, S. F., Sapp, J., and Tauber, A. I. (2012). A Symbiotic View of Life: We Have Never Been Individuals. *The Quarterly review of biology*, 87(4), 325–341, https://doi.org/10.1086/668166.

Gorz, A. (1980). *Ecology as Politics*. Montreal: Black Rose Books Ltd.

Graeber, D. (2004). *Fragments of an Anarchist Anthropology*. Cambridge: Prickly Paradigm Press.

Graeber, D. (2018). *Bullshit Jobs: A Theory*. New York: Penguin.

Gutwirth, S., and Stengers, I. (2016). Théorie du droit, Le droit à l'épreuve de la résurgence des Commons. *Revue juridique de l'Environnement*, 41(2), 306–343.

Hage, G. (2012). Critical Anthropological Thought and the Radical Political Imaginary Today. *Critique of Anthropology*, 32(3), 285–308, https://doi.org/10.1177/0308275X12449105.

Haraway, D. (2015). Anthropocene, Capitalocene, Plantationocene, Chthulucene: Making Kin. *Environmental humanities*, 6(1), 159–165, https://doi.org/10.1215/22011919-3615934.

Haraway, D. J. (2016). *Staying with the Trouble*. Durham, NC: Duke University Press.

Harrison, P. (2007). "How Shall I Say It...?" Relating the Nonrelational. *Environment and Planning A*, 39(3), 590–608, https://doi.org/10.1068/a3825.

Harrison, P. (2008). Corporeal Remains: Vulnerability, Proximity, and Living on after the End of the World. *Environment and planning A*, 40(2), 423–445, https://doi.org/10.1068/a391.

Heidegger, M. (1966). *Discourse on Thinking*. New York: Harper & Row Publishers.

Henare, A. (2007). 'Taonga Māori. Encompassing Rights and Property in New Zealand', in: Henare, A., Holbraad, M., and Wastell, S. (eds), *Thinking Through Things: Theorising Artefacts Ethnographically*, 57–77. London and New York: Routledge.

Hobbs, R. J., Arico, S., Aronson, J., Baron, J. S., Bridgewater, P., Cramer, V. A., and Norton, D. (2006). Novel Ecosystems: Theoretical and Management Aspects of the New Ecological World Order. *Global Ecology and Biogeography*, 15(1), 1–7, https://doi.org/10.1111/j.1466-822X.2006.00212.x.

Hobbs, R. J., Higgs, E., and Harris, J. A. (2009). Novel Ecosystems: Implications for Conservation and Restoration. *Trends in Ecology & Evolution*, 24(11), 599–605, https://doi.org/10.1016/j.tree.2009.05.012.

Illich, I. (1970). *Deschooling Society*. New York: Harper & Row.

Illich, I. (1978). *The Right to Useful Unemployment and Its Professional Enemies*. London: Marion Boyars.

Iordachescu, G. (2019). Wilderness Production in the Southern Carpathian Mountains. Towards a Political Ecology of 'Untouched Nature'. Unpublished PhD thesis, Scuola IMT Alti Studi, Lucca.

Ivan, O. (2017). 'We Make More Money Now, but We Don't Talk to Each Other Anymore': On New Tourism and Capitalism in the Danube Delta. *Journal of Tourism and Cultural Change*, 15(2), 122–135, https://doi.org/10.1080/147668 25.2016.1260102.

Jonas, H. (1979). Toward a Philosophy of Technology. *Hastings Center Report*, 34–43.

Jonas, H. (1984). Ontological Grounding of a Political Ethics: On the Metaphysics of Commitment to the Future of Man. *Graduate Faculty Philosophy Journal*, 10(1), 47–61.

Jonas, H. (1985). *The Imperative of Responsibility: In Search of an Ethics for the Technological Age*. Chicago: University of Chicago press.

Jordan III, W.R. (1990). Two Psychologies. *Restoration and Management Notes*, 8(1), 2.

Jordan, W. R. (2003). *The Sunflower Forest: Ecological Restoration and the New Communion with Nature*. Berkeley: University of California Press.

Jordan, W. R., and Lubick, G. M. (2011). *Making Nature Whole: A History of Ecological Restoration*. Washington, DC: Island Press.

Jørgensen, D. (2015). Rethinking Rewilding. *Geoforum*, 65, 482–488, https://doi.org/10.1016/j.geoforum.2014.11.016.

Prior, J., and Ward, K. J. (2016). Rethinking Rewilding: A response to Jørgensen. *Geoforum*, 69, 132–135, https://doi.org/10.1016/j.geoforum.2015.12.003.

Katz, E. (1996). The Problem of Ecological Restoration. *Environmental Ethics*, 18(2), 222–224.

Katz, E. (2009). 'The Big Lie: Human Restoration of Nature', in: Kaplan, M. D. (ed.), *Readings in the Philosophy of Technology*, 443–451. Lanham, MD: Rowman and Littlefield.

Katz, E. (2012). Further Adventures in the Case against Restoration. *Environmental Ethics*, 34(1), 67–97, https://doi.org/10.5840/enviroethics20123416.

Kawharu, M. (2010). 'Environment as a Marae Locale', in: Selby, R., Moore, P., and Mulholland, M. (eds), *Māori and the Environment: Kaitiaki. Huia, Wellington, Aotearoa, New Zealand*, 221–237. Wellington: Huia.

Kirchhoff, T., Trepl L., and Vicenzotti, V. (2013). What is Landscape Ecology? An Analysis and Evaluation of Six Different Conceptions. *Landscape Research* 38(1), 33–51, https://doi.org/10.1080/01426397.2011.640751.

Kirchoff, T., and Vicenzotti, V. (2014). A Historical and Systematic Survey of European Perceptions of Wilderness. *Environmental Values*, 23(4), 443–464, https://doi.org/10.3197/096327114X13947900181590.

Kohn, E. (2013). *How Forests Think*. Berkeley: University of California Press.

Kropotkin, P. (1903). *Mutual Aid: A Factor of Evolution*. New York: McClure, Phillips & Co.

Kutílek, M., and Nielsen, D. R. (2015). *Soil. The Skin of the Planet Earth*. Dordrecht: Springer.

Latour, B. (2007). Can We Get Our Materialism Back, Please? *Isis, 98*(1), 138–142, https://doi.org/10.1086/512837.

Latour, B. (2017). *Facing Gaia: Eight Lectures on the New Climatic Regime*. Hoboken, NJ: John Wiley & Sons.

Latour, B. (2018). *Down to Earth: Politics in the New Climatic Regime*. Hoboken, NJ: John Wiley & Sons.

Latour, B., and Weibel, P. (eds). (2020). *Critical Zones: Observatories for Earthly Politics*. Harvard, MA: MIT Press.

Lavelle, P., and Spain, A. V. (2002). *Soil Ecology*. Netherlands: Springer Science & Business Media.

L'Observatoire de l'évolution (2019). *Manifeste pour l'invention d'une nouvelle condition paysanne*. Paris: L'échappée.

Lorimer, J., and Driessen, C. (2014). Wild Experiments at the Oostvaardersplassen: Rethinking Environmentalism in the Anthropocene. *Transactions of the Institute of British Geographers, 39*(2), 169–181, https://doi.org/10.1111/tran.12030.

Lovelock, J. (1995). *The Ages of Gaia: A Biography of Our Living Earth*. New York: W. W. Norton.

Malm, A. (2018). *The Progress of this Storm: Nature and Society in a Warming World*. London: Verso Books.

Margulis, L., and Sagan, D. (2000). *What is Life?* Berkeley: University of California Press.

Martin, A., Myers, N., Viseu, A. (2015). The Politics of Care in Technoscience. *Social Studies of Science, 45*(5), 625–641.

Massey, D. (2005). *For Space*. London: SAGE Publications Ltd.

Massey, D. (2006). Landscape as a Provocation: Reflections on Moving Mountains. *Journal of Material Culture, 11*(1–2), 33–48, https://doi.org/10.1177/1359183506062991.

Merleau-Ponty, M., 2005 [1945] *Phenomenology of Perception*. London: Routledge.

Mitchell, T. (2013). *Carbon Democracy. Political Power in the Age of Oil*. London: Verso.

Mitchell, T (2020). 'The Body Politic that Captured the Future', in: Latour, B., Schaffer, S., and Gagliardi, P., *A Book of the Body Politic: Connecting Biology, Politics, and Social Theory*, 49–74. Venice: Fondazione Giorgio Cini.

Moore, J. W. (2017). The Capitalocene, Part I: On the Nature and Origins of Our Ecological Crisis. *The Journal of Peasant Studies*, 44(3), 594–630, https://doi.org/10.1080/03066150.2016.1235036.

Moore, J. W. (2018). The Capitalocene Part II: Accumulation by Appropriation and the Centrality of Unpaid Work/Energy. *The Journal of Peasant Studies*, 45(2), 237–279, https://doi.org/10.1080/03066150.2016.1272587.

Mulhall, S. (2008). *The Wounded Animal*. Princeton, NJ: Princeton University Press.

Oelschlaeger, M. (1991). *The Idea of Wilderness: From Prehistory to the Age of Ecology*. New Haven, CT: Yale University Press.

Oelschlaeger, M. (2007). Ecological Restoration, Aldo Leopold, and Beauty: An Evolutionary Tale. *Environmental Philosophy*, 4(1/2), 149–161.

Park, G. (1995). *Nga Uruora*. Wellington: Victoria University Press.

Patel, R., and Moore, J. W. (2017). *A History of the World in Seven Cheap Things*. Berkeley: University of California Press.

Pradeu, T. (2009). *The Limits of the Self: Immunology and Biological Identity*. Oxford: Oxford University Press.

Prelz Oltramonti, G., and Tanasescu, M. (2019). 'The Criminalization of Informal Practices in the Danube Delta: How and Why', in: Polese, A., Russo, A., and Strazzari, F. (eds), *Governance Beyond the Law*, 49–65. Cham: Palgrave Macmillan.

Proietti, P., Famiani, F., Pannelli, G., and Guelfi, P. (2008). *Manuale per una potatura semplificata ed agevolata*. Castello: Città di Castello.

Rackham, O. (2020). *Trees and Woodland in the British Landscape*. London: Hachette UK.

Salmond, A. (2017). *Tears of Rangi: Experiments across Worlds*. Auckland: Auckland University Press.

Sariola, S., Gilbert, S.F. (2021). Toward a Symbiotic Perspective on Public Health: Recognizing the Ambivalence of Microbes in the Anthropocene. *Microorganisms*, 8(5), 746.

Selosse, M. A. (2021). *L'Origine du Monde*. Paris: Actes Sud.

Sennet, R. (2008). *The Craftsman*. Bristol: Allen Lane.

Simard, S. (2016). Exploring How and Why Trees "Talk" to Each Other. *Yale Environment*, 360(1), https://e360.yale.edu/features/exploring_how_and_why_trees_talk_to_each_other.

Simard, S. W. (2018). 'Mycorrhizal Networks Facilitate Tree Communication, Learning, and Memory', in: Baluska, F., Gagliano, M., and Witzany, G. (eds), *Memory and Learning in Plants*, 191–213. Cham: Springer.

Simand, S. (2021). *Finding the Mother Tree: Discovering the Wisdom of the Forest*. Bristol: Allen Lane.

Schama, S. (1995). *Landscape and Memory*. New York: Vintage.

Sharma, N. (2020). *Home Rule*. Durham, NC: Duke University Press.

Sheldrake, M. (2020). *Entangled Life: How Fungi Make Our Worlds, Change Our Minds, and Shape Our Futures*. New York: Vintage.

Skafish, P. (2016). The Descola Variations: The Ontological Geography of Beyond Nature and Culture. *Qui Parle: Critical Humanities and Social Sciences*, 25(1–2), 65–93, https://doi.org/10.5250/quiparle.25.1-2.0065.

Squatriti, P. (2013). *Landscape and change in early medieval Italy: chestnuts, economy, and culture*. Cambridge University Press.

Steffen, W., Broadgate, W., Deutsch, L., Gaffney, O., and Ludwig, C. (2015). The Trajectory of the Anthropocene: The Great Acceleration. *The Anthropocene Review*, 2(1), 81–98, https://doi.org/10.1177/2053019614564785.

Stengers, I. (2015). *In Catastrophic Times: Resisting the Coming Barbarism*. London: Open Humanities Press.

Stengers, I. (2018). 'The Challenge of Ontological Politics', in: de la Cadena, M., and Blaser, M. (eds), *A World of Many Worlds*, 83–111. Durham, NC: Duke University Press.

Stengers, I. (2000). *The Invention of Modern Science* (Vol. 19). Minneapolis: University of Minnesota Press.

Tanas, A., and Gutwirth, S. (2021). Une approche «écologique» des communs dans le droit. Regards sur le patrimoine transpropriatif, les usi civici et la rivière-personne. *In Situ. Au regard des sciences sociales*, https://doi.org/10.4000/insituarss.1206.

Tănăsescu, M. (2017). Field Notes on the Meaning of Rewilding. *Ethics, Policy & Environment*, 20(3), 333–349, https://doi.org/10.1080/21550085.2017.1374053.

Tănăsescu, M. (2017) Responsibility and the Ethics of Ecological Restoration. *Environmental Philosophy*, 14(2), 255-274.

Tănăsescu, M. (2019). How Knowledge of the Golden Jackal (Canis Aureus) Is Formed: Report from the Danube Delta. *Environmental Values*, 28(6), 665–691, https://doi.org/10.3197/096327119x15579936382545.

Tănăsescu, M. (2019). Restorative Ecological Practice: The Case of the European Bison in the Southern Carpathians, Romania. *Geoforum*, 105, 99–108.

Tănăsescu, M. (2020). Evocative Representation. *Constellations*, 27(3), 385–396, https://doi.org/10.1111/1467-8675.12463.

Tănăsescu, M., and Constantinescu, S. (2020). The Human Ecology of the Danube Delta: A Historical and Cartographic Perspective. *Journal* of *Environmental Management*, 262, 110324, https://doi.org/10.1016/j.jenvman.2020.110324.

Tănăsescu, M. (2022). *Understanding the Rights of Nature: A Critical Introduction*. Berlin: Transcript Verlag.

Tauber, A. I. (2017). *Immunity: The Evolution of an Idea*. Oxford: Oxford University Press.

Tsing, A. L. (2015). *The Mushroom at the End of the World*. Princeton, NJ: Princeton University Press.

Tsing, A. L., Bubandt, N., Gan, E., and Swanson, H. A. (eds) (2017). *Arts of Living on a Damaged Planet: Ghosts and Monsters of the Anthropocene*. Minneapolis: University of Minnesota Press.

Turner, V. W. (1981). *The Drums of Affliction: A Study of Religious Processes among the Ndembu of Zambia*. London: International African Institute in association with Hutchinson University Library for Africa.

Vicenzotti, V. and Trepl, L. (2009). City as Wilderness: The Wilderness Metaphor from Wilhelm Heinrich Riehl to Contemporary Urban Designers. *Landscape Research* 34(4), 379–396, https://doi.org/10.1080/01426390903019841.

Western, D. (2020). 'Scaling up the Governance of the Commons to Sustaining our Planet', in: Latour, B., Schaffer, S., and Gagliardi, P. (eds), *A Book of the Body Politic: Connecting Biology, Politics, and Social Theory*. Venice: Fondazione Giorgio Cini.

Wilson, E. O. (2016). *Half Earth: Out Planet's Fight for Life*. New York: W. W. Norton.

Wittgenstein, L. (1991). *Philosophical Investigations*. Hoboken: Wiley-Blackwell.

Wittgenstein, L. (1960). *The Blue and Brown Books. Preliminary Studies for the Philosophical Investigations*. New York: Harper Torchbooks.

Wohlleben, P. (2016). *The Hidden Life of Trees: What They Feel, How They Communicate—Discoveries from a Secret World* (Vol. 1). Vancouver: Greystone Books.

Youatt, R. (2008). Counting Species: Biopower and the Global Biodiversity Census. *Environmental Values*, 17(3), 393–417, https://doi.org/10.3197/096327108X343149.

Youatt, R. (2015). *Counting Species: Biodiversity in Global Environmental Politics*. Minneapolis: University of Minnesota Press.

Youatt, R. (2020). *Interspecies Politics*. Chicago: University of Chicago Press.

Index

Abram, David 121–123
anarchism 17, 106, 156, 158, 161–163, 167
animals, reintroductions of 90, 96, 101–103, 164, 176
Anthropocene 8–10, 14, 36, 44, 61, 85–86, 105, 127, 129, 131, 140, 143
anthropology, critical 38, 45, 80, 84

balance 11, 67, 100, 118–120, 124–125
bifurcation of nature 2, 5, 7, 23–26, 35, 38, 44, 95, 111, 123, 132, 134, 140, 147–148, 159–161, 170

cartography 6, 29–32
  and power 6, 28–31
  history of 29–31
Coetzee, J.M. 83–84
colonialism 6, 74–75, 90, 110–112, 115, 119, 170, 176
commons 19, 168–169, 177–178
competition 156, 159–161, 163, 170
conservation. *See* nature conservation; *See* nature: convivial conservation
cooperation 71, 107, 156–157, 160

Danube Delta 6, 27, 29, 32, 35, 75, 177–179
Debaise, Didier vi, 2, 4, 23, 32, 35, 37, 111
de la Cadena, Marisol 39
Descartes, René vi, 5, 25–28, 32, 116, 134
  and space 23, 25, 28, 32
description 5–7, 9, 14–15, 21–25, 66, 69, 78, 109, 116, 155
Diamond, Cora 79–84, 105, 124, 145–147
Drury, William 12, 67–68, 75, 100, 116, 160

Ecocene 2, 9, 11, 13–14, 18, 21–22, 25, 37, 43, 56–61, 70, 73, 76, 78, 80, 84–87, 89, 92, 99, 109–110, 115, 125–127, 131, 133, 136, 141, 143–145, 155, 159, 180
ecology 9, 11–14, 16–18, 66–67, 72–73, 75–76, 80, 93, 100, 115, 122, 129, 134, 155–156, 163
  and baselines 93–97, 99–100, 136, 165
  and redundancy of habitat 1, 72–74, 76, 87, 137
  meaning of 9, 11, 17–18, 122
ecomodernism 14, 43–45
ecosystem 12–13, 94, 96, 100, 134
ecotourism 102, 178–179
embodiment 23–25, 28, 35, 37–39, 61, 65, 68–69, 74, 76–77, 79–83, 85, 90, 122, 133, 142, 150, 158, 171
emplacement 25, 34, 36, 102–103, 113
ethics vii, 7, 16–19, 22, 45, 78–80, 82–86, 93–95, 106, 110–111, 119, 121–122, 124, 126–129, 135, 147, 150, 155, 163–164, 173
evolution, theory of 5, 7, 11, 42, 69, 94, 106, 156, 158–162

flesh, concept of 66–67, 122–123

Gaia 15, 42–43, 61, 63–68, 76, 130, 146, 160
genealogy, also *whakapapa* 22, 28, 39, 70, 117–118, 125, 143, 145, 173
geology 4, 8–9, 11, 33–34, 44, 64–65, 166
Graeber, David 18–19, 105, 132, 162
Great Acceleration 15, 148
guardianship 120, 129, 140–144

hau 115–116, 118, 122, 171–172, 174
hermeneutics 90, 98, 101, 133–134, 148
holism 15, 67, 70
holobiont 17, 70–71, 75, 98, 157–158
hope 2–3, 14, 59–60, 81

humanity, concept of 8, 81, 105, 129, 131, 135, 140

ignorance 3, 10, 13–14, 17, 42, 68, 70, 78–79, 119, 124, 140, 145, 158

indigeneity 38, 110–114, 119, 125, 141, 173

individuals v, 2, 8, 17, 44, 53, 59, 63–64, 68, 70–72, 85, 103, 113, 120, 131, 140, 157, 159–161, 163, 172–173

Jonas, Hans 128–131, 136, 144
Jordan, William III 74, 94–95, 167, 175, 180

kauri 150–151, 153–154
Kropotkin, Peter 42, 106, 158–161, 163

Latour, Bruno 5, 12, 34–36, 43, 50, 61, 63–66, 68, 76
legal person 19, 141–142
literature 74–75, 79–82, 84–85, 91, 150, 174
locality 11–12, 14, 19, 40, 98, 135
Lovelock, James 12, 50–51, 61–65

Māori philosophy 16, 71, 114–115, 118–120, 124, 129, 140, 142–143, 145, 170–171
Margulis, Lynn 12, 50–51, 61, 63–64, 70, 156–157, 160, 163
Massey, Doreen 4, 34
Merleau-Ponty, Maurice 35–36, 39, 121–122
modernity 2, 12, 15–16, 23, 25–26, 28, 32, 37–40, 42–45, 52, 54–55, 57, 68, 70, 72, 89–90, 92, 94, 111, 126, 129, 146–147, 149, 151, 160, 162, 171
   and development 15–17, 32, 37–38, 42–44, 52, 54, 56, 58–60, 68, 73–75, 89, 92, 111, 126, 129, 131–133, 136, 146–147, 149, 151, 155, 162, 170–171
   and nature 15, 23, 37, 43, 53–55, 57, 68, 70, 72, 75, 89–90, 92, 94, 144, 146–147, 151, 160
   concept of 2, 12, 23, 25–26, 38, 61, 111
Mulhall, Stephen 79, 82–84
multinaturalism 38, 40–41, 68, 72, 82, 122

multiplicity v, 2, 4, 15, 17, 19, 21, 24, 32, 35, 37–38, 40–42, 57, 61, 68, 71–79, 84, 89, 98, 104, 113, 122, 125, 136, 140, 144, 149, 163, 167
mutual aid 158–164
mutual beneficence 17, 19, 53, 106, 155–156, 159, 162–165, 167–169, 174, 177, 180

nativism 18, 43–44, 78, 107, 111–114, 150
nature 2–3, 5, 19, 23–26, 31–32, 36–40, 42, 44, 47, 61, 64–65, 67, 70–72, 77, 89–92, 94–96, 98–102, 105, 111–113, 115–116, 123, 126, 128–137, 140–141, 143–144, 147, 151–153, 159–160, 167, 170, 175
   concept of 23, 25, 36–38
   convivial conservation 93, 104, 106, 178
   urban restoration 97, 137–138, 169, 175, 180
nature conservation 19, 31, 76, 90–94, 99–100, 102, 104–106, 112, 130, 136, 153, 168, 175–179
   and participation 95, 97, 102, 106, 122, 125, 137, 164, 176–177, 180
nature restoration 19, 93, 96, 136, 137, 138, 139, 167, 175. *See also* nature: urban restoration

olives 48–50, 52–60, 97, 126, 152, 172
   cultivation vi, 18, 28, 50–51, 53, 55–57, 59–60
   history of 52–53, 56, 58
   pruning 48–49, 51–52, 54–56, 58–59
ontology 15–16, 22–24, 32, 35–36, 39, 41–42, 71, 74, 78–80, 84, 94, 109–110, 115–119, 122, 128, 141–142, 155, 163–164, 167, 171–172, 174

pollution 96, 130, 135, 137, 143, 180
prescription 5–7, 9, 14, 24–25, 109

reciprocity
   and exchange 37, 45, 90, 109–110, 115, 118–121, 123, 125–126, 139–140, 148, 158–159, 163, 165–167, 170–175, 180

concept of 10, 16, 19, 86, 90, 109–110, 114, 120–121, 126–127, 129, 155, 159, 162, 169–170, 177
relationality 15–16, 19, 41, 47, 71, 86, 96, 101, 113, 115–118, 129, 140–143, 145, 150, 157
responsibility, concept of 10, 16, 19, 86, 89–90, 109, 117, 126–131, 133, 135–136, 140–141, 144–145, 148, 155, 162, 169–170, 177
reversibility of perception 121–124
rewilding vi, 19, 28, 87, 97, 99–102, 104, 164, 168, 175–179
ritualization 51, 56–57, 89–90, 98–99, 101–102, 116, 121, 128, 139, 151, 165–167, 169, 175, 177–180

scale 11–12, 17, 31, 45, 58, 63, 66–68, 85, 104, 107, 117, 125, 130, 132, 138, 159, 174, 180
small theory 18, 61, 162
soil vii, 13, 49–52, 54, 56, 59–60, 66, 73, 90, 106, 120–121, 138, 153, 159, 164–166, 172, 174
space vi, 2, 10, 15, 21–37, 39–42, 44, 65–66, 69, 72–73, 76–77, 84–85, 87, 90, 92, 94, 96, 106, 112–113, 115, 120, 136–137, 140, 146, 155, 160, 163–165. *See also* Descartes, René: and space
Stengers, Isabelle v, 7, 15, 23–24, 28, 32, 36–38, 56, 61, 64–65, 129, 155
symbiosis 63, 71, 91, 156–157, 163

taonga 171–172, 174
technology 14, 27, 34, 44, 48, 127–131, 133–134, 140
Te Urewera 125, 141
tragedy 1, 3, 54, 56, 59, 145, 154, 181
Tūhoe 125–126, 141

utopia 3, 17, 144, 163, 170, 181
utu 118–119

Valle D'Itria 124
vulnerability 10, 16, 77–87, 122–123, 146–148, 151, 155

whakapapa. *See* genealogy, also *whakapapa*
Whanganui River 141–143
Whitehead, Alfred North 2, 4, 23, 35, 77

Xylella fastidiosa 54–57, 59–60, 152–154

About the Team

Alessandra Tosi was the managing editor for this book.

Melissa Purkiss performed the copy-editing, proofreading and indexing.

Anna Gatti designed the cover. The cover was produced in InDesign using the Fontin font.

Luca Baffa typeset the book in InDesign and produced the paperback and hardback editions. The text font is Tex Gyre Pagella; the heading font is Californian FB. Luca produced the EPUB, AZW3, PDF, HTML, and XML editions — the conversion is performed with open source software freely available on our GitHub page (https://github.com/OpenBook Publishers).

This book need not end here...

Share

All our books — including the one you have just read — are free to access online so that students, researchers and members of the public who can't afford a printed edition will have access to the same ideas. This title will be accessed online by hundreds of readers each month across the globe: why not share the link so that someone you know is one of them?

This book and additional content is available at:

https://doi.org/10.11647/OBP.0274

Customise

Personalise your copy of this book or design new books using OBP and third-party material. Take chapters or whole books from our published list and make a special edition, a new anthology or an illuminating coursepack. Each customised edition will be produced as a paperback and a downloadable PDF.

Find out more at:

https://www.openbookpublishers.com/section/59/1

Like Open Book Publishers

Follow @OpenBookPublish

Read more at the Open Book Publishers BLOG

You may also be interested in:

Living Earth Community
Multiple Ways of Being and Knowing
Sam Mickey, Mary Evelyn Tucker, and John Grim

https://doi.org/10.11647/OBP.0186

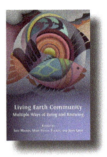

Global Warming in Local Discourses
How Communities around the World Make Sense of Climate Change
Michael Brüggemann and Simone Rödder

https://doi.org/10.11647/OBP.0212

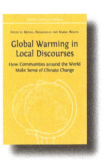

Negotiating Climate Change in Crisis
Steffen Böhm and Sian Sullivan

https://doi.org/10.11647/OBP.0265

Peak experience → valley experience